Women
and the
Word of God

A Response to Biblical Feminism

SUSAN T. FOH

BAKER BOOK HOUSE
Grand Rapids, Michigan 49506

Copyright 1979 by
Presbyterian and Reformed Publishing Co.

ISBN: 0-8010-3500-7

Reprinted 1980 by
Baker Book House Company
with the permission of the
copyright holder

PHOTOLITHOPRINTED BY CUSHING - MALLOY, INC.
ANN ARBOR, MICHIGAN, UNITED STATES OF AMERICA

Special thanks to Pennie Z. Burnett
of the Westminster Theological Seminary Library
for her generous help with regard to references and bibliography.

TABLE OF CONTENTS

INTRODUCTION

BEFORE speaking to a Sunday School class on Paul's views on women, I was asked if I was for or against women. I could not give a simple answer. The questioner was asking an inappropriate question, but one that expresses the popular approach to the so-called woman question. The position "for" women means women can do anything men can do, all possible distinctions are to be erased. "Against" women means women are restricted to a second grade status. Neither position is biblical. The Bible teaches that women, like men, bear the image of God and receive the benefits of salvation through faith in Christ (ontological equality) and that women are to submit themselves to their husbands and not to hold positions of ruling or teaching in the church (economic or functional subordination). But the Bible is for women; that is, it prescribes what is best for women. The difference between the feminist viewpoint and the biblical viewpoint is the difference between *all* we're meant to be and all we're *meant* to be.

For the Christian church, the "woman" question is a complex issue. In its most practical form, the question of the woman's role in the church implicates the role of the laity (can a layman exercise authority and teach in the church?), the format of worship (should only elders be allowed to speak? should there be more congregational participation?), and the use of spiritual gifts (do prophecy and tongue-speaking still exist?). In fact, one could say that the entire doctrine of the church is concerned and will be affected by decisions made about the woman's role. Such a complicated problem involving a major doctrine of the faith will take much time and study before resolution. And the issue is contemporary, going back only to the nineteenth century. Other doctrines of the faith, such as the Trinity, the person of Christ, and justification by faith, took time before the basics were worked out; and even now they must be studied, discussed, and refined. And so, such efforts as this book are not the final word, but only a beginning at understanding.

To add to the complexity of the problem, the biblical passages addressed specifically to women have exegetical difficulties that cannot and should not be whitewashed. For instance, in I Corinthians 11:3–16, the words translated "uncovered" and "covered" are unusual, and their precise meaning has not been indisputably established. The references to the angels and the "authority" (v. 10) the woman should have on her head appear mysterious to the modern Christian. These difficulties (and others) have not been conclusively resolved, and the tentativeness of proposed solutions should be recognized.

Several books about women and the Bible have been written by Christians known as neo-evangelicals (Letha Scanzoni and Nancy Hardesty, Virginia R. Mollenkott and Paul K. Jewett). The designation "biblical feminists" has been associated with this group. These authors have raised important issues and have rightfully drawn attention to the significance of women in the church.

The most crucial question the biblical feminists have raised is how to interpret the Bible. Deculturization is a part of the biblical feminists' hermeneutic; they think that since the Bible was written in a patriarchal culture, the biblical writers are prejudiced by that culture against women's rights. Therefore, patriarchal ideas in the Bible are not to be considered authoritative for all times and places. According to this approach, the Bible is fallible and it can contradict itself. In effect, this view exalts human reason, by which man then determines what is and what is not God's authoritative word. It also ignores the fact that *we* are products of *our* culture, which is moving in the direction of complete role interchangeability between the sexes. The question arises whether biblical feminists have been prejudiced by the thoughts and values of our own culture—a culture which is increasingly secularistic in spirit, which is called a post-Christian age by some historians. Are not biblical feminists themselves guilty of culturally determined interpretation? That question and their approach to Scripture will be further discussed in chapters 1–2.

Note: Throughout this book, a distinction is made between biblical feminists and Christian feminists. The latter is the more inclusive term, which includes the more radical feminists, such as Rosemary Ruether, Mary Daly, Dorothee Soelle; they still associate themselves with Christianity, but do not claim to believe in the Bible as God's inspired word. Biblical feminists claim to believe in the inspiration of the Bible, and they claim the Bible as the source for their views.

ONE

CAN WE BELIEVE THE BIBLE?

CAN we believe the Bible? This question may be dismissed by the "scholarly" as too literalistic or by the "sophisticated" as too simplistic. But the answer to this question is basic for considering what the Bible says about women. So we must begin by asking what we think of the Bible. How much of it do we believe? What is the extent of its authority over us?

Biblical feminists, as their name implies, claim that the Bible is the basis of their ideas; they do not deny its inspiration. For instance, Paul K. Jewett writes:

> ... the Spirit of God is the ultimate author of *all* Scripture. The Christian church, therefore, has rightly understood the phrase "the inspiration of Scripture" to indicate that in and through the words employed by the biblical writers God has given his word to mankind.[1]

Jewett affirms that Scripture is inspired. How is it inspired? God gives his word "in and through the words" that appear in the Bible. Thus Jewett allows for some discrepancy between God's eternal word and the words of the biblical writers; the two are not identical.

---

[1] Paul K. Jewett, *Man as Male and Female* (Grand Rapids: Eerdmans, 1975), p. 135.

Jewett clarifies his doctrine of Scripture: ". . . one must recognize
the human as well as the divine quality of Scripture."[2] When Jewett
says "human," he means fallible or subject to "human limitation."
The purity of God's word is discolored by the " 'dark glass' (I Cor.
13:12) of the 'earthen vessels' (II Cor. 4:7) who were the authors of
its content at the human level."[3] Jewett believes female subordination is contrary to the fundamental teaching of Scripture, and yet
Paul teaches it. How do we resolve the problem? According to
Jewett, Paul's human limitations are dominant in the passages that
teach female subordination. In cases of supposed contradiction, such
as the partnership of the sexes versus an hierarchy, Jewett chooses
the passage he judges to be most consistent with the rest of Scripture
(which constitutes the analogy of faith for him).

Though less explicit, Letha Scanzoni and Nancy Hardesty (*All
We're Meant to Be*) agree with Jewett's concept of Scripture. In their
terms, one has to get behind the "letter of the law" in matters that
are culturally conditioned, to the "spirit" of the law. Their intent is
to appeal only to those passages "which are theological and doctrinal
in content"—these constitute the analogy of faith (Jewett) and the
spirit of biblical teachings (Scanzoni and Hardesty). Such passages
govern the interpretation of the incidental references elsewhere
that deal with "practical local cultural problems."[4]

Virginia R. Mollenkott (*Women, Men and the Bible*) maintains
that "the Bible was not in error to record Paul's thought processes,"[5]
but her generous affirmation does not change the fact that, according
to her view, certain Pauline statements are not true and certain
Pauline commands are obsolete.

To summarize, the biblical feminists see irreconcilable contradictions in the Bible's teaching on women. These contradictions are

---

[2]Ibid., p. 134.
[3]Ibid., p. 135.
[4]Letha Scanzoni and Nancy Hardesty, *All We're Meant to Be* (Waco: Word Books, 1975,
c1974), p. 18.
[5]Virginia Mollenkott, "A Challenge to Male Interpretation: Women and the Bible," *The
Sojourners*, 5:2 (February, 1976), 22.

resolved by acknowledging that the Bible reflects human limitations. The culture in biblical times was patriarchal, and the men who wrote the Bible were inextricably influenced by their culture. That is why Paul sometimes places women in a subordinate position. Therefore, the biblical feminists reason, we must remove cultural elements from the Bible to recover God's truth; we must deculturize the Bible.

There are two problems inherent in the biblical feminists' concept of Scripture: (1) Once the possibility of inconsistency or cultural conditioning is admitted, how does one determine what parts or doctrines of Scripture are of abiding authority and value? What parts of Scripture constitute the analogy of faith which is to be the standard? (2) The biblical feminists do not account for the interpreter's human limitations. According to their understanding of the Bible, human reason becomes the judge of what is really God's word and what is not. But human reason is finite and affected by sin. The appearance of contradiction may result from a deficiency in our understanding.

Biblical feminists do not believe that God has given us his word true and trustworthy, the unchanging standard for beliefs and practice. Instead we have a hodgepodge of information (some of it is God's pure word, and some is only man's advice, molded by his male-dominated culture), and God has left us on our own to figure out which parts to obey and believe. Human reason becomes the final authority, the judge of Scripture.

What is at stake in the feminist controversy is the Bible. Mollenkott writes:

> Many biblical feminists fear that if they admit that some of Paul's arguments undergirding female submission reflect his rabbinical training and human limitations, the admission will undercut the authority of scriptures and the doctrine of divine inspiration. Things have come to a bad pass when we have to avoid seeing certain things in scripture (or avoid *admitting* that we see them) in order to preserve our preconceived notions about inspiration.[6]

---

[6]Ibid.

Mollenkott does not respond to the question: Will the idea that Paul's teaching on female subordination results from human limitation undercut the authority and inspiration of the Scriptures? (The answer is yes.) Instead she avoids the question of inspiration by creating doubts about the source of the traditional doctrine of Scripture. She implies that the traditional doctrine is preconceived and forced upon the Bible and that a "scholarly approach to Scripture" will reveal what is inspired and authoritative for all time and what is not.

What the Bible Says about Itself

Is the traditional view of the inspiration and authority of the Bible really preconceived? The traditionalists claim to derive their doctrine of Scripture from Scripture. This approach may seem to be circular and thus self-defeating. It is circular in that it trusts that what the Bible says is true,[7] but it is not self-defeating. On the contrary, it is the only conclusive argument for the authority and infallibility of the Scriptures. If the Bible is God's word, only God can testify to it[8]—in his word and by the internal witness of the Holy Spirit in believers. In addition, all other doctrines of Christianity are derived from the Bible. If we cannot believe what the Bible says about itself, how can we believe what it says about the nature of God, the way of salvation, etc.?

Our method of grounding our faith in the Bible as the word of God should be deductive, not inductive. We do not begin with the

---

[7]There are two corroborating lines of support for the Bible: (1) the characteristics of the Bible, i.e., "the heavenliness of the matter, the efficacy of the doctrine, the majesty of style, the consent of all the parts, the scope of the whole [which is, to give all glory to God], the full discovery it makes of the only way of man's salvation, the many other incomparable excellencies, and the entire perfection thereof" (Westminster Confession, I, v); and (2) the internal testimony of the Holy Spirit, by which the Christian is enabled to recognize the divine origin and nature of the Bible (I Cor. 2:14-15).

[8]"The authority of the Holy Scripture, for which it ought to be believed, and obeyed, dependeth not upon the testimony of any man, or Church; but wholly upon God (who is truth itself) the author thereof: and therefore it is to be received, because it is the Word of God" (Westminster Confession, I, iv).

data or facts of Scripture and try to show that every detail is accurate, true, and consistent. What the Bible says about its own origin and character is the only proper basis for our faith in it.

What does the Bible teach about itself? There are two passages that expressly deal with the nature of Scripture.

(1) All scripture is inspired by God and profitable for teaching, for reproof, for correction, and for training in righteousness, that the man [person] of God may be complete, equipped for every good work (II Tim. 3:16-17).

The word translated "inspired" is literally God-breathed ($\theta\epsilon o\pi\nu\epsilon\nu\sigma\tau o\varsigma$). Scripture is not in any way breathed into by God, nor does God breathe into Scripture's human authors. The idea of II Timothy 3:16 is *not* that the human product is so interpenetrated with God's influence that it can be called the word of God. Rather the idea is that every scripture is breathed *out* by God; they are the result of the creative breath of God.[9] The whole of Scripture is authored by God; Paul makes no distinctions among portions of Scripture. Therefore, all of the Bible is profitable; that is, its teaching is trustworthy and true, even Paul's teaching regarding women.

"Scripture" undoubtedly refers to the Old Testament here. Nonetheless, what Paul says in II Timothy 3:16 applies to the New Testament, even though it probably did not yet exist as a collection. Paul's point concerns the nature of Scripture, all Scripture. So, if the New Testament is Scripture, it is God-breathed and profitable for teaching, reproof, correction, and training in righteousness.

If there are any doubts, parts of the New Testament expressly witness that other parts of the New Testament are Scripture.[10] In defense of Paul, who is a primary target of feminist disrepute, Peter testifies that Paul's letters qualify as Scripture; he says:

So also our beloved brother Paul wrote to you according to the wisdom given him, speaking of this as he does in all his letters. There

---

[9]Benjamin Breckinridge Warfield, *The Inspiration and Authority of the Bible* (Philadelphia: Presbyterian and Reformed Publishing Company, 1948), p. 133.

[10]Luke 10:7 with I Timothy 5:18.

are some things in them hard to understand, which the ignorant and unstable twist to their own destruction, as they do the other scriptures (II Pet. 3:15–16).

The New Testament writers were aware that the Scriptures were being augmented by the Holy Spirit, and the same inspiration and authority that belonged to the Old Testament belong to all the Scriptures.

In II Timothy 3:16 Paul does not tell us about the human authors of the Scriptures or how God breathed out the Scriptures. Peter, on the other hand, is explicit in this area.

(2) First of all you must understand this that no prophecy of scripture is a matter of one's own interpretation, because no prophecy ever came by the impulse of man, but men moved by the Holy Spirit spoke from God (II Pet. 1:20–21).

Peter asserts that no prophecy of Scripture is the result of human initiative, will, determination, investigation, thought processes, or imagination. This verse eliminates *all* human contamination, cultural or individual. However, human agency is recognized. The relationship of human agency and divine authorship is explained in the phrase "men moved by the Holy Spirit spoke from God." What the men spoke was from God because they were borne by the Holy Spirit.[11]

John Murray summarizes II Timothy 3:16–17 and II Peter 1:20–21:

. . . human authorship or instrumentality is fully recognized and yet human agency is not conceived of as in any way impairing the divine origin, character, truth, and authority of Scripture. It is divine in its origin because it is the product of God's creative breath and because it was as borne by the Holy Spirit that men spoke from God. For these reasons it bears an oracular character that accords it an authority as real and divine as if we heard the voice of God speaking from heaven.

---

[11]Edward J. Young, *The Word Is Truth; Some Thoughts on the Biblical Doctrine of Inspiration* (Grand Rapids: Eerdmans, 1957), pp. 65–70; Warfield, p. 155–158. God providentially prepared the authors of Scripture so that they spoke God's words but not through mechanical dictation.

This oracular character is a permanent feature and so Scripture has an abiding stability and application—it is unbreakable and indissoluble.[12]

Christ's Witness to the Old Testament

The "proof" of the inspiration (the God-breathing) and authority of the Bible does not rest on these two passages alone. Though the Old Testament witnesses to its own divine origin and authority,[13] the most powerful and convincing witness to its character is Christ himself.

In a familiar verse, Christ says:

Think not that I have come to abolish the law and the prophets; I have come not to abolish but to fulfill them (Matt. 5:17).

Jesus denotes the Old Testament by the phrase, "the law and the prophets." His assertion that he does not come to annul the Old Testament, including the levitical law with its so-called "patriarchal" bias, is a recognition of its validity and authority. In verse 18 Jesus makes it clear that he means every single word (every jot and tittle) of the law and the prophets, not simply the gist or the broad theological concepts behind the particulars. Such indissolubility could not be attributed to the Old Testament law if it were in any detail fallible, because, if fallible, it would someday come to nothing.[14] Here Christ implies the verbal inspiration (words as well as thoughts) of the Old Testament. Christ's witness to the divine trustworthiness of the Scriptures was constant, detailed, and intimate throughout his ministry.[15]

---

[12]John Murray, "The Attestation of Scripture," in *The Infallible Word: a Symposium* by the members of the faculty of Westminster Seminary (Philadelphia: Presbyterian and Reformed Publishing Co., 1946), p. 33.

[13]Consider the frequent occurrences of "Thus saith the Lord." Malachi 4:4 provides a striking witness to the Mosaic law.

[14]Murray, "Attestation," p. 22.

[15]For example, in Matthew 19:4–5, Christ attributes the authorship of Genesis 2:24, a statement not recorded as a saying of God but simply the word of Scripture, to God. See Murray, "Attestation," p. 27.

Does Christ mean that we should keep all of the Old Testament law? Christ has fulfilled or completed the law in every respect without invalidating it; and in the case of what is usually designated the ceremonial law, he has fulfilled it in such a way that we no longer observe it. Fulfillment rather than abolition of the Old Testament means that its entire contents are profitable to us. Though many of the Old Testament laws were temporary and provisional (cf. Lev. 11:1–23 and Acts 10:9–16), they are of divine origin and had divine authority for the Old Testament era.

The Biblical Feminists and the Old Testament

The attitude of the biblical feminists towards the Old Testament is remarkably different from Christ's. Scanzoni and Hardesty comment on Genesis 1–2:

> On the surface they [Gen. 1 and Gen. 2] are contradictory. So the temptation has been to build one's theology on one and ignore the other. Paul, for example, seldom refers to the first story at all. According to biblical scholarship, the second chapter is older, imbedded in Jewish folklore from more primitive times. Genesis 1 is a more recent account and may be seen as an editorial attempt to counter some of the more anti-feminine and anthropomorphic interpretations which chapter 2 had occasioned. Read as a unit, however, the first three chapters of Genesis seem to answer different questions that people have always pondered. . . .[16]

Scanzoni and Hardesty seem to imply that a profound reading of Genesis 1 and 2 shows that the two chapters are harmonious, and that they should be read as a unit to get the whole picture. However, they do not harmonize the two. They state that "Genesis 1 and 2 vary in the matter of order."[17] They use this "discrepancy" to undermine the significance of the woman's being created after the man.

---

[16]Scanzoni and Hardesty, p. 25.
[17]Ibid., p. 28.

Scanzoni and Hardesty also accept the critical view of the Pentateuch, which sees Genesis 1 and 2 as being two separate traditions, written by different authors or schools.[18] Their language, "imbedded in Jewish folklore from more primitive times," and their association of Genesis 2 with the purely fictional story of Lilith (in their footnote 2) detracts from the credibility of Genesis 2, the account that gives the historical basis for the subordination of the woman to her husband.

Scanzoni's and Hardesty's critical view of Scripture extends to Paul and his interpretation of Genesis 2. They consider Paul an example of tempting but faulty theology, which is based only on half of the story, only on Genesis 2, because he seldom refers to Genesis 1 (see quotation above, number 16). In I Corinthians 11:8-9, Paul, according to Scanzoni and Hardesty, makes a "theological leap" to "woman's subordination" that is "a traditional rabbinic (and one might add 'Christian') understanding that is not supported by the text."[19] However, the text does support Paul's argument; he bases it on the fact that the woman was created after, from, and for the sake of the man.

Mollenkott concedes:

> It is of course possible to harmonize Genesis 1 and 2 by seeing the second chapter as a symbolic and poetic expansion on the first, while viewing the first account as authoritative concerning the simultaneous creation of Adam and Eve—but if we do that, then Paul's argument falls flat.[20]

---

[18]Jesus regards Genesis 1-2 as a unity (Matt. 19:1-6) with God as the author. For a detailed defense of the unity of the Pentateuch, see Oswald T. Allis, *The Five Books of Moses* (Nutley, N.J.: Presbyterian and Reformed Published Co., 1949). No attempt is made to discount the historical processes by which Scripture is recorded, such as the possible use of sources by Moses in the writing of Genesis. However, Allis points out basic problems with the approach of the documentary hypothesis. (1) It denies the unity and harmony of God's word. It seizes upon slight variations of diction, style, point of view, and subject matter as indicative of difference in author, date, and source. Often these differences are magnified into contradictions, which are impossible if the Bible is God's word. (2) This method minimizes or rejects the supernaturalism of biblical history and attempts to reconstruct it in terms of natural evolution. The miraculous elements are considered suspect and indicative of an unreliable passage.
[19]Scanzoni and Hardesty, p. 28.
[20]Mollenkott, "Challenge," p. 22; cf. Virginia Ramey Mollenkott, *Women, Men, and the*

Mollenkott does not take Genesis 2 "literally." She does not say what she means by symbolic and poetic (most probably she means non-historical, not factual), and she does not say what makes Genesis symbolic and poetic. But she obviously rejects its teaching that God created the man before the woman. So a real contradiction between Genesis 1 and Genesis 2 exists in her thinking.

The biblical feminists criticize the Old Testament and question its authority. In contrast, Jesus believed the Old Testament to be completely reliable. Yet, some biblical feminists cite Jesus' behavior in Matthew 19:3-9 as justification for their deculturization of the Bible.

> And the Pharisees came up to him and tested him by asking, "Is it lawful to divorce one's wife for any cause?" He answered, "Have you not read that he who made them from the beginning made them male and female, and said, 'For this reason a man shall leave his father and mother and be joined to his wife, and the two shall become one'? So they are no longer two but one. What therefore God has joined together, let no man put asunder." They said to him, "Why then did Moses command one to give a certificate of divorce, and to put her away?" He said to them, "For your hardness of heart Moses allowed you to divorce your wives, but from the beginning it was not so. And I say to you: whoever divorces his wife, except for unchastity, and marries another, commits adultery" (Matt. 19:3-9).

Bible (Nashville: Abingdon, c1977), p. 101-102. A better case can be made for the opposite view, that Genesis 1 is the poetic version of creation. Genesis 1 is a stylized, schematic presentation ("And God said . . ."); it has "a poetic quality reflected in the strophic structure" (Meredith Kline, 'Genesis," in *The New Bible Commentary: Revised,* edited by D. Guthrie *et al* [Downers Grove: InterVarsity Press, c1970], p. 82). Genesis 2 is more descriptive, even journalistic, more detailed (it includes geography, vv. 10-14), and less majestic than Genesis 1. In addition, Genesis 2 is introduced by the formula, "These are the generations of . . . ," a formula which determines the structure of the whole book of Genesis (5:1ff.; 10:1ff.; 11:10ff.; 25:12ff.; 36:1ff.). "The placing of the entire Genesis narrative in this genealogical framework is a clear sign that the author intended the account to be understood throughout as a real life history of individual men, begotten and begetting" (ibid., p. 80); and this includes Adam and Eve. However, no case can be made for the symbolic or mythological character of Genesis 1 in correlation to its poetry, as Mollenkott suggests for Genesis 2. Genesis 1 is not a scientific textbook; but where it touches on science, it is accurate, and its language is that of simple observation of reality.

The feminist reasoning is this: Jesus pitted his teaching against the Mosaic law (Deut. 24:1–4), so why can't we?[21] Even if Jesus did annul a Mosaic law, it does not follow that we can. We are not Jesus, whose judgment and knowledge are righteous and perfect; we, limited and sinful, should not presume to put our reasoning above God's revelation in the Bible. But Jesus does not contradict the Old Testament at this point. As in Matthew 5:21–48, Jesus is teaching the true meaning of the law. He points out that divorce was prohibited from the beginning and quotes Genesis 2:24 as proof.

The Pharisees, consciously or unconsciously, twist the meaning of the law in the wording of their question; Moses did not command divorce in certain cases. The law the Pharisees have in mind is Deuteronomy 24:4. Some translations seem to indicate that divorce was mandatory in cases of "indecency" in a woman. However, the concern of the law is to prevent remarriage in the case that the wife has married another man in the mean time and then become free again; the more profound concern of Deuteronomy 24:4 is to discourage divorce. Verses 1–3 establish the situation (form the protasis) and verse 4 gives the command (forms the apodosis).[22] This law presupposes divorce has taken place and regulates what happens after that. The passage does not make divorce mandatory in any case; in fact, it discourages divorce (see p. 76). God's command controls a sinful practice without sanctioning it.

Jesus corrects the Pharisees' interpretation of the law. Moses *allowed* divorce, and Jesus tells them why—for their hardness of heart, or because of their depraved nature. Jesus' point is that humanity's fallen condition necessitated divorce legislation which would have been irrelevant before the fall. Deuteronomy 24:1–4 does not contradict Genesis 2:24; rather it "provided direction for just requittal when God's commandments were violated."[23] According to William Hendriksen:

---

[21]Jewett, p. 137; Mollenkott, *Women,* p. 119.

[22]John Murray, *Divorce* (Philadelphia: Presbyterian and Reformed Publishing Co., 1972), pp. 3–7.

[23]Greg L. Bahnsen, *Theonomy in Christian Ethics* (Nutley, N.J.: Craig Press, 1977), p. 103.

> Here, by means of a few simple words, Jesus discourages divorce, refutes the rabbinical misinterpretation of the law, reaffirms the law's true meaning (cf. Matt. 5:17, 18), censures the guilty party, defends the innocent, and through it all, upholds the sacredness and inviolability of the marriage bond as ordained by God.[24]

If we follow our Lord's lead, we will regard the Old Testament as God's inspired word and treat it accordingly.

The Attitude Toward Scripture in the New Testament

The New Testament writers regarded the Scriptures in the same way Jesus did. They justified the message they preached in every detail by appealing to the Scriptures (I Cor. 15:3–5; cf. Acts 8:35; 17:2–3; 26:22–23). The significance of events is found in the Scriptures (Rom. 8:36; 9:33; 11:8; Acts 1:16–17). The words of the Scriptures are undoubtedly considered God's (Heb. 1:1).[25]

How do we know that the New Testament has such authority? The New Testament writers considered one another's writing as Scripture. They also considered their own work divinely authoritative.[26] Consider how Paul viewed his own ministry when questioned by the Corinthians (II Cor. 2:17; 3:5b–6a). He stated that the form and content of his teaching were from the Holy Spirit.

> And we impart this in words not taught by human wisdom but taught by the Spirit, interpreting spiritual truths in spiritual language (I Cor. 2:13).

At one point (I Cor. 7:12), Paul seems to be distinguishing between the authoritative teaching of Christ and his own, as some suppose, nonauthoritative, uninspired opinion on marriage and separation. This verse has been appropriated by those who deny the

---

[24]William Hendriksen, *New Testament Commentary: Exposition of the Gospel According to Matthew* (Grand Rapids: Baker Book House, 1973), p. 306.

[25]Warfield, pp. 145–147.

[26]For a full treatment of the authority of the New Testament, see N. B. Stonehouse, "The Authority of the New Testament" in *The Infallible Word*, p. 92–140.

inspired, authoritative teaching of Paul as proof of their position. Paul emphatically declares, "To the rest, I say, not the Lord . . ." in contrast to verse 10, in which he says, "not I but the Lord." It is certain that Paul is making a distinction, but it is not between inspired and uninspired commands. Such a distinction would contradict his own view of his apostolic authority (as exemplified in v. 17: "So I command all the churches"). The distinction is between what Christ explicitly taught during his earthly ministry and what he did not explicitly state. In verses 12–16 Paul is dealing with a case on which Jesus did not give a ruling. He regulates this case as one "who by the Lord's mercy is trustworthy" (v. 25) and who has the Spirit of God (v. 40). There is no distinction between the binding character of the commands in verses 10–11 and verses 12–16. Paul is just as emphatic and mandatory in language and terms in the second instance as the first, because he knows he speaks God's word.[27]

In summary, the Bible as a whole and in parts witnesses to its own inspiration and consequent authority and inerrancy. Its thoughts and words are God's.

An Historical Note

Until the eighteenth century (when the Age of Enlightenment exalted human reason above God's word and made man's mind the ultimate judge instead of the almighty creator and sustainer of the universe), the church universal considered the Bible the authoritative and inerrant word of God.[28]

In the nineteenth century, the Bible was a target for attack by the first feminist movement. Their hermeneutic was not so sophisticated as the present day biblical feminist's, but they held some of the same ideas: the customs of one group or age should not be imposed on all; there are contradictions in the Bible; the levitical legislation

---

[27]Murray, "Attestation," p. 38.

[28]See Warfield, chapter 2; Harold Lindsell, *The Battle for the Bible* (Grand Rapids: Eerdmans, 1975), chapter 3.

is not inspired; God may be addressed as Mother as well as Father. But the nineteenth century feminists' doctrine of Scripture was more consistent. They made no pretensions about their opinion of the Bible. ". . . We have made a fetich of the Bible long enough. The time has come to read it as we do all other books, accepting the good and rejecting the evil it teaches."[29] It was not considered inspired or authoritative. Like any other book, it was to be judged on its own merits, by human reason. So the nineteenth century feminists rewrote the Bible to make women equal to men. In a similar manner, today's biblical feminists use human reason to pick which parts of the Bible are authoritative for all times and which parts are culturally determined.

The Woman's Bible (1895, 1898) denied that Jesus is God ("He commands far more love and reverence as a true man with only human possibilities, than as a God . . .").[30] Biblical feminists, in contrast, believe in Jesus as God, Lord, and Savior. As a result, their teaching that Scripture is not inerrant has more influence and is more easily accepted by Christians than the ideas of the original feminists were.

In this century, there has been a movement in the evangelical community (organizations and denominations that believe the Bible to be the word of God) towards a view of limited inerrancy; in other words, there are those who believe that the Bible is the word of God and that it is infallible in matters of faith and practice but not necessarily in matters of science, geography, and history.[31] The biblical feminists have taken one step further away from the biblical concept of the trustworthy Scriptures. They maintain that the Bible is defective concerning at least one matter of faith and practice. The Bible is defective when it says, "The husband is the head of the wife as Christ is the head of the church . . ." (Eph. 5:23) and "I permit no woman to teach or to have authority over men; she is to keep silent"

---

[29]Elizabeth Cady Stanton, *The Original Feminist Attack on the Bible (the Woman's Bible)*, part 2 (New York: Arno Press, 1974), p. 8.

[30]Ibid., p. 117.

[31]This position is not tenable. See Lindsell, p. 113.

(I Tim. 2:12). John Alexander, who is sympathetic to the biblical feminists, writes:

> The central issue about the Bible is whether we live it. . . . Theories of inspiration are nothing compared to obedience. . . .[32]

Such a statement sounds noble, but in light of the biblical feminists' view of the Bible, it is impossible to know what to obey, at least in the area of male-female relationships. A correct doctrine of inspiration is essential, so that we may know what to believe and what to obey.

The Consequences of Errancy

The biblical feminists have abandoned the biblical and historic position of the God-breathed, inerrant Scriptures. What are some of the consequences of this incorrect doctrine of Scripture? If we cannot rely on what the Bible says about itself, the basis for all other doctrines is undercut. How can we know whether or not Paul's firm belief in the resurrection is merely the result of his pharisaical indoctrination against the Sadducees' denial of resurrection?

Murray explains:

> If human fallibility precludes an infallible Scripture, then by relentless logic it must be maintained that we cannot have any Scripture that is infallible and inerrant. All of Scripture comes to us through human instrumentality. If such instrumentality involves fallibility, then such fallibility must attach to the whole of Scripture. For by what warrant can an immunity from error be maintained in the matter of "spiritual content" and not in the matter of historical or scientific fact? Is human fallibility suspended when "spiritual truth" is asserted but not suspended in other less important matters?[33]

If God is able to convey theological truth through human agency without error, he is able to convey truth in all other areas through

---

[32]John F. Alexander, "Some Incoherent Thoughts on Scripture," *The Other Side,* 12:3 (May–June, 1976), 9.
[33]Murray, "Attestation," pp. 4–5.

human agency as well. And if he cannot convey truth through human agency in "non-theological" areas, he cannot in theological areas.

To introduce the possibility of error or of cultural conditioning, as the biblical feminists would say, in matters of doctrine and life means that all biblical teaching must come under scrutiny. The burden of infallibility then falls on our shoulders (and the shoulders of generations to come); we must make infallible decisions on what parts of the Bible are God's word and what parts are only man's. We become the final authority. If fallible human authors have given us a fallible Bible, how can we, who are surely fallible, detect what is true and what is false (culturally determined and irrelevant to us)? With the biblical feminists' concept of the Bible, there is no end to subjectivity.

A faulty conception of Scriptures produces apostasy. This is the opinion of Harold Lindsell. He writes:

> It is my opinion that it is next to impossible to stop the process of theological deterioration once inerrancy is abandoned. . . . I am saying that whether it takes five or fifty years any denomination or parachurch group that forsakes inerrancy will end up shipwrecked. It is impossible to prevent the surrender of other important doctrinal teachings of the word of God when inerrancy is gone.[34]

History supports Lindsell's contention; the Unitarian Universalist denomination and the first feminist movement with its doctrine of Christ as only a man are prime examples.

The Bible states that it is God's word, trustworthy and true. It can be relied upon and believed in every detail. To concede that it contains error, whether that be of science or history or a contradiction resulting from the culturally determined opinions of one of its human authors, leads to serious consequences. It produces uncertainty and doubts about the other doctrines of the faith and about the character of God. A doctrine of Scripture that admits error eventually results in apostasy or heresy. The first feminist movement is a vivid

---

[34]Lindsell, pp. 142–143; cf. pp. 159–160; Warfield, p. 181.

illustration of this departure from the truth. It is significant that the first woman minister, Antoinette Brown Blackwell, ordained in 1853 in a congregationalist church, "gave up her ordination because of her increasing theological liberalism."[35]

---

[35]Gayle Graham Yates, *What Women Want: The Ideas of the Movement* (Cambridge: Harvard University Press, 1975), p. 29.

TWO

HOW TO INTERPRET THE BIBLE

NOW that we have established the nature of the Scriptures (God-breathed), we can consider how to interpret them—the problem of hermeneutics.

The Bible shares some principles of interpretation with other literature.

(1) The literary context, including an understanding of the idioms and structure of the biblical languages and a recognition of to which literary genre a passage belongs, must be considered. For instance, we know from the context that God's command to Hosea ("Go, take to yourself a wife of harlotry . . . ," 1:2) applies only to Hosea and not to all Christians. In other words, the Bible should be interpreted in the sense intended by the authors. Poetry is to be interpreted as poetry, prose as prose. Figures of speech and metaphorical and symbolic expressions must be acknowledged. The aim of exegesis is to discover the meaning the Holy Spirit intended to convey.

Such an evaluation of the context forestalls the criticism Scanzoni and Hardesty level against those who take the Bible "literally," those who say the Bible means what it says.[1] The Bible does mean

---

[1] Scanzoni and Hardesty, p. 19.

what it says, but to determine "what it says," one must understand its verbal context. To assert "Scripture means what it says" counters interpretations that make a passage say the opposite of what it means, such as Karl Barth's exposition of Ephesians 5:21-33. Though he believes the woman is subordinate to the man, Barth so qualifies the subordination of the woman and the position of her husband as head that it is hard to tell the difference in roles. Jewett describes Barth's view:

> The man's preeminence is such as involves his humiliation; the wife's relation to her husband is such that she is really greater than he, not second but first; the headship of the man as leader finds its meaning in the mutual subordination expected of all who are in Christ.[2]

Biblical feminists carry Barth's reasoning further: they say there is no difference between the husband's and the wife's roles. There is total reversibility. The meaning of Ephesians 5:21 is taken out of context, and the result is that the rest of the passage loses its natural meaning.

The consideration of the verbal or literary context has special application for Scripture because the very words are inspired by God, so that careful attention must be paid to the choice of words, the grammar, etc.

(2) Knowledge of the situation, historical and geographical, aids in understanding the text. The biblical narrative covers centuries during which great changes occurred. For example, an understanding of the historical background illuminates the biblical text describing the arrest and trial of Christ. The Sanhedrin was unable to execute the death sentence legally under Roman dominion, so that the Jews were forced to bring Jesus before the Roman governor to secure Christ's legal execution.

This second principle is not to be misused (as the biblical feminists have misused it) in order to free ourselves from biblical commands. Knowledge of the cultural situation does not legitimize deculturization

---

[2] Jewett, p. 83.

of the biblical text. The biblical culture was patriarchal, and the Bible contains commands for wives to submit to their husbands. This concurrence does not automatically make the biblical commands suspect as mere products of the culture.

There are also special rules of interpretation that apply only to the Bible because it is the inspired and authoritative word of God.

(1) The Bible is to be interpreted under the guidance of the Holy Spirit (I Cor. 2:14). The unregenerate mind cannot understand God's truth. His disposition is opposed to God. He who is indwelt by the Holy Spirit has the mind of Christ (I Cor. 2:16), but even he must humbly and prayerfully seek the Holy Spirit's guidance in the interpretation of Scripture.

(2) The Bible, though written over a long period of time by many individuals, is a unity, because God is its author. The unifying principle is Jesus Christ (Luke 24:27; II Cor. 1:20; I Pet. 1:10–12). Another way to designate the unity of the Bible is by the term "redemptive-historical." This term expresses both the focus on Christ and the progressive nature of biblical revelation. The Bible records the history of redemption, of God's redemptive acts and his explanation of them, in his word. It is a process that culminates in Christ.

> In many and various ways God spoke of old to our fathers by the prophets; but in these last days he has spoken to us by a Son . . . (Heb. 1:1).

The progressive nature of biblical revelation accounts for the preparatory (typological and symbolic), externalized character of the Old Testament and the real difference Christ's coming made in the lives of God's people, i.e., the Holy Spirit's permanent residence in each believer (John 14:17; I Cor. 6:19) and the consequent internalized emphasis of the New Testament (Matt. 15:11, 17–20; Heb. 9–10).

The biblical feminists do not comprehend this principle. Consequently, their approach to the Old Testament is critical, as noted earlier. They also deny the unity of the Bible when they pit Paul against Jesus, as many feminists do. For example, Arlene Swidler writes:

> But what impressed us most is the fact that in none of these passages
> [I Cor. 11:7-16; 14:26-35; I Tim. 2:9-15], nor in any dealing with
> the male-dominated family structure, is there any reference to the
> teachings and practice of Jesus.[3]

The implication is that Jesus would not have gone along with Paul's
commands to women. The feminists want Jesus on their side and
blame Paul, or more precisely Paul's rabbinic indoctrination, for his
alleged discrimination against women.

Another indication that the biblical feminists do not comprehend
the redemptive-historical nature of revelation is that they apparently
do not accept the New Testament as the culmination and end of
God's revelation to his people. They want to do for it what the New
Testament did for the Old Testament. They want to point out its
temporary provisions, its concessions to a culture that no longer
exists.

The more radical Christian feminists (not included in the term
"biblical feminists") and the nineteenth century feminists have a
better understanding of the unity of the Bible than the biblical
feminists. They realize that if you change one biblical doctrine,
changes must occur in other doctrines. If you exchange the sexual
hierarchy for equal partnership, changes in the basic Christian
doctrines will follow. For example, Mary Daly quotes Elizabeth
Cady Stanton and then continues Stanton's reasoning:

> "Take the snake, the fruit-tree and the woman from the tableaux, and
> we have no fall, nor frowning Judge, no Inferno, no everlasting
> punishment—hence no need of a Savior. Thus the bottom falls out of
> the whole Christian theology. Here is the reason why in all Biblical
> researches and higher criticisms, the scholars never touch the position
> of women." The distortion in Christian ideology resulting from and
> confirming sexual hierarchy is manifested not only in the doctrines
> of God and of the Fall but also in doctrines concerning Jesus. A great
> deal of Christian doctrine has been docetic, that is, it has not seriously
> accepted the fact that Jesus was a limited human being.

As the idolatry and the dehumanizing effects of reifying and

---

[3]Arlene Swidler, *Woman in a Man's Church* (New York: Paulist Press, 1972), p. 36.

therefore limiting "God" become more manifest in women's expanded consciousness, it will become less plausible to think of Jesus as the "Second Person of the Trinity" who "assumed" a human nature in a unique "hypostatic union." Indeed it is logical that the prevalent emphasis upon the total uniqueness and supereminence of Jesus will become less meaningful.[4]

For Daly, sexual equality leads to beyond God as the Father, to the humanity without divinity of Jesus, to a religion far removed from true Christianity.

(3) A corollary of the unity of the Bible is the principle that Scripture does not contradict Scripture. For instance, Paul says, "For by grace you have been saved through faith; and this is not your own doing, it is the gift of God—not because of works, lest any man should boast" (Eph. 2:8-9); and James says, "You see that a man is justified by works and not by faith alone" (James 2:24). To some, these two verses seem to contradict one another—to such a degree that Luther was inclined to exclude James from the New Testament canon. However, we know that the Scriptures agree with one another because God is their author. In the case of faith and works and in other cases where apparent contradictions exist (such as I Cor. 11:3-16 and I Cor. 14:34-35), further study has produced solutions.[5]

Many biblical feminists frankly disregard this principle because of their incorrect concept of Scripture. Their understanding of the Bible includes the possibility of contradiction. Jewett illustrates this:

Because these two perspectives [in Paul]—the Jewish and the Christian—are incompatible, there is no satisfying way to harmonize the Pauline argument for female subordination with the larger Christian vision of which the great apostle to the Gentiles was himself the primary architect.[6]

---

[4]Mary Daly, *Beyond God the Father; Toward a Philosophy of Women's Liberation* (Boston: Beacon Press, 1973), pp. 69-70.

[5]Paul does not ignore good works, as Ephesians 2:10 illustrates. Both James and Paul would agree that one cannot be saved by good works and that only through faith in Christ is one saved but that saving faith necessarily produces good works. James' point is that one who says he has faith but produces no good works does not have faith (2:14, 17-18), whereas Paul is concerned about persons who try to earn their own salvation through works.

[6]Jewett, pp. 112-113.

To repeat, Scripture cannot contradict Scripture; therefore, Scripture must explain Scripture. Because the Scriptures agree, no verse or passage is to be understood in isolation from the rest of Scripture. This rule of interpretation is called the analogy of Scripture or the analogy of faith.

Jewett explicitly refers to this principle:

> To put matters theologically, or perhaps we should say hermeneutically, the problem with the concept of female subordination is that it *breaks the analogy of faith*. The basic creation narratives imply the equality of male and female as a human fellowship reflecting the fellowship in the Godhead; and Jesus, as the perfect man who is truly in the image of God, taught such equality in his fellowship with women so that one may say—must say—that "in Christ there is no male and female."[7]

Jewett himself breaks the analogy of faith by setting Scripture against Scripture. Apparent contradictions (antinomies) in Scripture are to be resolved by a proper understanding of both sides, as in the case of Paul and James on faith and works. However, Jewett admits that a proper understanding of Paul includes his belief in the subordination of women. Jewett's answer is to consider that teaching "human" and nonauthoritative, an expression of Paul's cultural conditioning. It is therefore to be disregarded. To use the analogy of faith correctly, one should use Scripture to interpret Scripture so that seeming contradictions are harmonized, rather than excluding one side from deliberation and from authority over us.

Essentially, Scanzoni and Hardesty have the same approach as Jewett. They designate certain passages to be the norm by which other passages are to be judged; if the other passages do not say the same thing, they are considered culturally conditioned and therefore not binding. They speak of following the spirit (equivalent to Jewett's analogy of faith) rather than the letter of the law; in their opinion the letter and the spirit do not agree. "By theology, then, we mean an attempt to go behind the letter to the spirit of biblical

---

[7]Ibid., p. 134.

teachings."[8] This statement is based on a misunderstanding of II Corinthians 3:6: "for the letter killeth, but the spirit giveth life" (KJV), which is one of the most misused sentences in the entire Bible. J. Gresham Machen's comment on it applies to Scanzoni's and Hardesty's use of it and the biblical feminists' hermeneutic in general.

> [II Corinthians 3:6 is] constantly interpreted to mean that we are perfectly justified in taking the law of God with a grain of salt; they [the words] are held to indicate that Paul was no "literalist," but a "Liberal," who believed that the Old Testament was not true in detail and the Old Testament law was not valid in detail, but that all God requires is that we should extract the few great principles which the Bible teaches and not insist upon the rest. In short, the words are held to involve a contrast between the letter of the law and "the spirit of the law"; they are held to mean that literalism is deadly, while attention to great principles keeps a man intellectually and spiritually alive.
>
> Thus has one of the greatest utterances in the New Testament been reduced to comparative triviality—a triviality with a kernel of truth in it, to be sure, but triviality all the same. The triviality, indeed, is merely relative; no doubt it is important to observe that attention to the general sense of a book or a law is far better than such a rendering of details as that the context in which the details are found is ignored. But all that is quite foreign to the meaning of the Apostle in this passage, and is, though quite true and quite important in its place, trivial in comparison with the tremendous thing that Paul is here endeavoring to say.
>
> What Paul is really doing here is not contrasting the letter of the law with the spirit of the law, but contrasting the law of God with the Spirit of God. When he says, "The letter killeth," he is making no contemptuous reference to a pedantic literalism which shrivels the soul; but he is setting forth the terrible majesty of God's law. The letter, the "thing written," in the law of God, says Paul, pronounces a dread sentence of death upon the transgressor; but the Holy Spirit of God, as distinguished from the law, gives life.[9]

---

[8]Scanzoni and Hardesty, p. 19.
[9]J. Gresham Machen, *What Is Faith?* (Grand Rapids: Eerdmans, 1925), pp. 187–189.

Machen repeats:

> . . . He [Paul] does not mean "the spirit of the law" as contrasted
> with the letter; he certainly does not mean the lax interpretation of
> God's commands which is dictated by human lust or pride. . . .[10]

Paul's contrast is not between a ceremonial or external religion and
an internal or "spiritual" religion, but between a religion of merit
that means death and a religion of grace that means life.

Biblical feminists do take God's word with a grain of salt when
they attempt to deculturize it. They extract a few principles and say
the rest is invalid because it is only the result of social conditioning.
They set Scripture against Scripture, rather than allowing Scripture
to interpret Scripture. II Corinthians 3:6 does not permit a hermeneutic that upholds the general idea, the theology or doctrine, the
general thrust of the Bible or the analogy of faith as Jewett defines it,
at the expense of the details or practice. Such a hermeneutic denies
what Scripture says about itself; all of Scripture is profitable and
God-breathed. Since God is its author, all of Scripture works together
to present God's truth to us. Any general idea or thrust that does not
allow room for the particulars of Scripture is not valid.

The Biblical Feminists' Hermeneutic

> Because patriarchy is the cultural background of the scriptures, it is
> absolutely basic to any feminist reading of the Bible that *one cannot
> absolutize the culture in which the Bible was written.* We must make
> careful distinctions between what is "for an age" and what is for all
> time. We cannot assume that because the Bible was written against
> the backdrop of a patriarchal social structure, patriarchy is the will of
> God for all people in all times.[11]

Mollenkott's statement is a good summary of the feminist approach
to the Bible. Her statement also suggests that God is not consistent

---

[10]Ibid., p. 190.
[11]Mollenkott, "Challenge," p. 21.

(patriarchy was his will only some of the time, when the Bible was being written); her God is not sovereign or all-powerful (he could not speak without cultural contamination or pick the best time for Christ's coming, when the culture would better reflect his ultimate will, such as now when women have almost gained "equality").

It is true that "one cannot absolutize the culture in which the Bible was written," if by culture, one means that which is only cultural as opposed to that which is commanded by God in his word as well as reflected in the biblical culture. For instance, Christians have no obligation to wear sandals or tend sheep just because such things were done in Christ's day. However, the biblical feminists mean more than this when they employ the hermeneutic of deculturization (or de-absolutization of the biblical culture). Regardless of how the Bible presents a subject, even if it is directly commanded, it could be the result of cultural contamination if it also appears in the biblical culture, according to the biblical feminist. This concept of deculturization is possible only in conjunction with an incorrect doctrine of Scripture.

The biblical feminists try to support their hermeneutic by appealing to cases in which "deculturization" has already been accomplished, namely monarchy and slavery. Monarchy is a good example of an institution present in Scripture as a cultural, historical and perhaps typical phenomenon, but not as the fulfillment of God's command or revealed will. A good part of the Old Testament deals with kings, but monarchy is not commanded in Scripture. In fact, part of the reason the Israelites asked for a king was the result of cultural contamination; the Israelites wanted to have a king *like the other nations* (I Sam. 8:5). God said that the Israelites' desire for a king was a rejection of *his* kingship over them (I Sam. 8:7–9), and the consequences of demanding a king were disastrous for national Israel, as the Lord warned in verse 9. In a sense, God's allowing Israel to have a king is judgment for their rejecting God as their king. Though *all* governing authorities (kings, presidents, prime ministers) rule by God's appointment (Rom. 13:1–2), it is not true that "most biblical authors assumed that . . . absolute monarchy was the divinely ordained form of government as long as direct national obedience to God was not possible."[12] Monarchy is not commanded in the Scriptures. Though it illustrates the absolute sovereignty and glory of God's rule, the Bible does not present monarchy as God's will for nations. The only absolute monarchy ordained for all times is God's kingdom. In contrast, the wife's submission to her husband and the woman's subordination in the church are commanded in the Bible. It should be noted that the biblical injunctions are not concessions to patriarchy with its potential for domination and abuse. The biblical concepts of marriage and church government forbid misuse of authority; the one in authority is to perform his role with love, humility, and a desire to serve.

Slavery is a more difficult and complicated case. One observation must be made at the beginning. The issues of slavery and racism should not be confused. Slavery in biblical times was not limited to one race of people, nor was race the basis for slavery. The relationship of Simon Legree and Uncle Tom is not the paradigm for slavery in biblical times.

Biblical feminists make two assumptions: (1) although slavery is not openly condemned in the New Testament, the New Testament implies that the institution of slavery is intrinsically evil; and (2) as New Testament principles work themselves out, their logical consequences, including the abolition of slavery, are effected. The feminists consider the headship of the husband analogous to slavery; both were firmly entrenched in first century culture, and both are contrary to God's will. Since Paul could not overturn the whole social order, he cautiously mentioned principles that would eventually abolish these institutions, as the Christian vision is implemented in society. Jewett adds that Paul's vision was less clear concerning slavery than Jew-Gentile relations and even less clear concerning husband and wife.[13]

Both of the above feminist assumptions can be challenged. Is slavery intrinsically evil? John Murray responds:

---

[12]Mollenkott, *Women*, p. 92.
[13]Jewett, pp. 144–145.

If the institution is the moral evil it is alleged to be by abolitionists, if it is essentially a violation of basic human right and liberty, if slave-holding is the monstrosity claimed, it is, to say the least, very strange that the apostles who were so directly concerned with these evils did not overtly condemn the institution and require slaveholders to practice emancipation. . . . It seems hardly enough to say that the New Testament quietly establishes principles which would in due time expose the iniquity of the institution and by their irresistible force stamp it out. If it is the evil it is stated to be, we should expect more. The apostles were not governed by that kind of expediency; they openly assailed the institutions of paganism that were antithetical to the faith and morals of Christianity. What could be more outright and severe than the denunciation quoted above, 'Go to now, ye rich, weep and howl for your miseries that are coming upon you' (James 5:1). And without doubt, the economics of that day were to a large extent bound up with the evils that were the occasion for such denunciation. The apostles were not afraid to upset an economic *status quo* when it violated the fundamental demands of equity.[14]

If slavery is wrong, why didn't someone—Jesus or the apostles—say so? Instead of condemnation of slavery *per se,* in the New Testament we find the clear denunciation of the abuses resulting from and associated with slavery. A distinction should be made between the institution itself and the abuses associated with it; denunciation of the abuses related to slavery does not concern the legitimacy of slavery itself.

One of the misuses of slavery is to consider the slave the property of the owner in the sense that the slave is treated as a thing rather than a person. However, slavery should be defined as "the property of man in the *labour* of another."[15] This definition of slavery relieves the institution of the horrors usually connected with it. There are cases in which ownership in the labor of another would be beneficial. For instance, if one person became greatly indebted to another, wouldn't it be better for the debtor to owe his creditor his labor until the debt is paid rather than go to prison or lose his home?

---

[14]John Murray, *Principles of Conduct* (Grand Rapids: Eerdmans, 1957), pp. 94–95.

The Old Testament regulations on slavery state that a Hebrew slave must be freed after six years (Deut. 15:12). But the regulations also include a provision for the slave's desire to remain with his master (Deut. 15:16–17), because he loves his master and fares well there. When the institution is not misused, it may be desired above freedom. When slavery is voluntarily chosen, it seems inappropriate to label it an inhuman monstrosity *per se.*

Both Old and New Testaments condemn the abuses of slavery. "Whoever steals a man, whether he sells him or is found in possession of him, shall be put to death" (Exod. 21:16). This law alone censures the entire practice of Negro slave trade. When the New Testament says, "Masters, treat your slaves justly and fairly . . ." (Col. 4:1), it attacks the root of the evils connected with slavery. What Paul means is that slaves, bond and free, are to be properly compensated for their work. The principle involved is "The laborer is worthy of his hire" (Luke 10:7; I Tim. 5:18).

The biblical feminists claim that Paul wants masters to treat slaves more nearly as equals.[16] What does treating another as an equal mean? Basically, it means treating someone as you wish to be treated. It is the golden rule. It means treating someone kindly and respectfully. Undoubtedly, Paul desired masters to treat slaves kindly and respectfully, or as we would say today, to treat them as *persons.* Scanzoni and Hardesty state the feminist approach to slavery more explicitly:

> Once Christian masters would begin viewing slaves as persons valuable in God's sight and as fellow members of Christ's family, an atmosphere would be created for recognizing an *equality* of personhood and rights.[17]

The equality of personhood is what we were just discussing. Equality of personhood is a contemporary term that covers such biblical ideas as that all persons bear the image of God, all have sinned, the way of salvation is the same for all, and all who believe are children of God and heirs with Christ. Paul reminds masters that they stand in the

[16]Mollenkott, "Challenge," p. 21.
[17]Scanzoni and Hardesty, p. 107.

same relationship to God as their slaves (Eph. 6:9) and so ought to treat their slaves well. The command to "in humility count others better than yourselves" (Phil. 2:3) applies to Christian masters as well as anyone else. And a recognition of equality of personhood is to manifest itself in action (cf. James 2:1–9).

However, "equality of rights" is another question. There is little emphasis on obtaining rights in the Bible. The biblical direction is always the fulfillment of your obligation, not the assurance of your rights. Equality of personhood does not necessarily imply the equality of rights. One can be equal to one in one respect and not equal in others. Masters and slaves could be Christian brothers and love each other accordingly; but the master has the right to obedience from the slave, and the slave has the right to appropriate and just compensation for his services. Perhaps the right of the master and the right of the slave are "equal," but they are different. The authority structure can exist in harmony with the Christian principle of loving your neighbor as yourself or acting in accordance with equality of personhood as defined above. In short, it would be possible for the institution of slavery to exist in accord with the Christian ethic, if the biblical commands concerning it were obeyed. And slavery is not dead today. Many employer/employee relations (consider the army) can be seen as a form of legitimate slavery.

Although the Bible does not renounce slavery or state that it should be abolished, the Bible does not insist on the continuation of slavery. There is no "There shalt be slavery." Jewett remarks, "it is impossible to suppose that slavery is an ordinance of God manifesting his will for the Man-to-Man relationship."[18] That is true. God did not ordain slavery as a permanent institution; the Bible regulates a man-made institution, which, since invented by man, could be removed by man. Possibly, the temptation to abuse slavery was too great for that institution to continue. Certainly, in the case of American slavery of blacks, the only way to remove the injustices and atrocities was to destroy the institution of slavery.

---

[18]Jewett, p. 139.

In the case of slavery, deculturization or de-absolutizing the biblical culture is not the hermeneutic employed. Slavery is not commanded by God; it is only regulated by God. In that sense, its existence was never an absolute, whose abolition needed biblical justification. Nor was slavery an intrinsically evil institution tolerated by Paul because of his own human limitations or cultural conditioning or because of his hesitancy to upset the social order. Slavery could be an acceptable state if Paul's injunctions were followed.

Since slavery has bad connotations for us, a comparable institution may help our thinking. Consider a factory. In many ways management and labor are like masters and slaves. God has not commanded the existence of factories but that does not mean that their existence is necessarily wrong. Nevertheless, factories increase the likelihood of certain injustices (at least before unions) such as management's paying low wages, requiring long hours and allowing hazardous working conditions or labor's working at a slow rate. Consequently, the employers and employees, to fulfill their duties as Christians, must observe certain rules, like those addressed to masters and slaves.

The examples of monarchy and slavery do not help justify the biblical feminists' hermeneutic. Biblical feminists cannot legitimately call for the de-absolutization of biblical culture in the area of sexual politics just because deculturization (in its narrow sense, p. 30) is appropriate in the area of national politics. Monarchy, slavery and male-female relationships cannot be lumped together in the same category in the name of deculturization, because they are not presented in the same way in the Bible. Each area must be examined individually, and biblical passages must be exegeted carefully before applications can be made. In the case of God's commands to women, we hope to demonstrate that they apply to women for all time.

To support the deculturization of the Bible, biblical feminists also cite other Pauline commands that are no longer taught and obeyed. In the words of Scanzoni and Hardesty:

Most Christians do not feel that they are breaking a divine command by not following the "letter of the law" in regard to some matter seen to be culturally conditioned. Men wear longer hair styles in spite of I Corinthians 11:14. Few Christian women feel they are sinning if they wear jewelry, attractive clothing, robes or braided hair—even though 1 Timothy 2:9 and 1 Peter 3:3 are on the pages of Scripture. Churches do not require men to lift their hands while praying (1 Tim. 2:8). Modern translations have not hesitated to change the "holy kiss" of 1 Corinthians 16:20 into a handshake. This is interpretation and application.[19]

Some of the applications in the above quotation are questionable, and these questionable applications explain why some of the above practices (such as not wearing jewelry) are not observed. Other biblical feminists point out that women no longer cover their heads in church because that was only a first century custom and people no longer come to church with a hymn, lesson, revelation, etc., so why should women have to observe silence in the churches or to refrain from teaching men? In other words, we have stopped obeying certain commands, presumably because they are thought to be only customs of culture, such as feet washing. However, some commands have fallen into disuse without any theological justification. The "covering" for women is a good example. Women stopped wearing something on their heads to church (in most Protestant churches) only within this century, and the reasons were financial (hats became too expensive) and cultural (hats went out of style). In fact, the biblical background behind women's wearing hats to church had been lost to most of the laity long before the hats came off.

The biblical feminists reason, since we do not obey certain commands, why do we enforce those that "keep women in their place"? The question deserves consideration, but our response should be to look again at those exhortations that are being overlooked with an intent for further, greater obedience. Perhaps the holy kiss should be reinstated. Perhaps each Christian should come with his own contribution to the worship service. The Christian's mind set should

---

[19]Scanzoni and Hardesty, p. 18.

not be to look for release from God's commands but for greater obedience.

The biblical feminists have *chosen* a principle by which they judge the rest of the Scriptures. If a particular section of Scripture does not agree with their self-imposed standard, they explain it as a reflection of the culture in which it was written and therefore it is not binding.

The principle they have chosen can be labelled equality[20] (in particular, with regard to men and women). This principle breaks the analogy of Scripture as correctly understood, because it does not account for large portions of Scripture. What can be termed "equality" represents only one side of the biblical picture of human relations; to represent God's will as revealed in the Bible, it must be balanced by the principle of subordination or submission; justice must be done to both sides of the antinomy. In spite of the frequent coordination of these two supposedly contradictory principles in the Bible, the biblical feminists insist on following their own reasoning and eliminating one of them. (Chapters 3 and 4 will demonstrate that both ideas run throughout the Scriptures and are not just a matter of isolated proof texts and that they can be coordinated.)

An Excursus on Equality

The choice of "equality" as the standard is interesting. The word itself immediately raises the question, equal in terms of what. When the constitution says, "All men are created equal," it is concerned with equality in terms of the law; the enforcement of the law with its rights and punishments applies to all equally. It is ridiculous to suppose that "created equal" means that there are no differences in abilities, intellect, temperament, etc., at birth. Because of the great variety in people (no two are quite the same), when one speaks of "equality," it must be defined; or else the term becomes vague and

---

[20]Jewett, pp. 14, 171; Scanzoni and Hardesty, p. 107.

meaningless. In addition, differences in definitions of "equality" can cause misunderstandings.

A uniform definition of the biblical feminists' standard of equality is difficult to formulate. Jewett speaks of "the equality of male and female as a human fellowship reflecting the fellowship in the Godhead; and Jesus, as the perfect man who is truly in the image of God, taught such equality in his fellowship with women. . . ."[21] In the first instance, Jewett could mean that man and woman share equally in the image of God as taught in Genesis 1:26–27. In the second instance, he could mean that Christ treated men and women equally, with equal love, respect, concern, attention, instruction, etc., in his personal relationships with them. Yet neither of these interpretations of "equality" between men and women (both are in the image of God and both are to be treated kindly, etc. in personal relationships) conflicts with the commands to wives to submit themselves to their husbands. In other words, men and women are equal in some respects (i.e., in being or personhood) and not in others (in function); they are the same in some respects and different in others. And so, equality and subordination are not necessarily contradictory, despite what the biblical feminists assert. Equality in one area does not contradict subordination in another.

The problem with the above explanation for the biblical feminists is that the distinctions the Bible makes between men and women are made on the basis of sex. Women cannot teach and exercise authority over men in the church because they are women, regardless of ability.

When the biblical feminists speak of equality between men and women, they mean "role-interchangeability," no specialization on the basis of sex.[22] They mean no distinctions between men and women, other than biological ones. As Krister Stendahl puts it, "Any reasoning that limits a maximum of equality must be

---

[21]Jewett, p. 134.

[22]Scanzoni and Hardesty, p. 110.

considered suspect."[23] Role-interchangeability is the standard by which they judge biblical texts concerning men and women.

Our question is: Can this concept of "equality" (role-interchangeability) be found in the Bible?

"Equality" seems an inappropriate choice for a major theme in the Bible. A quick look at a concordance will demonstrate its infrequent usage,[24] and a reading of the few verses listed will reveal that even fewer of them (Ps. 55:13; Col. 4:1) refer to relationships between people. "Equality" also seems inappropriate because it, with its modern connotations and as the feminists employ it, smacks of demands for rights. Women are demanding their rights. Though the Bible definitely commands justice and giving others their due ("Give justice to the weak and the fatherless; maintain the right of the afflicted and the destitute," Ps. 82:3), it does not frequently speak of rights (other than our "right" to God's presence through Christ), not even the rights of life, liberty and the pursuit of happiness. It more often speaks of the Christian's responsibilities, even to the point of selflessness or rights-lessness (cf. Matt. 16:24ff.).

> But if any one strikes you on the right cheek, turn to him the other also; and if any one would sue you and take your coat, let him have your cloak as well; and if any one forces you to go one mile, go with him two miles . . . (Matt. 5:39–41).

> Everything is clean, but it is wrong for any one to make others fall by what he eats . . . let each of us please his neighbor for his good, to edify him (Rom. 14:20b; 15:2).

> Clothe yourselves, all of you, with humility toward one another, for "God opposes the proud, but gives grace to the humble" (I Pet. 5:5b).

Ephesians 5:21–6:9 (cf. Col. 3:18–4:1; I Pet. 2:13–3:12) is an example of the emphasis on responsibilities, rather than rights. It begins with the heading, "Be subject to one another out of reverence

---

[23]Krister Stendahl, "Women in the Churches: No Special Pleading," *Soundings*, 53:4 (Winter, 1970), 375.

[24]Ps. 55:13; Matt. 20:12; John 5:18; Phil. 2:6; Rev. 21:16; Job 28:17, 19; Lam. 2:13; Isa. 46:5; Ezek. 18:25, 29; 33:17, 20; Col. 4:1; II Cor. 8:14.

to Christ." Under this heading, Paul instructs different groups concerning their duties to one another, that is, he tells them just how they are to submit themselves to one another. Wives are to submit themselves to their husbands. Husbands are to love their wives. Children are to obey their parents. Fathers are not to provoke their children but to discipline and teach them of the Lord. Slaves are to obey their masters. Masters are to treat slaves justly and fairly. No one's *rights* are mentioned. Paul does not say, "Wives, your husband should love you" or even, "Husbands, you are the head of your wife." He teaches each group its duties.

The concept of submission or subordination, in contrast, frequently appears on the pages of Scripture. Christianity renovates the position of those in authority (husbands, masters, parents, elders) with the idea of mutual submission, but it does not destroy the authority structure.

Our culture has been moving away from authority structures (including the idea of absolute truth) and emphasizing individual's rights, self-sufficiency, subjectivism, and relativism. Only in such a climate could abortion be legalized and gays find advocates. This atmosphere is also responsible for the low view of Scripture held by the biblical feminists and others. In an interview, Lois Snook commented:

> But I think it's almost anachronistic, in a society in which the loss of authority is prevalent that there are these segments of the church in which clinging to the authority of both scripture and of the pastor is absolutely essential for a person's sanity or his contribution to the church.[25]

When we reject the biblical teaching of divinely ordered authority structures, we are only giving in to our cultural conditioning.

The Bible requires submission in many areas:

> Let every person be subject to the governing authorities (Rom. 13:1).

> Likewise you that are younger be subject to the elders (I Pet. 5:5).

---

[25]James H. Burtness, "An Interview with the Rev. Barbara Andrews," *Dialog*, 10 (1971), 127, Lois Snook speaking.

> Obey your leaders and submit to them . . . (Heb. 13:17).

> Submit yourselves therefore to God (James 4:7).

Submission was required of Christ himself (Phil. 2:5–11); God the Son submits himself to God the Father. Christ's relationship to God the Father has been compared to the woman's relationship to her husband (I Cor. 11:3). To buttress their argument that there is no chain of command implied in I Corinthians 11:3 or "in Christ," Scanzoni and Hardesty claim that Christ is no longer subordinate to the Father. Christ subordinated himself only in the incarnation and resumed full equality with the Father at his ascension.[26] This theory is necessary to their logic, because they maintain that subordination and equality are contradictions. Yet, I Corinthians 15:27–28, which Scanzoni and Hardesty amazingly cite in support of their theory, states:

> But when it says, "All things are put in subjection under him [Christ]," it is plain that he [God the Father] is excepted who put all things under him. When all things are subjected to him, then the Son himself will also be subjected to him [God the Father] who put all things under him, that God may be everything to every one.

At the end of the age, when Christ returns in glory, we shall see all things subjected to him (Heb. 2:8). Even when all things are subject to Christ, he will be subject to the Father. "Chain of command" is a polemical choice of words; authority structure is more accurate. There is an authority structure within the Trinity; God has established his church as a benign oligarchy (not a democracy) with elders to rule over the congregation (I Tim. 3:5; 5:17); and God has established the husband as the head of his wife. Authority structures are not antithetical to God's will.

Back to the original question: Does the Bible teach role-interchangeability (equality) between men and women? Where is this notion to be found in the Bible? The passages the biblical feminists cite on the side of equality are: Genesis 1:26–28; I Corinthians 11:11–12; Galatians 3:28; Ephesians 5:21; I Peter 3:7; Philippians

---

[26]Scanzoni and Hardesty, p. 22.

4:3. These passages will be exegeted in the following chapters, but permit a few generalizations at this point. None of these passages teaches as much as the biblical feminists claim. Genesis 1:26–28 teaches that men and women are both Man in the image of God and that they are co-regents over God's creation; but Genesis 1 says nothing about the relationship between man and woman. I Corinthians 11:11–12 teaches the mutual dependence of man and woman. Woman's dependence on man is founded on the original creation of the woman from the man. Man's dependence on woman is demonstrated by the woman's giving birth to children. One cannot exist without the other. Nonetheless, interdependence does not imply complete equality. Galatians 3:28 does not say that all are equal in Christ but that all are *one* in Christ. This oneness does not suggest uniformity or role-interchangeability. We have only to look at the body metaphor of I Corinthians 12 to see the diversity of functions, and I Corinthians 12:28–30 indicates that positions in the church are not interchangeable. Believers are one in the body of Christ, and each has his or her own gift(s) to exercise.

> Now there are varieties of gifts, but the same Spirit; and there are varieties of service, but the same Lord; and there are varieties of working, but it is the same God who inspires them all in every one (I Cor. 12:4–6).

In Ephesians 5:21–6:9, Paul explains the different modes of submission required of different groups. The mutual submission required of individual Christians to one another does not obliterate the different modes of submission for different groups. I Peter 3:7 states that men and women are joint heirs of the grace of life. Like it or not, the "equality" taught in I Peter 3:7 is in the spiritual realm. Man and woman share equally in salvation, in its benefits now and when it is completed by the resurrection of their bodies. In Philippians 4:3, Paul mentions two women who have struggled with him in the gospel. Whereas there is no doubt that women have an important and active place in the work of the gospel, this verse cannot by any stretch of the imagination be considered sufficient evidence that women could or did everything that men did in furthering the gospel.

If the biblical feminists did not get their concept of equality from the Bible, where did they get it? Elisabeth Elliot Leitch has said:

> Ideas such as "equality," "social justice," and "human rights," regarded in our times as unarguable imperatives, may in the end prove to be pseudo-Christian and provincially Western in their definition. We prostrate ourselves before these idols, muttering the required mumbo-jumbo of the sociologists without ever suspecting that we have surrendered to secularism.[27]

Ironically, the biblical feminists derive the idea of equality from our culture. Virginia Mollenkott admits this route; she began with secular concepts and then looked at the Bible. She says:

> I was into the feminist movement from a secular point of view, but I had been afraid to look at the Bible.[28]

She was afraid to look at the Bible because she feared, "I would see a God who is so unjust to my sex that I would have to give him up, and I couldn't do that."[29] She was in an intolerable position: she was convinced of women's rights, as defined by the world, and she believed in the God of the Bible, who makes some distinctions between men and women. From her candid statement, it appears that her commitment to women's rights had top priority—she did not consider giving that up. Her resolution is to adjust the Bible to her thinking, to the world's standards.

Martin Luther said:

> If I profess with the loudest voice and clearest exposition every portion of the truth of God except precisely that little point which the world and the devil are at that moment attacking, I am not confessing Christ. Where the battle rages, there the loyalty of the soldier is proved, and to be steady on all the battle front besides is mere flight and disgrace if he flinches at that point.[30]

---

[27] Elisabeth Elliot Leitch, speaking at Wheaton College, May 2, 1975, *The Other Side,* 12:3 (May–June, 1976), 50.

[28] John F. Alexander (interviewer), "A Conversation with Virginia Mollenkott," *The Other Side,* 12:3 (May–June, 1976), 26.

[29] Ibid., p. 25.

[30] Martin Luther quoted by Francis Schaeffer, "Schaeffer on Scripture," *Christianity Today,* 19:23 (August 29, 1975), 29.

The "little point" being attacked by the world and the devil now is the position of women in the home and in the church. Christians must stand up for God's truth against the rhetoric, reasoning, and pride of the world.

The Problems of Deculturization

Once this false standard of equality is set up as the Christian ideal, the hermeneutical principle of deculturization becomes all-important as the means by which passages that make distinctions between men and women can be removed.

A major problem results from this approach. How do we know what parts of the Bible are culturally conditioned and therefore non-authoritative? Or, how can we determine the essential content, the norm of Scripture, if Scripture as a whole is no longer considered the standard? What is the standard?

Once authority is taken away from the canon of Scripture, which is a well-defined and objective standard, the new standard must be the following:

(1) It must be external to the Scriptures. Even if the idea can be found in the Scriptures, it cannot claim the Scriptures as its source if it does not include the full scriptural teaching. The biblical feminists found a type of equality in the Bible; but their definition of equality came from secular sources, not the Bible, and they have tried to force biblical concepts into secular molds. The result is that the creator's word is judged by his creatures, a topsy-turvy state of affairs.

(2) It must be subjective. The standard will vary from person to person. Authority is transferred from the Scriptures to the interpreter. If the Scriptures are affected and infected by culture, how does the interpreter hope to escape the effects of his/her culture? And so, any absolute standard is impossible.

Mollenkott expressly favors the shift from Scripture to the interpreter.

> Even if the biblical evidence were 50 percent in support of female subordination and only 50 percent in favor of the equality of mutual submission, ordinary kindness and decency should lead modern Christians to choose in favor of equality.[31]

If the "ordinary kindness and decency" of modern Christians were able to make ultimate decisions concerning what God's will is, the Bible would not be necessary. Mollenkott neglects the deceitfulness of the human heart (Jer. 17:9) and the tendency towards sin still present in the mortal bodies of Christians.

A claim to be Spirit-led in the editing of the Scriptures is not valid. According to the biblical feminists, God cannot speak through human beings without his word being contaminated; but then, how would any modern Spirit-led deciphering avoid the same contamination? Here we see the self-defeating nature of the feminist hermeneutic and the endless subjectivity it would produce. In addition, according to the Bible, every spirit must be tested to see if it is from God. The only way to examine the spirits is to compare them to the Scriptures. The person who is truly led by the Spirit of God will not contradict the Scriptures. The Holy Spirit's speaking now and having spoken then will agree; God does not contradict himself.

How does "deculturization" affect our interpretation of the Old Testament? It does not cause so much difficulty in practice because as we have said before, the New Testament interprets the Old so that we can know which commandments no longer apply to us. However, in response to the biblical feminists' approach to the Old Testament, which nullifies rather than explains the fulfillment and meaning of some Old Testament sections, we should remember that all of those laws were given by God for a purpose and had complete authority over the Israelites until they were fulfilled in Christ. No Old Testament law can be termed the result of cultural conditioning (merely a reflection of the patriarchal culture) in spite of the fact that God intended them to be valid only for a certain period of

---

[31]Mollenkott, "Challenge," p. 22.

history. This understanding of the Old Testament is consistent with the doctrine of Scripture developed in the first chapter.

But what about the New Testament? We interpret the Old Testament by the New Testament. What criteria can the biblical feminists use to "deculturize" the New Testament since we have no further written revelation? If Paul's teaching about women in the church is cultural, maybe his teaching on justification or his faith in God is, too. Once we start amputating parts of the New Testament, how do we know when to stop? The biblical feminists' answer is "good, careful, scholarly exegesis."[32] This sounds good, but the biblical feminists have not reached their conclusions concerning women through scholarly exegesis. This is not to say they have never exegeted passages carefully and well. For example, Jewett concludes that Paul's statements about women imply that he thought of the woman as subordinate to the man,[33] that "the marriage relation is not a matter of mutuality as between equal partners,"[34] that the "customs" of I Corinthians 11:3–16 (long hair and/or veiling) were not merely customs but symbolic expressions of the absolute will of God.[35] These conclusions illustrate Jewett's sound exegesis. Then on the basis of his presuppositions and his thought processes, not on the basis of any biblical text, Jewett adds that subordination necessarily implies inferiority, that Paul contradicts himself and that certain Pauline texts suffer from human limitations and therefore are not binding for the Christian today. In Jewett's case it is clear that his conclusions about women are not based on the exegesis of biblical passages about women.

Jewett's approach is not really what Mollenkott intended when she said sound exegesis should determine what is culturally determined and what is not. Scanzoni's and Hardesty's exegesis of I Corinthians 14:34–35 better illustrates Mollenkott's idea. Paul appeals to the "law" to support his command to women to be silent

---

[32]Alexander (interviewer), "Conversation," p. 30.
[33]Jewett, p. 51.
[34]Ibid., p. 59.
[35]Ibid., p. 118.

in the church. Scanzoni and Hardesty correctly observe that the "law" cannot be either Genesis 3:16 or I Timothy 2:11–12, as some cross-references note. They then propose another possible meaning for "law" ("law" is used in different senses in the New Testament); they define it as what is proper or what is assigned to someone, one's role. They consider Paul's appeal to "law" an appeal to social custom. If so, Paul is only asking the women to observe the customs of their culture so that Christian meetings would be orderly.[36] According to Scanzoni and Hardesty, Paul's real point, arrived at through deculturization, is that Christian meetings should be orderly; he does not really mean to limit the ministry of women.

Scanzoni and Hardesty reach their conclusions through exegesis but is it correct? In I Corinthians 14:34, "law" does not refer to social customs. To my knowledge, Paul never uses "law" to refer to a social custom. Almost always, by law Paul means either God's law in general or particularly the Mosaic law. The exceptions are Romans 7:2–3 and Romans 7:21–8:2. In the first instance, Paul has a specific law, prohibiting adultery, in mind; it is one of God's commandments and so Paul speaks of it as having absolute authority. In Romans 7:21–8:2, Paul mentions "the law of sin and death"; here "law" means an active principle or an impulse to sin in human nature. It is a compelling force from which God must free us. Thayer explains the use of νομος in this context: "the mention of the divine law causes those things even which in opposition to this law impel to action, and therefore seem to have the force of a law."[37] When Paul employs the word "law," he intends a permanent, binding, authoritative principle. Paul does not use νομος when referring to temporal, social rules or customs. In I Corinthians 14:34, Paul appeals to ὁ νομος, the law, with no other identification. In all other cases in which Paul refers to the law, he means the law of God, the only ultimate authority.

---

[36]Scanzoni and Hardesty, p. 69.

[37]Joseph Henry Thayer, tr. & rev., *Greek-English Lexicon of the New Testament Being Grimm's Wilke's Clavis Novi Testamenti* (Grand Rapids: Zondervan, 1962), p. 427.

The teaching of the law referred to in I Corinthians 14:34 is not that women are to be silent, as some assume. Some commentators see I Corinthians 14:34 as the reflection of Paul's rabbinic training;[38] the "law," they say, is from the Talmud, "It is a shame for a woman to let her voice be heard among men." The law to which Paul refers commands the subordination, not the silence, of women. Scanzoni and Hardesty state that there is no verse in the Old Testament that specifically says the woman should be in subjection. This statement is true; nonetheless, the Old Testament does teach the subordination of the woman. Genesis 2, when correctly interpreted by the God-breathed words of I Corinthians 11:3, 8-9, establishes the headship of the husband. Old Testament legislation, such as Numbers 30 on vows, demonstrates the subordination of wives to husbands. In Numbers 5:19, 20, the woman is spoken of as "under her husband." Genesis 3:16, which is a judgment rather than a prescription or commandment, implies the subordination of the wife to her husband; the "curse" of Genesis 3:16 is that the woman will resist the headship of her husband and so marriage will involve struggle. In short, "law" in I Corinthians 14:34 refers to the whole Old Testament teaching concerning women. In addition, there is nothing in the context of I Corinthians 14:34-35 to suggest that social customs are in view. To the contrary, Paul's appeal to "the law" is one that is expected to silence all objections; only an appeal to God's law could have such an effect.

Though Scanzoni and Hardesty support their conclusions with exegesis, their conclusions were decided beforehand. They and other biblical feminists approach the Bible with the preconceived idea that God neither could nor would make distinctions between women and men; God would not prohibit women from certain activity in the church on the basis of sex. This preconception depends on another more basic one: that God did not sovereignly speak his word; God spoke through finite, culturally determined people, whose finiteness and culture discolored God's words. Man's words,

---

[38]Mollenkott, "Challenge," 21.

commands and theology are intermixed with God's. It is only with the latter presupposition that Scanzoni and Hardesty could suppose that Scripture could base commands purely on social customs, as they say is the case in I Corinthians 14:34–35.

Sound exegesis, which includes a biblically derived doctrine of Scripture, will demonstrate that each New Testament passage dealing with women is not a concession to first century culture, that the commandments to women rest on unchanging principles, and that they consequently apply to women today.

THREE

WHAT THE OLD TESTAMENT SAYS ABOUT WOMEN

OF all places to look for guidance in understanding who woman is, the Old Testament seems most unlikely. Today, feminists reject most of the Bible as hostile to women, with the possible exception of Jesus. Jesus seemed to break with the Old Testament view of woman, but his followers, Paul in particular, seemed to miss his point and revert to the Old Testament tradition: the woman is subordinate even as the law says (I Cor. 14:34).

In Old Testament times, Sheila Collins infers:

> . . . women were regarded as an inferior species to be owned like cattle, an unclean creature incapable of participating in the mysteries of the worship of Yahweh. For whatever historical reason . . . ancient Hebrew society was blatantly misogynist and male dominated.[1]

The Old Testament, it is argued, "discriminates against" women. Eve is created second, some say as an afterthought; she is the first to sin, and this makes her the "devil's gateway"[2] in the eyes of Tertullian, a church father. The same critique attacks the writer of Ecclesiastes

---

[1] Sheila D. Collins, "Toward a Feminist Theology," *Christian Century*, 89 (August 2, 1972), 796.

[2] Tertullian, "On the Apparel of Women," *The Ante-Nicene Fathers*, Alexander Robert and James Donaldson, eds., IV (Grand Rapids: Wm. B. Eerdmans, 1956), 14.

who finds only one man out of a thousand who has found wisdom, but not one woman (Eccl. 7:28).

The Old Testament is said to be full of male chauvinism, and yet it claims to have the authority of God's word. How can these two aspects of the Old Testament be reconciled? How much of it, if any, is the product of a patriarchal society? Is it to be erased by the New Testament with its teaching of freedom in Christ? What does the Old Testament really teach about women?

In the Garden

In Genesis 1 and 2, there are two accounts of the creation of humanity. In Genesis 1:27, "so God created man (*adam*) in his own image, in the image of God he created him; male and female he created them." In Genesis 2, the man is created first; he names the animals, and no helper for him is found among them. Then the woman is built from the man's rib to be a helper fit for him. Each story has been misinterpreted: chapter 1 has been thought to teach the absolute and unequivocal equality of the sexes, and chapter 2, the inferiority of the woman.[3] Neither extreme is correct; the true picture of the creation of woman emerges only when both narratives are put together. Chapters 1 and 2 complement each other.

On the sixth day God created humanity, Man in the generic sense, in two sexes. There is no indication that there is any difference between male and female in Genesis 1:26ff. This passage expresses in what way man and woman are equal. Both man and woman are in the image of God in exactly the same way. Some state that man was created in God's image and woman in man's image so that the image of God in woman is a second hand, reflected image.[4] Or, some suggest that since God reveals himself as male, God the Father and

---

[3]Phyllis Trible, "Eve and Adam: Genesis 2-3 Reread," *Andover Newton Quarterly,* 13:4 (March, 1973), 251.

[4]Rousas J. Rushdoony, "The Doctrine of Marriage," *Toward Christian Marriage: a Chalcedon Study,* Elizabeth Fellersen, ed. (Nutley, N.J.: Presbyterian and Reformed Publ. Co., 1972), p. 14.

God the Son, woman must be excluded from participation in his image.[5] However, Genesis 1:27 makes no distinction. Both are blessed by God and told to multiply and to subdue the earth. The stewardship of creation is given to both man and woman; they are jointly responsible for the care of the earth.

An Excursus on the Image of God

Because the Bible does not say what the image of God is in so many words, the definition of the divine image in man is still a subject of discussion. Paul Jewett has brought this question into prominence by his adoption and development of what many have called a "novel" position, "that understands the distinction between man and woman as itself a manifestation of the *imago Dei.*"[6] Jewett's argument is this:

> While I do not reject the classical view of the image as having to do with Man's unique powers of self-transcendence by which he exercises dominion over creation as God's vice-regent, I do insist that Man's creation in the divine image is so related to his creation as male and female that the latter may be looked upon as an exposition of the former. His sexuality is not simply a mechanism for procreation which Man has in common with the animal world; it is rather a part of what it means to be like the Creator. As God is a fellowship in himself (Trinity) so Man is a fellowship in himself, and the fundamental form of this fellowship, so far as Man is concerned, is that of male and female. This view of Man's being, I argue, implies a partnership in life. . . .[7]

So Jewett considers this interpretation the basis for his rejection of an hierarchical male-female relationship and for his espousal of male-female partnership (of equals in every respect).[8]

---

[5]Collins, p. 796.
[6]Jewett, p. 33.
[7]Ibid., pp. 13–14.
[8]"Since men and women are equally in the image of God, what is true for one is true for the other" (ibid., p. 131). Interchangeability rather than equality may be a more accurate description of Jewett's opinion.

Though novel, Jewett's theory is not original. Karl Barth was the first major theologian to promote the idea that "Man in the image of God is Man as male and female."[9] However, Barth does not push this view to Jewett's conclusion.

> He [Barth] seeks to maintain the traditional subordination of the woman to the man without acknowledging the traditional theological grounds on which this subordination is based, namely, the superiority of the man. . . .[10]

Jewett criticizes Barth for not following his own theology of the divine image in Man as male and female to its clear conclusion, a fellowship of equals. Jewett and Barth agree that their understanding of the divine image in Man implies that man and woman are equal as human beings. The main point of disagreement is not about the implications of the divine image; it is whether or not the subordination of the woman depends on her inferiority. Jewett says emphatically yes, but his only argument is that subordination without inferiority does not make sense. And to maintain his thesis of equal partnership, Jewett must explain away several biblical passages. (These will be discussed in the New Testament chapter.) The point of this critique is that Jewett's theology of the divine image in itself is not "inimical to a doctrine of sexual hierarchy."[11] His theory is inimical to the doctrine of sexual hierarchy only when buttressed with the argument that subordination necessarily involves inferiority.

On what grounds does Jewett base his theory of God's image in Man? Though he does not expend many words on the exegesis of Genesis 1:26–27, he appeals to two exegetical facts: (1) the proximity of the phrase "male and female"; and (2) the use of the plural when God speaks, "Let us make. . . ."

Jewett reasons, ". . . the text of Genesis 1:27 makes no direct comment on Man in the image of God save to observe that he exists as male and female."[12] Undoubtedly, the phrase "male and female"

[9]Ibid., p. 35.
[10]Ibid., p. 85.
[11]Ibid.
[12]Ibid., p. 36.

must be accounted for in discussions of the image of God; it cannot be ignored, as Jewett maintains it has been.[13] Nonetheless, error must not be made in the opposite direction; the phrase must not be given too much weight, as Jewett seems to do.

It should be noted that in verse 26, God speaks of creating humanity in his image without reference to Man as male and female; instead dominion over the earth is closely associated with humanity in God's image. The close association in the text between image and dominion has led some theologians to define image in terms of dominion. Like most theologians, Jewett appears to regard dominion as only an expression or result of Man's being in the image of God. Jewett, then, must agree that mere proximity in the text does not imply definition.

In verse 26 God states his intent, and in verse 27 the author of Genesis describes the result of God's word in three parallel but not identical clauses:

(A) So God created man in his own image,
(B) in the image of God he created him,
(C) male and female he created them.

What is the relationship of these three clauses? Parallelism is a characteristic of Hebrew poetry and occurs frequently in biblical narratives. There are three types of parallelism: (1) synonymous parallelism, in which the same idea is stated in different phrases; (2) antithetic parallelism, in which the idea in the first part is clarified in the second part by contrast; and (3) synthetic parallelism, in which the second part develops the idea in the first part.[14] In Genesis 1:27 clauses A and B are clearly synonymous. Clause C develops the idea in A and B. There are two changes: a new element, "male and female," is introduced, and the plural pronoun "them" replaces the singular "Man" and "him." The change from a singular to a plural reference to Man occurs also in verse 26. When God spoke of creating Man, he did not intend to make one individual, but

---

[13]Ibid., p. 19.
[14]Artur Weiser, *The Old Testament: Its Formation and Development,* (New York: Association Press, 1961), p. 24.

he spoke of Man as a species, humanity (Gen. 5:2). The singular noun for mankind (אָדָם) suggests the unity of the species, a fact of theological significance (Rom. 5:12–21). So there is no problem understanding how "them" in clause C relates to "Man" in clause A and "him" in clause B.

But how does the phrase "male and female" relate to clauses A and B? Its position is parallel to the image of God. But we have suggested that in synthetic parallelism, development in thought occurs, so that each element in the first clause need not have an exact parallel in the following clause. Neither Jewett nor Barth supposes that the phrase "in his own image" and "in the image of God" are synonymous in meaning to "male and female."

There are two possibilities: "male and female" explains the image of God (Jewett's choice); or "male and female" describes, elucidates "them." I prefer the latter view for the following reasons:

(1) In what way God created Man as "them" (v. 26) must be stated. God created Man the species on the sixth day, but more specifically he created a man and a woman, the two basic types of Man.

(2) The words "male" (זָכָר) and "female" (נְקֵבָה) denote gender only; they do not refer exclusively to humans but can refer to animals (Gen. 6:19; 7:16). Their use here suggests that they describe Man.

(3) The most conclusive evidence for not associating "male and female" with the image of God is other biblical material. God's image in Man is only alluded to in the Old Testament (Gen. 5:1–3; 9:6). However, in the New Testament, several direct references are made to the image of God and its relationship to humanity. No connection with the male-female relationship is made in these verses; the only relationship in view is person-God. The major emphasis in the New Testament is that the divine image must be renewed in humanity through faith in Christ.[15] The traditional

---

[15]That the image of God must be restored does not imply that it was totally lost at the fall, though it was distorted. Genesis 9:6 and James 3:9 (which prohibit killing and cursing men because they are created in God's image) indicate that the image is not completely lost.

concept of the image of God in man, that man is like God in his moral and rational capacities, is based on the following verses.

> . . . and put on the new nature, created after the likeness of God in true righteousness and holiness (Eph. 4:24).

> . . . and have put on the new nature which is being renewed in knowledge after the image of the creator (Col. 3:10).

Humanity must be renewed in true righteousness and holiness (moral) and knowledge (rational). This view of the image of God commends itself because the verses themselves explicitly state what being like God involves and because we know that this idea of the divine image corresponds precisely to what God is like as revealed by the Scriptures—perfect knowledge, righteousness, and holiness. In contrast, a view which associates "male and female" with the image has difficulty seeing in what way being male and female is like God. Jewett refrains from pressing his analogy of the male-female fellowship to the fellowship of the Trinity "so as to suppose a sexual distinction in God."[16] Jewett leaves us with a mystery—the mystery of the Trinity (how Father, Son, and Holy Spirit relate to one another) and the mystery of the eternal masculine and the eternal feminine, the ontology of sexuality (a subject he cannot tackle because he cannot define it).[17]

Conformity to the image of Christ (Rom. 8:29; I Cor. 15:49; II Cor. 3:18) who is the express image of God (Col. 1:15; Heb. 1:3) is another New Testament expression of the need for renewal of God's image in Man. Conformity to Christ can easily be understood in terms of righteousness, holiness, and knowledge, but it would be hard to comprehend how male-female fellowship can reflect likeness to Christ.

The only New Testament text in which the image of God is mentioned in the same context as the male-female relationship is I Corinthians 11:7. If the male-female relationship itself reflects the image of God, Paul missed a golden opportunity to say so in this

---

[16]Jewett, p. 165.
[17]Ibid., pp. 178–179.

passage. Instead he says only that man is the image of God. (He does not deny that woman is the image of God; see discussion in chapter 4.) The interdependence of man and woman (a conclusion Jewett draws from Gen. 1:27) is not based on the fact that man and woman are created in the image of God but on the facts that woman was created from the man (Gen. 2:21–22) and that man is now born from woman (I Cor. 11:11–12). Jewett eliminates this passage from his consideration of the divine image in man because he thinks Paul at this point is showing the bias of his rabbinic training; he accuses Paul of ignoring the thrust of Genesis 1:27[18] and of teaching that the woman does not bear the image of God to the same degree as the man.[19] The absence of any connection between the image and "male and female" in this passage, which mentions both, supports the idea that "male and female" is not an exposition of God's image in Man.

There is also one passage which indicates that the male-female relationship does not have the eternal significance that Jewett assigns to it when he associates it so closely with the image of God—Galatians 3:28. Jewett points out that the wording "male *and* female" (as opposed to "nor") obviously mirrors the language of Genesis 1:27.[20] Here is a verse clearly referring to Genesis 1:27 that apparently abolishes the distinction upon which Jewett's whole theology rests. Jewett hastens to explain that sexuality is not abolished in Christ and that the goal for Christians is "a fellowship of male and female."[21] For Jewett, the image of God is expressed in the male-female fellowship particularly, not in human-human fellowship. This distinction implies a difference between men and women, which Jewett admits is metaphysical, fundamental, mysterious, and indefinable. For Jewett, Galatians 3:28 removes all distinctions between man and woman (any sinful hostilities and all social, as in marriage, and ecclesiastical regulations distinguishing between men and women); it leaves only that mysterious, metaphysical difference

---

[18]Ibid., p. 119.
[19]Ibid., p. 165.
[20]Ibid., p. 142.
[21]Ibid., pp. 143–144.

that makes male-female fellowship so special. This sort of difference between men and women is not suggested in any biblical passage; comparatively few commands are addressed to either men or women as groups; most are directed to believers. In addition, the "fellowship" emphasis seems to be among the members of Christ's body (I Cor. 12–13; Eph. 4–5:20; Col. 3:12–17; I Pet. 3:8; I John 3:11–18), not between men and women.

The cumulative effect of these objections may show that the image of God is not reflected specifically in the male-female relationship. But "male" and "female" should not be entirely disassociated from God's image in Man. "Male and female" specifies the extent of the image. If that phrase were missing from the account, it would be difficult to prove that women are also in God's image. As the account stands, God created Man in two sexes in his image. Both male Man and female Man are in God's image.

The use of the plural in Genesis 1:26 is probably an allusion to the Trinity, as Jewett supposes. The problem with incorporating an analogy between the fellowship of man and woman and the Trinity into one's doctrine of Man is that such an idea makes too much of too little. When the Lord speaks in the Old Testament, he occasionally refers to himself in the plural (Gen. 3:22; 11:7; Isa. 6:8; 41:22). We cannot see the significance of the plural in these references, and so it seems unlikely that we should put too much emphasis on the plural in Genesis 1:26. In addition, the doctrine of the Trinity is undeveloped in the Old Testament.

As in the discussion of "male and female," the main reason for rejecting the analogy between the male-female fellowship and the intertrinitarian relationship is that there is little scriptural support for it. The only comparison between the two is in I Corinthians 11:3, in which the analogy is indirect. And it is only an analogy; it is not an essential doctrine of the faith. The unstated comparison is between "the head of a woman is the man" and "the head of Christ is God." Understanding the one relationship illuminates the other, but that is as much as can be said. (Note the common element is headship; rather than suggesting an equal partnership, as Jewett maintains, the only analogy in Scripture between the male-female relationship and the intertrinitarian relationship suggests the opposite—an hierarchical arrangement.) The much more common comparison in the Bible is between husband-wife and God-his people (Jer. 2:33–3:10; Ezek. 16, 23; Hosea 1–3; Eph. 5:25–32; Rev. 21:2).

Some of Jewett's points are well taken. For instance, the fact of human sexuality should not be omitted from theologians' discussions of anthropology; and men and women are dependent on one another (I Cor. 11:11–12). However, Jewett's concept of the divine image is not a necessary presupposition for these conclusions nor for the thesis that man and woman are equal in being; and his theory does not have sufficient support in Scripture.

In Genesis 1:26–31, we see humanity (male and female) in relation to God (they are in his image) and to nature (they are to fill the earth and subdue it). Men and women have the same relationship to God and to nature. Genesis 2 depicts the relationship between the man and woman and yet underlines their equality as human beings.

God created man from the dust and breathed the breath of life into him. Man is commanded not to eat of the tree of the knowledge of good and evil. Then God says it is not good for man to be alone; when he says "not good," he does not mean that he made a mistake or forgot something. The helper for man is not someone whose place could conceivably have been filled by the animals. Even before God brought the animals to Adam for naming, he had planned to make a helper fit for man (Gen. 2:18). God, the Almighty, knows exactly what he is doing. His work is unfinished until he makes the woman.

But in Genesis 1, the creation of man and woman is simultaneous. Does not Genesis 2, in picturing woman as a late-comer, contradict it? No, the creation of man and woman is relatively simultaneous; Genesis 1 tells us that man and woman were created in the same day. Genesis 1 gives us a day-by-day account of creation, whereas Genesis 2:4bff. gives us a blow-by-blow account of the creation of humanity on the sixth day.

Woman enters the world designated as *ezer kenegdo,* "helper fit for him." The response to this designation varies, but many, like John Calvin, take it to mean an "inferior aid."[22] Thomas Aquinas in *Summae Theologica* brings out the feminist in all of us women when he writes:

> Woman was made to be a help to man. But she was not fitted to be a help to man except in generation, because another man would prove a more effective help in anything else.[23]

Perhaps in reaction to this low opinion of women, many modern theologians try to find connotations of superior help in the Hebrew word *ezer* (helper). Clarence Vos cites the other Old Testament references to *ezer:* 15 times it refers to God as the helper and 3 times, to the help of man, which is ineffectual. He concludes, "Thus if one excluded Gen. 2:18, 20 it could be said that only God gives effectual help ($^c\bar{e}zer$) to man."[24] This conclusion may overstate the case. Nonetheless, it can safely be said that *ezer* does not imply inferiority. More importantly, the helper of man is *kenegdo,* that is, corresponding to or like him, neither inferior nor superior. She corresponds to him in that she, like him, is made in the image of God.

In addition, the woman is made because she is needed. She is not extraneous or a luxury, but a necessity for the welfare of the man. The man is not self-sufficient; he needs the woman's help.

The mode of the woman's creation is puzzling. How can the man's rib be a suitable helper for him? Why does God create her from Adam's body, and why a rib?

The woman is created from the man, as opposed to a separate creation from the dust, for several reasons. (1) It is a part of her corresponding-ness to him; she is made of the same substance without inferiority or superiority. She is the very bone of his bone and flesh of his flesh. Why God selected the man's rib from which to

---

[22]John Calvin, *Commentaries,* vol. I (Grand Rapids, Wm. B. Eerdmans Publ. Co., 1948), p. 69.

[23]Collins, p. 797.

[24]Clarence J. Vos, *Woman in Old Testament Worship* (Delft: N. V. Verenigde Drukkerijen Judels & Brinkman, n.d.), p. 16.

build the woman is difficult to say. If it is possible to explain at all, it seems likely that the woman is made from the rib or side of man to reinforce the equality of being and substance and their being like one another. An old adage may have captured a truth quaintly:

> . . . Eve was not taken from Adam's head that she should rule over him, not from his feet, to be trampled under foot, but she was taken from his side that she might be his equal; from under his arm that she might be protected by him; near his heart, that he might cherish and love her.[25]

(2) God's creation of humanity is one act which begins with the man and ends with the woman. (3) The human race, including the first woman, comes from one source, Adam. He, as the beginning of humanity, is the actual head and thereby representative of humanity. This is why I Corinthians 15:29 says, "As in Adam all die." (4) The woman was created from man to set up the basis for the one-flesh principle in marriage. There is a real biological and historical foundation for the oneness that should be between husband and wife (Gen. 2:24).[26] Reasons (3) and (4) prepare us for the principle of inequality between the man and the woman. (5) Though the woman's being created second and from and for the man does not indicate inferiority, it does indicate a difference in the way they are to function. The woman is created to be a help to her husband; her function is dependent on him. The temporal priority of the man is significant. The woman followed his lead in the creation process, and she is to follow his lead as her husband.

This sort of reasoning may not be convincing; it obviously has not convinced many Christian women. It has been said that in the garden before the fall, there was a 50–50 partnership between husband and wife, and that the headship of man is a consequence of the curse. There is no direct statement to the contrary, and the modern notion of paradise would have liberty, equality, and fraternity. However, the order of creation is significant according to the New Testament (I Cor. 11:8–9; I Tim. 2:13). Scripture must be

---

[25]Russell C. Prohl, *Woman in the Church* (Grand Rapids: Eerdmans Publ. Co., 1957), p. 46.
[26]See I Corinthians 7:4; the one-flesh principle is expressed in that the husband rules the wife's body and she rules his.

allowed to interpret Scripture. God, through Paul, has given the proper interpretation of creation. I Corinthians 11:8–9 states that man is the head of the woman because she was created from him (made from his rib) and she was created for his sake, rather than the reverse. The plausibility of this interpretation of the order of creation of Man (male and female) is increased if we remember that it is a purposeful and powerful God who created the categories male and female and who could have created man and woman in any way or order he chose.

God's assignment of functions may sound like job discrimination to us. Men get to be bosses, and women have to be secretaries. We feel a twinge (or maybe a pang) of resentment because we do not know what a sin-free hierarchical arrangement can be like. We know only the arbitrariness, the domination, the arrogance that even the best boss/underling relationship has. But in Eden, it was different. It really was. The man and the woman knew each other as equals, both in the image of God, and thus each with a personal relationship to God. Neither doubted the worth of the other nor of him/herself. Each was to perform his/her task in a different way, the man as the head and the woman as his helper. They operated as truly one flesh, one person. In one body does the rib rebel against or envy the head?

The man's reaction to the woman's entry into existence is note-worthy. His poem should not be passed over as simply a recognition of identity and equality. The man is enraptured with the woman. He has been eagerly waiting for the helper corresponding to himself; his thought is "Now, finally, she is here." He has not been in existence for a whole day, and still he has longed for his counterpart. The woman is a part of himself, and he lovingly welcomes her and cleaves to her. Love is the original relationship between husband and wife.

Before the fall, there were several principles, which, corroded by sin, continue to operate after the fall. (1) Both man and woman are in the image of God; they are equal in being. (2) The man's priority in creation corresponds to his headship of his wife, to which he is appointed by God. The wife is to help her husband. There is a functional subordination of the wife to her husband. In the New

Testament, the woman is called upon to fulfill her created function. The idea of the woman as a helper to her husband corresponds to her submission to him in Ephesians 5:22–23. (3) Husband and wife are one flesh.

The first question that comes to mind as we begin Genesis 3 is: why did the serpent, "more subtle than any other wild creature," approach the woman first? The answer may not be satisfying but it is simple. We do not know why the serpent approached the woman rather than the man. The Bible does not tell us. Speculation regarding an answer ranges from the chauvinist to the feminist. On the male side, Luther suggests:

> The subtlety of Satan showed itself also when he attacked human nature where it was weakest, namely in Eve, and not in Adam. I believe that had Satan first tempted the man, Adam would have gained the victory.[27]

There is nothing in Genesis 1–3 to suggest that the woman was inferior to the man in any way or more susceptible to temptation than he; she was a part of him (one flesh). The cleverness of the serpent consists in his method of temptation, his half-truths, his slight distortion of God's truth, *not* in his choice of victims.

At the other extreme, some hypothesize that the serpent goes to the woman because she is the perfecting element (creation was incomplete without her).[28] The serpent knew that once the woman fell, the man was sure to fall; but if the man fell, the woman, the perfection, might have remained obedient to God's commandment. Once more, we repeat that the account gives no indication that the man would respond differently than the woman did; they are on equal footing regarding their susceptibility to sin.

A more biblical theory is suggested by Geerhardus Vos:

> The tempter addresses himself to the woman, probably not because she is more open to temptation and prone to sin, for that is hardly the

---

[27]Martin Luther, *Luther's Commentary on Genesis*, vol. I (Grand Rapids: Zondervan Publ. House, 1958), p. 68.

[28]George H. Tavard, *Woman in Christian Tradition* (Notre Dame: University of Notre Dame Press, 1973), p. 13.

conception of the O.T. elsewhere. The reason may have lain in this, that the woman had not personally received the prohibition from God, as Adam had; cpr. 2:16, 17.[29]

The idea is still speculative, and the woman was aware of God's command. The Bible does not tell why the serpent selects the woman, and guessing produces a variety of plausible answers.

The woman listens to the serpent, disobeys God's command, and eats the forbidden fruit. What is the exact nature of her sin? Walter Maier suggests:

> Disregarding her concreated subjection to Adam, she took leadership into her own hands and urged her husband to violate the commandment of the Lord.[30]

Many consider the woman's sin primarily as that of insubordination to her husband, usurpation of his authority. A variation of this theme is that her sin was acting independently, without first asking her husband whether or not she should eat the fruit. According to this view, the woman either could or should not make a decision on her own.

The woman, however, knew God's commandment, even though under pressure she exaggerated it; she did not need to ask her husband whether or not to eat, to spell out God's law. Her sin was primarily against God, as are all of our sins (Ps. 51:4). She exalted herself above her creator when she discussed with another creature whether or not God's law was fair.

The woman sinned against her husband too, but not by taking the lead or by acting without his consent. The woman was created to help the man. She helps him in Genesis 3:6b, but she helps him badly, to do the wrong thing. In Genesis 3:17, God tells Adam why he is being judged. It is not because he listened to his wife *per se*, but because he heeded her bad advice—to disobey God.

---

[29]Geerhardus Vos, *Biblical Theology* (Grand Rapids: Wm. B. Eerdmans Publ. Co., 1971), p. 45.

[30]Walter A. Maier, "Some Thoughts on the Role of Women in the Church," *The Springfielder*, 33:4 (March, 1970), 36.

Not much is said about how Adam sinned, although many assume as quoted above that the woman "urged" him or enticed or seduced him into sin. So, the woman becomes the temptress; she is "the one who persuaded him whom the devil was too weak to attack."[31] All of these derogatory ideas are drawn from the simple narrative: ". . . she took some of its fruit and ate; and she also gave some to her husband, and he ate" (Gen. 3:6). The verse gives no hint that the woman had to convince her husband of anything. There is only one hint as to the nature of Adam's sin in the Bible. In I Timothy 2:14, we are told that Adam was not deceived (he knew what he was doing), but the woman was utterly deceived. The serpent's cunning confused and manipulated the woman, but not the man who, apparently, sinned with full awareness of his disobedience to God.

Yet, too many distinctions should not be made between the respective sins of the man and woman. In the narrative, they sin almost simultaneously, as if Adam's sin were a reflex act of the woman's (remember before the first sin, husband and wife were perfectly one flesh); and the results of their sins occur at the same time. After Adam eats, *"Then* the eyes of *both* were opened . . ." (Gen. 3:7). The consequences are the same for both; they know they are naked, make aprons for themselves and hide from God when he walks in the garden. The man and woman are equal in their sin and guilt.

When God addresses them he calls to the man because he is the appointed head. The first-created is addressed first. Nonetheless, the woman is treated as a responsible being; God requires an explanation from her, as well as the man. In contrast, God does not allow the serpent, once so eloquent, to explain himself.

The parity of the man and woman is shown by their responses. Essentially, both shift the blame rather than acknowledge their guilt. The man blames God for giving him the woman and blames the woman for giving him the fruit, and the woman blames the serpent. The hierarchy here (man, the head of his wife; his wife, a

---

[31]Tertullian, p. 14.

co-ruler with him over creation; and the serpent, part of creation) has often been noted. The significance of the hierarchy is usually connected with the nature of the fall, which is said to be usurpation of initiative by the ruled from the ruler. Yet, as we have said before, the major emphasis of the passage is on disobeying God's command not to eat of the tree.

The appropriateness of the "curses" has also frequently been pointed out. The major areas of concern for both man and woman are noted. The woman's punishment revolves around husband and children, and the man's around his work. In other words, the woman feels the effects of sin in her roles as mother and wife and the man in his role as provider. Does this sound like sexual stereotypes? Does this support 'the woman's place is in the home'?

Phyllis Trible suggests that the judgments are culturally conditioned. The woman is defined in terms of her husband and work (child-bearing) and the man in terms of his wife and work (farming). Just as the man has moved beyond farming in his work, so the woman has moved beyond childbearing as her only work.[32]

To limit the judgments in terms of the culture or of what we now know are sexually stereotyped roles is to obscure the point. The judgments of God, who is Lord of time *and* culture, are universally applicable to the fallen (sinful) world. Understanding what the "curses" mean will help us better understand the world, including men and women, today.

The judgment of the woman affects her physical being; pregnancy and the bearing of children will be accompanied by great hardship. No advance in modern medicine can ease the toil (which results in pain for many) of childbearing. Giving birth is very aptly termed labor; it is hard work.

The sentence of the man is one of hard labor also. The equality of the judgments is reinforced by the use of the same word in verse 16

---

[32]Phyllis Trible, "Good Tidings of Great Joy: Biblical Faith without Sexism," *Christianity and Crisis,* 34:1 (February 4, 1974), 14.

(translated "pain"[33] in RSV) and verse 17 (translated "toil" in RSV). Both sentences involve pain/toil, and both affect the bringing forth of life, human and otherwise. Death, which is the consequence of sin, affects the reproduction of life; because death rules all things, childbirth and the growth of food are infected with hardship.

Relationships are marred by sin. The harmony and order of Eden have been replaced by domination and struggle. Humanity wrecked its relationship to God and also the relationship between men and women and between humanity and creation.

Perhaps the most enigmatic part of the curse is Genesis 3:16b: "Yet your desire shall be for your husband, and he shall rule over you." How to understand "desire" (תְּשׁוּקָה) is perhaps the most pressing question. The following are common but unsatisfactory interpretations of "desire."

(1) "Desire" is frequently equated with sexual desire. The woman's craving for her husband is so strong that she desires marital intercourse, though its results, conceiving and bearing children, involve pain. This explanation closely links verse 16b with verse 16a, and so fits the immediate context. This interpretation has two unsatisfying features. The Hebrew word for desire occurs only three times in the Old Testament. One of these (Gen. 4:7) is obviously nonsexual, and so we can conclude that the word itself has no sexual denotations.[34] The etymology of "desire" supports a nonsexual understanding of it. In addition, experience does not corroborate this theory. The man usually has stronger, more easily aroused sex drives—or is this a sexist myth?

---

[33]Some advocates of natural childbirth (such as Helen Wessel, *Natural Childbirth and the Christian Family* [New York: Harper & Row Publishers, 1963]) object to the translation of *itsebon* as pain, and it is misleading to find the same word in verse 16 and verse 17 translated differently. Nonetheless, *itsebon* connotes hardship, labor that distresses, becomes grievous, sorrowful, so that one should not exclude pain from its field of meaning. Toil that is so great can produce pain.

[34]Cf. G. R. Driver, "Notes and Studies: Theological and Philological Problems in the Old Testament," *Journal of Theological Studies*, 47 (1946), 158. Brown, Driver and Briggs have related שׁוּק to the Arabic root *šāqa*, to desire, excite desire. This meaning would associate תְּשׁוּקָה with sexual desire. However, the phonemic equivalent of the Hebrew *š* is *s* in Arabic. The proper etymology in Arabic for שׁוּק is *sāqa*, to urge or drive on. This meaning need not have sexual connotations.

(2) According to John Calvin, the clause means that the woman will desire only what the husband desires and that she will have no command over herself.[35] "And he shall rule over you" is a restatement of "yet your desire shall be for your husband." This repetition may seem redundant to us, but it often occurs in Hebrew poetry. However, if the wife so loses her will that she does not disagree with her husband, the hardship of his rule, which is the punishment for sin, is lost.

(3) A very appealing and more true-to-life solution is suggested by Gini Andrews.

> I'm wondering if this immense, clinging, psychological dependence on man which is part of us as women is not something we should face as part of our fallenness. . . . We'll jettison any plans, rearrange our lives or our hair-dos; we'll work our fingers to the first joint, throw up a promising career, and too often even undercut our best friend—all for some man we find compellingly attractive.[36]

All three of these interpretations agree that through the woman's desire for her husband, he rules her. Because the woman desires her husband in some way, he is able to rule over her. This area of agreement makes all three views unacceptable. Genesis 3:16b is God's judgment against sin; therefore, the desire of the woman in no way contributes to the rule of the husband, which is God's original intent for marriage. Her desire does not make it easier for her husband to rule, contrary to the three interpretations above. If her desire does enable her husband to rule over her (as the usual indicative translations, "and he shall rule over you," suppose), why do so few husband's rule their homes?

A comparison of Genesis 3:16b and Genesis 4:7b will give us the answer. The Hebrew of these two verses is exactly the same, except for appropriate changes in person and gender. Notice the entirely different translation of 4:7b: "its [sin's] desire is for you [Cain], but you must master it." Sin's desire for Cain was one of possession or

---

[35] Calvin, *Commentaries,* vol. I, p. 1972.
[36] Gini Andrews, *Your Half of the Apple; God and the Single Girl* (Grand Rapids: Zondervan, 1972), pp. 51–52.

Many consider the Hebrew wife one of her husband's possessions. One proof text cited is Exodus 20:17. The neighbor's wife is listed after his "house" as one of the things one should not covet, along with his servants, oxen, or asses. However, this verse does not prove that wives are chattel. It seems clear that desiring another's wife (or husband) is wrong, and that is the point of Exodus 20:17. The ten commandments are addressed to women as well as men.[43] In Exodus 20:17, the word "house" refers to the whole household, and the wife is a member of the household, so she is mentioned. Husbands are not listed because, just as it has been the custom in our culture to use the pronoun "he" when either male or female persons are in view, the Old Testament laws are in masculine terms. It is appropriate to use masculine terms when both men and women are included because the husband is the head of his wife, and she is thereby represented in and by him. The Hebrew woman listening to the ten commandments would know she was not to covet her neighbor's husband.

Another argument for the wife as possession is the bride price (*mohar*). *Mohar* is the price paid by the fiancé to the father of the bride. Some assume that this payment is a virtual purchase of the woman, that wives were bought and sold. There is another explanation. This price could be compensation paid to the family for the loss of a daughter.[44] But, it seems to me, too much is made of *mohar*. It occurs only three times in the Old Testament, and these instances do not indicate that it is the norm or even the common practice in Israel. In Genesis 34:12, a non-Israelite offers to pay any sum as *mohar*, a marriage gift; and in I Samuel 18:25, Saul, from whom the Lord had departed, asks David for a hundred Philistine foreskins as *mohar*. His purpose is not to set up a marriage for his daughter but to get rid of David or show him up. These two instances would not establish a standard because one is offered by a non-Israelite and one

---

[43]The command to keep the sabbath does not specify wives as it does sons, daughters, and male and female servants. She still must keep the sabbath. So the command is addressed to both men and women.

[44]Vaux, p. 27.

is required by a sinful king. The only time *mohar* is required by God's law is Exodus 22:16; if a man seduces an unbetrothed virgin, he must pay her father *mohar*. In the parallel passage, Deuteronomy 22:29, *mohar* is not mentioned, just the price, 50 shekels. God commands payment of *mohar* only in cases of rape, and this price seems to be compensation for the irreparable loss of virginity.

In addition, there is Old Testament material that indicates that the wife is not mere chattel. She cannot be sold, even if she has been captured in war (Deut. 21:14). The definition of marriage, which also defines monogamy as God's intention, in Genesis 2:24 demonstrates that the wife is not to be considered property. The husband is to leave his family and cleave to his wife.[45] She is not said to cleave to him, but he to her.

Some think that the widow was willed to the heir of her husband's property. The cases referred to as proof (Gen. 35:22; 49:4; II Sam. 16:21ff.) are unacceptable as proof because they are historical events which the Bible reports without condoning. The Bible expressly forbids sons (heirs) to lie with their fathers' concubines (Lev. 18:6ff.). In Genesis 49:4, Reuben loses his place of honor as firstborn because he slept with his father's concubine. Absalom's behavior was intended to insult his father David; it was a political move to demonstrate that he was powerful enough to offend his father.

Scanzoni and Hardesty criticize the levirate law because it prevents a woman from being her own person; they see it as one more law to keep a woman under the jurisdiction of a man all her life. Scanzoni and Hardesty misrepresent the law when they say that Deuteronomy 25:5–10 *requires* a childless widow to marry her husband's brother.[46] The levirate law emphasizes the duty of the husband's brother (v. 7), rather than the widow's. It is not just any brother who is involved but a brother who has been living with the deceased. And even he has the option of refusing though that means

---

[45]Samuel Terrien, "Toward a Biblical Theology of Womanhood," *Religion in Life,* 42:3 (Autumn, 1973), 329.

[46]Scanzoni and Hardesty, p. 40.

shame for him. Deuteronomy 25:5-10 is expressly intended to protect the deceased, to give him an heir to perpetuate his name and to inherit the land. These were important matters to the Israelites. Note the intensity of the phrase, "that his name may not be blotted out of Israel" (v. 6). This law assumes that the widow will want the marriage, out of a concern for her dead husband's name or out of concern for herself. Widows occupied a vulnerable position in Israel; that is why Old Testament legislation is solicitous for them (Exod. 22:22-24; Deut. 14:29; 24:17). It is the brother-in-law who is more likely to object to the levirate law. The widow has the *right* to bring a reluctant brother-in-law before the elders; it is the widow who performs the ceremony of disgrace if the brother-in-law continues to refuse. If the widow did not want to marry her brother-in-law, she would not have to exercise her rights.

The widow's (and divorcee's) independence of a man's authority is shown by her ability to make her vows without interference (Num. 30:9), whereas the married or betrothed woman is under the authority of her husband and the daughter is under the authority of her father. The husband or father can cancel a vow; however, he has only 24 hours in which to do so. The authority to nullify vows is an expression of the headship of the husband and makes sense if we consider how the wife's vows might affect her husband. He might have to pay for his wife's extravagance in money or goods or have to suffer from deprivation of his conjugal rights for a time.[47] It is not women *per se* who cannot make their own vows. It is only if their position is under the God-established authority of husband or father. So, it seems the principle of submission does not apply for all women under all men but only within the family structure. In the Bible "nowhere outside of the husband and wife relationship in marriage [and parent/child] do we find such a demand" for submission.[48]

The daughters, unlike wives, could be sold into slavery, and so

---

[47] I Corinthians 7:5 expresses the mutuality and accord that should be present in marriage in the making of vows of abstinence.

[48] Prohl, p. 46.

could the sons. The conditions of bondage were different for sons and daughters; the daughter received special treatment. She was sold as a slave but was usually designated as someone's wife. If not, she would be redeemed, that is, bought back by her father. She could not be sold to foreigners, or if her owner took another wife, he could not decrease her food, clothing, or marital rights (Exod. 21:7–11). Also, the father could not employ his daughter as a prostitute (Lev. 19:29).

Daughters had the right to inherit if there were no sons (Num. 27:8). Daughters could inherit even if there were sons (Job 42:15). The provisions (sons had first claim to the inheritance, and daughters had to marry within their own tribe, Num. 36:6–9) had a purpose. God gave each tribe a fixed portion of the land, and God's division of the land was to be permanent. In the year of jubilee, all land was to return to its original owner to remind the Israelites that "the land is not to be sold in perpetuity, for the land is mine," says the Lord; "for you are strangers and sojourners with me" (Lev. 25:23). The land was not the possession of the Israelites to do with it as they pleased.

As mother, the wife was on equal footing with her husband. Honor is commanded for both father and mother (Exod. 20:12; Lev. 19:3). The penalty for striking or cursing father or mother is the same, death (Exod. 21:15, 17; cf. Deut. 21:18–21). Proverbs has frequent references to the importance of honoring parents; references to father and mother are parallel (Prov. 6:20; 10:1; 15:20; 17:25; 19:26; 20:20; 23:22, 25). What the mother says is as important as what the father says. "Hear, my son, your father's instruction and reject not your mother's teaching" (Prov. 1:8). In cases of naming children, the mother names the child 26 times, God four times, and the father 14 times. In Israel, naming was significant; it involved the exercise of authority and the discernment of the nature of what was being named. So mothers are respected in the Old Testament, but motherhood has always been exalted. What about the wife as a person in her own right?

Perhaps in the legislation for divorce and adultery, the woman's position appears weakest. It has been said that the Hebrew law offers no restraints for the husband regarding extra-marital inter-course.[49] Yet the wife is severely punished for sex outside marriage. Her husband can even request a trial by ordeal for her if he suspects her of infidelity (Num. 5:11ff.). The wife has no such recourse. Nonetheless, the ordeal of "bitter waters" in Numbers 5:11ff. is not severe, in contrast to those of other cultures where the test itself was almost certain death. This law protects the woman against a jealous husband. If the woman were considered her husband's private property or a subhuman being, his being suspicious of infidelity would probably be enough to convict and punish her. It may be of little comfort to some in favor of women's rights that the wife could not be convicted without a trial (a noteworthy condition in Old Testament times), but it is comforting to us Christians to know that the Lord, who established the form of the ordeal, was in control of such trials and assured the correct outcome.

The husband's headship is referred to in Numbers 5:19–20. The wife is "under" her husband (תַּחַת אִישֵׁךְ). It is an explicit statement of the wife's subordinate position.

The wife had no laws to keep her husband faithful to her. The man is punished only if he lies with another's wife (Lev. 20:10–12). The two principles, the husband's headship and the one-flesh idea in marriage, may explain the Old Testament adultery laws. The status of the woman, single, engaged, or married, determines the fate of the offenders. If the woman is unattached, the man, whether married or not, marries her (Deut. 22:18ff.). However, if the woman is betrothed or married, both are put to death (Lev. 20:10; Deut. 22:22) because she is not free to marry him. The exception is cases of rape in which the girl could have called for help but could not have been heard (Deut. 22:25–27). In such a case, only the man is killed. The girl is given the benefit of the doubt. The one-flesh principle God established (cf. I Cor. 6:16) is taken seriously; violation of it is punished severely. When a man and a woman have sexual intercourse

---

[49]E. Neufeld, *Ancient Hebrew Marriage Laws* (London: Longmans, Green & Co., 1944), p. 163.

they become one flesh. It is something that cannot be changed. They will always be of one flesh. As such, they should be permanently joined together in marriage. If they cannot be married because the woman is one flesh with another, their sin is punished.

As mentioned before, Deuteronomy 24:1ff. appears to give the husband only the right to divorce. Any "indecency" in a wife seems to be the only grounds needed by the dissatisfied husband for a divorce. It is hard to determine what "indecency" referred to during the time of Moses. Later (first century A.D.), Hillel, a rabbinic school, thought the phrase meant any trivial thing, such as a badly cooked dish.[50] However, it is not necessary for us to determine what an "indecency" is, because God is not establishing the conditions mandatory or necessary for a divorce here. The rabbis misunderstood the point of Deuteronomy 24:1ff. God through Moses is regulating a sinful procedure (divorce). This command restrains the sinful tendencies that seek a divorce and also provides a deterrent to divorce. Deuteronomy 24:1–3 presupposes that a divorce has already taken place (see chapter 1, pp. 15–16). The question at hand is: Can the divorced couple remarry? The purpose of Deuteronomy 24:1–4 is to prevent the remarriage of a man and woman if the woman has married another in the meantime and then become free. This "defiled" remarriage is an "abomination" to the Lord. Deuteronomy 24:1–4 also deters divorce. Since there was a good possibility of not being able to remarry his wife, the husband would be less likely to divorce his wife hastily. God's true judgment of divorce is stated in no uncertain terms: "I hate divorce" (Mal. 2:16). In Old Testament times, easy divorces were not God's will for men. God opposes divorce. God "permitted" divorce only in the sense that he did not punish the offenders. Moses allowed it for their hardness of heart (Matt. 19:3–9); see also p. 15). It cannot be said that Old Testament laws gave only men the right to divorce, easy or not, because Old Testament legislation, truly interpreted, discourages divorce initiated by anyone.

---

[50]Vaux, p. 34.

Old Testament marriage legislation still seems to favor men. Why? As a result of the fall, the God-established headship of the husband is challenged. Both husband as head and wife as helper are no longer content; marriage has become a battlefield. Still, the headship of the husband is a part of God's intention. Perhaps God established laws in the Old Testament'that were to reestablish and maintain the husband's headship.

Though marriage laws undergird the husband's headship, the Hebrew wife usually occupied a position of dignity and respect. She was loved by her husband (Gen. 24:67; I Sam. 1:4–8). She had a great deal of independence. Hannah's husband told her to do what seemed best to her (I Sam. 1:23). Abigail wisely reversed her husband's decision not to help David (I Sam. 25:14ff.). A woman told her husband they should set up a guest room for Elisha because he was a holy man (II Kings 4:9–10).

A good wife was greatly valued and considered difficult to find. She was a gift from God (Prov. 18:22; 19:14). The Old Testament ideal, found in Proverbs 31:10ff., is very different from the typical American housewife or what is becoming the typical American career-woman. She is neither chained to the kitchen sink and buried in dirty diapers nor leaving her family to fend for themselves.

Is she a homebody? One commentator emphasizes that she is a wise business manager of the *home;* but he criticizes her for remaining a housewife since nothing is said about any intellectual interests or religion.[51] Her circle of interests should be broadened. Matthew Henry says that it is good that her only desire and chief happiness is to please her husband because she conforms to the curse (Gen. 3:16):

> Though she is a woman of spirit herself, yet *her desire is to her husband,* to know his mind, that she may accommodate herself to it, and she is willing that *he should rule over her.*[52]

---

[51]Crawford H. Toy, *A Critical and Exegetical Commentary on the Book of Proverbs,* International Critical Commentary (New York: Charles Scribner's Sons, 1916), p. 542.

[52]Matthew Henry, *Commentary on the Whole Bible,* III, (New York: Fleming H. Revell Co., n.d.), Proverbs 31:10ff.

This commentator confuses the headship of the husband established by God at creation with the difficult "rule" of the husband that is a result of God's judgment on sin.

Proverbs 31:10ff. paints the picture of the good wife, a scarce and precious person. She is not just a "good wife" (RSV); she is literally a woman of *hayil,* might, capacity or virtue. She is made strong by the fear of the Lord. Contrary to the interpretations referred to above, the ideal wife is mainly concerned with pleasing God; primarily she is a woman who knows and fears the Lord (v. 30). The woman who fears God is the one who is to be praised and who is motivated to do things worthy of praise. Caring for and loving (seeking their good, v. 12) her husband and family is a result of her faith in God. To enhance her husband's reputation (v. 23) is not the goal of her activities nor the guiding principle; it is one by-product. People think well of him because they know his wife and respect her. He is not the only one known in the gates, where the leaders of the people gathered; she is known there also (v. 31) because her works praise her. The good woman is respected and valued for her own merits.

Does this passage justify the career wife/mother? It has been said that the woman of Proverbs 31 does not employ herself with scholars' or statesmen's business but with woman's work;[53] you would not find her husband helping her with the dishes. She works her fingers to the bone to provide food and clothing so that he can sit around at the gates and talk politics. However, the wife, not the husband, is in view; we are not told what he does. He is mentioned incidentally, whereas, all the major jobs of the ideal wife are enumerated.

Whether or not her work is limited to "woman's work" is hard to say. The particulars of her activities are determined by the cultural setting. The passage does not mean all women should go into real estate (v. 16); and few of us women today know the difference between a "distaff" and a "spindle," or what to do with either one.

---

[53]Ibid.

The activities of Proverbs 31:10-31 have great variety; and though they are performed for the benefit of the household, they show that the wife is a person in her own right. She is not confined to the house or the neighborhood store; she has freedom of movement (v. 14). She buys land and plants a vineyard on it (v. 15). This sounds like hard work, and it is. She has to gather up strength to do it, roll up her sleeves (the expression then was to gird up her loins). She also gives to the poor. She does not leave charitable works to the United Fund or to the deacons in the church, nor does she just put money in the offering plate or write a check to her favorite charity. She "reaches out her hands to the needy"; she seeks them out and gives them what they need. She makes garments and sells them to travelling merchants. She is strong, dignified, unafraid of the future, and wise. On her tongue is the law of mercy. Mercy is the word used to designate God's covenant love, his favor towards his people. This woman is familiar with God's law. She deserves admiration and imitation, not in the particulars, but in her fear of the Lord.

Whose Rite?

Some say the whole Hebrew ceremonial system accommodates a prejudice against women.[54] Women could not receive the sign of the covenant, circumcision, and there were a number of laws that seemed to discriminate against them.

To begin with, the woman is unclean after she bears a child, and to top it off, she is unclean longer if she has a girl than if she has a boy (Lev. 12). Why is she considered unclean after childbirth, and why does the uncleanness last longer after a girl-child? Motherhood is an honorable profession, is it not?

Being "clean" means being qualified for the worship of the Lord in the tabernacle. Cleanness is a prerequisite for holiness, but being clean is not being holy. The life of the Israelite consisted in continual

---

[54]Nancy Hardesty, "Women: Second Class Citizens?" *Eternity*, 22:1 (January, 1971), 25.

service to the Lord, so a constant distinction had to be made between persons who were clean and who were unclean.[55] This necessity for daily distinguishing was meant to bring the law to mind, to remind them to distinguish between right and wrong. The point of the clean/unclean laws was "to imbue the mind of Israel with moral distinctions,"[56] and to teach them that their God was a holy God who required a holy people (Lev. 20:24-26).

God established very specific and concrete laws for cleanness to make the Israelite conscious of a distinction between moral cleanness and uncleanness, which is not easy to discern. Instead of just telling them about right and wrong, God had his people act it out; God set up pictures of clean and unclean things to teach a nonphysical truth. In the Old Testament God taught his people as children (cf. Gal. 3:23-24) in pictures and symbols. After Christ came, God's people came of age and no longer need to be taught as babes. This change accounts, at least in part, for why God's people no longer are required to observe the clean/unclean laws.

In some cases of uncleanness, there is a parity between man and woman (Lev. 15). Both are considered unclean if they have a discharge, with the same communicability and the same requirements for restoration to cleanness. These regulations were to make the Israelites conscious of sin as something defiling. It was also a reminder of the perfection of God; no person with a physical (also a result of sin) or ethical defect was allowed to come into the tabernacle.

But why is the law so hard on mothers? Perhaps because the child is born a sinner[57] (Ps. 51:5). But it is the mother who is unclean. Is she considered to have sinned to have brought a sinner into the world? That is impossible since God commanded reproduction. Others have suggested that the uncleanness of the mother is related to the fall. But how? Part of God's judgment is that the woman

---

[55]G. Vos, p. 191.

[56]Andrew Bonar, *A Commentary on Leviticus* (London: The Banner of Truth Trust, reprint, 1972), p. 211.

[57]Ibid., p. 235.

should bear children in hardship. Perhaps because God specifically indicated that difficulty in childbirth is a result of or punishment for sin, the process is considered defiling and declared unclean, as are dead bodies, another result of sin.

In the case of the male child, the mother is unclean for seven days and then the boy is circumcised, he is received into the covenant community. Then the mother continues in the blood of her purifying and is effectively unclean for 33 more days. For the daughter, the time periods are doubled. The difference in time may be to mark the difference between the sexes from birth. In connection with the headship of the man, the boy is received into the covenant community before the girl (as Adam was created first), and this time difference affects the mother's ceremonial cleanness. Whatever the reasons, no greater worth or less sinfulness can be attributed to the son because the same burnt offering and sin offering are made for both.

Another case of alleged "discrimination" is the dedication of the first-born males to the Lord; they had to be redeemed or bought back (Exod. 13:2, 13). First-born females were not redeemed, nor were second- or third-born males. More than male chauvinism is involved here. The consecration of the first-born male points to a future event: God redeemed his people through his first-born son Jesus.

Male animals were specified for the major offerings. The burnt offering, which represented complete consecration to the Lord,[58] had to be male. The sin offering for priests, rulers or the whole people, which was offered to restore fellowship with God,[59] had to be male; however, the sin offering for an individual man or woman was the same, a female. All had to be without blemish. The male sacrifice without blemish is a type of Christ. But why is a female used for individuals? Maybe the reason is practical: the male/female aspect may have had no significance, except that bulls and male goats are more valuable (for breeding) than the females. This

---

[58]Robert B. Louthan, *The Atoning Efficacy of the Mosaic Legislation,* a thesis submitted to the faculty of Westminster Theological Seminary, Philadelphia, 1959, p. 5.

[59]Ibid., p. 14.

principle does not carry over to human beings. An individual could not afford a male animal for his sin offering.

The peace offering, which was a thank offering (Lev. 7:11ff.) for the peace the offerer had with God because of atonement,[60] could be male or female. Possibly no sex is specified to show that both sexes have free access to God through the Son of God's atonement.

Leviticus 27 evaluates women and girls as worth less than men and boys, at least as far as being released from a vow is concerned.

	Male	Female
20–60 yrs.	50 shekels	30 shekels
5–20 yrs.	20	10
over 60	15	10
a mo.–5 yrs.	5	3

One interpretation suggests that those capable of most service are valued most, males more than females, prime years more than old or young. Men did participate in war (Num. 1:1ff.), a service woman did not perform. Another factor may be the ability to pay. This theory is supported by verse 8; if a man is too poor to pay the normal fee, the priest must reevaluate him according to his ability to pay. Men in their prime may have had more financial resources. In addition, the headship of the husband, jeopardized after the fall, could be involved. God's legislation may be concretely setting this principle before the people. The man is valued more because God has appointed him to a position of headship.

Lastly, women could not be priests. Once more, the explanation is probably that the priest is a type, a prefiguration of Christ, who is a high priest forever.

In view of all these limitations, what could the woman do in the cult? Was she, lacking circumcision, even considered a part of the covenant community? Only men were required at the three annual feasts (Exod. 23:17).

---

[60]Bonar, p. 53.

Nonetheless, women did participate; they did attend the three feasts usually (I Sam. 1:1ff.). They were expected (Deut. 16:11, 14). God's law did not *require* their presence because of their periodic uncleanness.

Women brought sacrifices themselves (I Sam. 2:19; Lev. 12; 15). They participated in the ceremonial feasts (Deut. 12:12-18).

> . . . and you shall rejoice before the Lord your God, you and your son and your daughter, your manservant and your maidservant, the Levite who is within your towns, the sojourner, the fatherless, and the widow who are among you . . . (Deut. 16:11).

Wives are included in such a way that they are not mentioned as are sons, daughters, man- and maidservants and widows. They, with their husbands are addressed directly by the Lord. If wives were not included, there would be no need to state that *males* are *required* at the three annual feasts (Deut. 16:16).

The women were permitted to do more than weave cloth for the tabernacle or give gold offerings for the building of the tabernacle (Exod. 35:22). There was a group of women who "ministered" at the door of the tent of meeting (Exod. 38:8; I Sam. 2:22b); no more information is given about them. Today scholars debate whether or not this group was an official body and what was the nature of their service. The verb translated "ministered" is the same used of the Levites, the priestly caste (Num. 4:23, 30).[61] The women were not priests, as the preceding references show, but they did have a recognized function at the tabernacle, possibly prayer.

Women could take the vow of a Nazirite (Num. 6), just as a man could, with the restrictions imposed in Numbers 30 regarding vows in general. The Nazirite vowed to separate him/herself to the Lord; he or she was considered a holy person.

Women were required to be present during the reading of the law (Deut. 31:12; Neh. 8:2). It was as important for them to hear it as for the men.

---

[61]Ismar J. Peritz, "Woman in the Ancient Hebrew Cult," *Journal of Biblical Literature*, 17 (1898), 145.

So we see that in relation to the ceremonial law, there is an equality and nonequality between men and women. The laws that seem to discriminate against women may have been intended to undergird the headship of the husband or to prefigure the coming Son of God, who would fulfill the law. The status of the woman was different in Hebrew law to point out the difference between the sexes. Women are not men, and God requires different things from men and women in some areas. On the other hand, the woman stands in the same relation to God as the man. When a man or woman sins, the guilt is the same (Num. 5:6). She is responsible for her own obedience; she is to know and obey God's law. She prays to God without mediation of husband or priest (Gen. 16:7–13; I Sam. 2:1ff.). God spoke to women directly (Gen. 25:22–23; Judg. 13:3–5). She offers her own sacrifices. The woman is a full-fledged member of the covenant community.

In the Public's Eye

The woman's role in public worship, the cult, was limited in the Old Testament; she could not be a priest; she could minister only at the door to the tent of meeting (only priests could go inside). But women could be prophetesses and queens (Esther, Bathsheba), and Israel's history claims one woman judge. Apparently, there was less discrimination outside the church than in it.

Some want to limit the woman in public life. Calvin writes:

> We know that the gift of prophecy is sometimes though rarely allowed to women, and there is no doubt that female prophets existed whenever God wished to brand men with a mark of ignominy as strongly as possible. I say as much as possible, because the sister of Moses enjoyed the prophetic gift, and this never ceased to be the reproach of her brother (Ex. XV.20). But when Deborah and Huldah discharged the prophetic office (Judges IV.4 and 2 Kings XXII.14), God doubtless wished to raise them on high to shame the men and obliquely to show them their slothfulness (*Corpus Reformatum*).[62]

---

[62]G. Vos, p. 196.

All of this is pure inference; the texts very matter of factly state that "Deborah, a prophetess, the wife of Lappidoth, was judging Israel at that time" (Judg. 4:4) and that Hilkiah the priest et al consulted Huldah about the book of the law (II Kings 22:14). There is no indication that the men were slothful in Deborah's or Huldah's time. Deborah, speaking authoritatively as God's prophet, tells Barak to lead his men against Sisera, their enemy. He does not respond with obedience to God's word; instead he adds a conditional clause: "if Deborah will go with him." She, better than we, understands his motive in asking her to go (v. 9); he wants a sure ticket to glory, but it will not be his. The triumph over Sisera goes to another woman (Judg. 4:6-9). From this point on, all we see is cooperation between prophetess Deborah and commander Barak (she speaks God's word and he obeys it); both praise the Lord in a victory song (Judg. 5:1ff.).

The case of Huldah is even more straightforward. King Josiah finds the long-lost book of the law and directs the high priest, his secretary and several other important men to "inquire of the Lord for me . . . concerning the words of this book that has been found . . ." (II Kings 22:13). So these men go to Huldah, the prophetess, and she authoritatively speaks God's word to them. There was not even a lack of prophets at that time. Jeremiah and Zephaniah were available. King Josiah, who had been diligently repairing the Lord's temple, and his faithful servants are neither guilty of sloth nor in need to be humbled by a woman's prophesying.

Miriam was a prophetess too, but her record has a blemish (as does Aaron's and Moses'). She initiates a rebellion against Moses, and Aaron goes along with her. They are upset about Moses' mixed marriage and jealous of his status. The Lord breaks up the attack on his servant Moses and punishes Miriam, not Aaron, because she began the attack. She is afflicted with leprosy and sent outside the camp for seven days. Israel waits for her and then moves on (Num. 12). Afterwards, we hear of no more trouble from her. She was not a reproach to her brother Moses, except in this one incident; she did not dishonor him when she publicly praised the Lord after his victory over Pharoah at the Red Sea (Exod. 15:20-22). Apparently, it was a custom for the women to welcome the Lord's triumph with music and dance (Judg. 11:34; I Sam. 18:6-7; Ps. 68:11 [feminine noun]; Isa. 40:9).

The prophet Joel confirms the propriety of prophetesses:

> And it shall come to pass afterward,
> that I will pour out my spirit on all flesh;
> your sons and your daughters shall prophesy,
>> your old men shall dream dreams,
>> and your young men shall see visions.
> Even upon the menservants and maidservants
>> in those days, I will pour out my spirit (Joel 2:28-29).

In conclusion,

> Whenever a woman prophesies or rules, the Old Testament does not speak disapprovingly of her in her position of leadership because she is a woman. Disapproval is expressed only when she uses her influence against God's will.[63]

Hebrew women were not known just for their cooking; they were also known for their wisdom. Abigail is introduced to us as a woman "of good understanding" (I Sam. 25:3), and her conduct proves it true. Then there is the "wise woman" from Tekoah (II Sam. 14:2). Her actions and her story are hard to understand, but she is designated as a wise woman. Another wise woman saves a city from destruction by her wisdom (II Sam. 20:16-22).

If there were "wise women" around, why couldn't Qoheleth find one? When he hunted for those who had found wisdom, "One man among a thousand I found, but a woman among all these I have not found" (Eccl. 7:28). Is Qoheleth saying that wise men are scarce but wise women do not exist?[64] Is Qoheleth talking about a certain kind of wisdom that women do not have? For instance, no woman wrote a book of the Old or New Testament. (But inspired songs of women, such as Deborah, Miriam, Hannah, and Mary, are recorded.) H. C. Leupold and Ernest W. Hengstenberg comment respectively:

---

[63]*Acts of Synod* (Grand Rapids: Board of Publications of the Christian Reformed Church, 1973), p. 537.

[64]George Aaron Barton, *A Critical and Exegetical Commentary on the Book of Ecclesiastes,* International Critical Commentary (New York: Charles Scribner's Sons, 1909), p. 147

Nor, for that matter, has it ever been the province of women to produce by constructive wisdom works or systems of thought that are truly creative in the realm of revealed truth. Koheleth, therefore, speaks no slander but utters what our present-day observation still substantiates.[65]

It lies beyond the degree of woman, whose characteristic is in these respects predominantly receptive, not productive, and whose real sphere of independent action is quite another [the home].[66]

Both of the above writers conclude from Ecclesiastes 7:28 (and experience?!) that women's minds are inferior to men's. That is, women's minds do not produce but only receive. In other words, women, by nature, cannot produce systematic theologies.

Let us look again at what Qoheleth said:

Behold, this have I found, saith the Preacher, *laying one thing to another,* to find out the account; which my soul still seeketh, but I have not found: one man among a thousand have I found; but a woman among all those have I not found (Eccl. 7:27–28, ASV, 1901).

Qoheleth is not talking about the nature of woman; he is talking about empirical findings, what he himself has experienced. Verse 27 indicates that his search for wisdom has not been exhaustive; he is still looking. Qoheleth himself has not met a woman who has wisdom, but that does not mean that there is none.

What was the life of the ordinary woman, who was not a prophetess, judge, queen, or wise woman, like? Was she confined to the home? We have already seen the extensive territory covered by the "Wonder Woman" of Proverbs 31. She did not stay at home.

Women could plead their own cases in court. The wise woman of Tekoah had direct access to the king (II Sam. 14:4) as did the two mothers with the one living child (I Kings 3:16ff.). Mahlah, Noah, Hoglah, Milcah, and Tirzah, the daughters of Zelophehad made

---

[65]H. C. Leupold, *Exposition of Ecclesiastes* (Columbus: The Wartburg Press, 1952), p. 177.
[66]Ernest W. Hengstenberg, *A Commentary on Ecclesiastes* (n.p., Sovereign Grace Publishers, 1960), p. 185.

their plea for the right to inherit before Moses and all the people (Num. 27:1–2).

The Shunammite woman sought out Elisha to restore her dead son; she left her husband at home. All along, she, not her husband, had taken the initiative in their relationship with Elisha; it was her idea to set up a guest room for him.

Hebrew women, though they were not soldiers, were not excluded from war. Deborah celebrates (Judg. 5:24ff.) Jael, a woman, for killing Israel's enemy, Sisera. In Psalm 68:12, the women at home divide the spoil of their defeated enemies.

Women were not kept out of public life; and they do appear to have been treated as individuals of worth. If they were not, we would never have heard of Ruth or Esther.

Women were not treated as men in the Old Testament. God created man and woman in his image but for different functions. The husband is the head of his wife, and she is his helper; together they are one flesh. After the fall, this relationship, both the equality in being and the inequality in function, is threatened and would have been lost without God's revelation in the Old Testament. Consequently, many Old Testament laws distinguish between women and men to maintain the husband's headship. The Hebrew woman is also pictured as a capable and worthwhile being—in relation to God and to her husband (if she has one). The Old Testament's teaching about women is not the prejudice of a patriarchal society.

FOUR

WHAT THE NEW TESTAMENT
SAYS ABOUT WOMEN

DOES the coming of Christ radically change the woman's status as a member of the community of the Lord? Are all Old Testament laws that distinguish women from men abolished in the New Testament so that men and women are equal in every way?

> Any view which subordinates the woman to the man is not analogous to but incongruous with this fundamental teaching of both the Old and the New Testaments.[1]

Or are women still subordinate as "the law" says?

> In fact, her inferior position is more clearly and emphatically set forth by the Apostles than by the Prophets and Patriarchs. There are no such specific directions for woman's subordination in the Pentateuch as in the Epistles.[2]

Elizabeth Cady Stanton, an original feminist, thought the New Testament went even further than the Old in subjugating women.

How can two people, such as the two quoted above, come up with

---

[1]Jewett, p. 134.
[2]Stanton, part 2, p. 113.

such different understandings of the Bible? The reason is that there is some truth on both sides. Seemingly contradictory principles concerning men and women exist in the New Testament as well as the Old.[3] Like the Old Testament, the New Testament teaches both equality in being and the subordination of the woman to her husband and both the value of woman's participation in the church and certain restrictions on her activity. Stanton is right in her analysis of the relationship of the Old Testament to the New: both say the same thing, but the New Testament clarifies and develops the Old.

How to Treat a Lady

There is only one area where most students of the New Testament agree regarding women: Jesus treated women as they should be treated. Dorothy Sayers summarized Jesus' attitude.

> They [women] had never known a man like this Man—there never has been such another. A prophet and teacher who never nagged at them, never flattered or coaxed or patronised; who never made arch jokes about them, never treated them either as "The women, God help us!" or "The ladies, God bless them!"; who rebuked without querulousness and praised without condescension; who took their questions and arguments seriously; who never mapped out their sphere for them, never urged them to be feminine or jeered at them for being female; who had no axe to grind and no uneasy male dignity to defend; who took them as he found them and was completely unself-conscious. There is no act, no sermon, no parable in the whole Gospel that borrows its pungency from female perversity; nobody could possibly guess from the words and deeds of Jesus that there was anything "funny" about women's nature.[4]

There is no doubt that Jesus' treatment of women was a radical break with the status quo. In first century Palestine, the men, especially rabbis, did not speak to women in public. Jesus not only

---

[3](1) Men and women have the same relationship to God. (2) The woman is to submit herself to her husband. (3) Husband and wife become one flesh in marriage.

[4]Dorothy Sayers, *Are Women Human?* (Downers Grove: InterVarsity Press, 1971), p. 47.

talked with women, he healed them (Matt. 15:21–28), he taught them[5] (John 4:7ff.), and he called on them to witness to their faith in him (Mark 5:25–34). In this last case, Jesus publicized the fact that a ritually unclean woman had touched him. This incident demonstrated Christ's effect on the ceremonial law—it is fulfilled in him. Jesus taught women individually as well as in mixed groups, and he revealed some of the most important truths to them. He told the Samaritan woman that God is spirit and must be worshipped in spirit and truth (John 4:23); he told Martha that he is the resurrection and the life (John 11:25). After he had risen from the dead, Jesus told Mary Magdalene about his ascension to God the Father (John 20:17) and she was sent to tell his disciples about his resurrection (Matt. 28:7; Mark 16:7; John 20:17–18). Note that she was *not* sent "abroad" with the news, as Scanzoni and Hardesty state,[6] but to the disciples.

In Luke 10:38–42 (involving Mary and Martha), Jesus defended a woman's right to learn about the gospel against any who would deny her religious education, even against another woman who placed too great a value on maintaining and managing the home. The first priority, the only needful thing, for men and women, is to hear and obey Jesus' word. In Luke 11:27–28, Jesus did not give motherhood undue sentimental praise but affirmed the common requirement for his male and female disciples—to obey God's word.[7]

In this public teaching and preaching, Jesus spoke to the needs and concerns of both men and women; he refers to both sexes. For example, he came to set son against father, daughter against mother. Whoever loves father or mother or son or daughter more than him is not worthy of him (Matt. 10:34ff.). Women are his sisters and

---

[5]The significance of Christ's teaching women is enhanced by a first century rabbinical saying, "Whoever teaches his daughter the Torah is like one who teaches her lasciviousness," cited by Leonard Swidler, "Jesus Was a Feminist," *Southeast Asia Journal of Theology*, 13:1 (1971), 102.

[6]Scanzoni and Hardesty, p. 59.

[7]Calvin's comment on Luke 11:27–28 adds another dimension. "For it is a better thing to be born again by Christ than to conceive the flesh of Christ in her womb, to have Christ spiritually living in her than to suckle Him at her breast," John Calvin, *A Harmony of the Gospels: Matthew, Mark and Luke*, vol. II (Grand Rapids: Eerdmans, 1972), p. 54.

mothers, and men are his brothers; "whoever does the will of my Father in heaven is my brother, and sister, and mother" (Matt. 12:50). In his parables, he made the same point with several different metaphors so that people of different backgrounds could identify with them. And so, he included illustrations from women's experience: the woman leavening bread to depict the growth of God's kingdom (Matt. 13:33); and the woman rejoicing because she had found her one lost coin (Luke 15:8–10).

Perhaps the most startling aspect of Jesus' relationship with women is the band of women who followed him wherever he went, and it happend in a day when women only appeared in public when absolutely necessary.[8] The women, several of whom are mentioned by name (Matt. 27:55–56; Luke 8:1–4), travelled with him from the beginning of his earthly ministry in Galilee to the end in Jerusalem. They, unlike the male disciples, did not flee Jerusalem when Christ was crucified. These women obeyed Jesus' command in Matthew 10:34–39.

In short, Jesus relates to women as human beings of worth. To treat women as persons is the model to follow, but it is difficult to induce specific principles from Jesus' behavior. Did he treat men and women in the same way all the time? What inferences can be drawn from his silence on women's role in the church, from his exclusion of women from the apostolate, from the feminine illustrations in his parables? Can we reason from Jesus' healing and teaching women, as Georgia Harkness does, that "no specific words of his are required to demonstrate his belief in the equality of women"?[9] Or is it more accurate to suppose that if women were to have equal rights, Jesus, to combat the contemporary trend, would have had to stand up in the synagogue and so declare?

Krister Stendahl is correct when he says, "It is clear that not everything that was an 'event' in Jesus' life is binding in a normative

---

[8]Joseph A. Grassi, *The Teacher in the Primitive Church and the Teacher Today* (Santa Clara: University of Santa Clara Press, 1973), p. 117.

[9]Georgia Harkness, *Women in Church and Society* (Nashville: Abingdon Press, 1972), p. 158.

way."[10] His point that an appeal to the all-male apostolate is not a sufficient argument against the ordination of women is well-taken. However, Christ's omission of women apostles is significant. It is not merely a matter of concession to the social conventions and prejudices of his time. To argue that Jesus' choice of apostles was determined by culture is to ignore the fact that God chose the culture and time in which his Son was to be born. No detail escapes God's consideration. Jesus' choice is consistent with the Old Testament teaching that a woman submits herself to her husband; the explicit application of the principle which relates directly to the choice of the male apostolate is stated in I Timothy 2:11–12. In Jesus' entourage, women were welcome and undoubtedly had many essential duties, but not one is described as preaching or teaching publicly. To have had women with him is "an unprecedented happening in the history of that time. . . . Jesus knowingly overthrew custom when he allowed women to follow him."[11] It is unconvincing to acknowledge that Jesus radically broke custom in this regard but conceded to it by not allowing women to preach or teach.

The parable of the women with the lost coin (Luke 15:8ff.) forms the shaky basis for another conclusion: that "Jesus did not shrink from the notion of God as feminine."[12] The woman in the parable represents God. But a parable is not an allegory; not every detail of the parable has significance. Jesus taught in parables that his audience could identify with; Jesus could include a woman who has lost something in this series of parables about the lost in order to evoke the interests and empathies of the women among his listeners. The point of these parables centers on the relationship of God to the lost individual, not on who God is. Jesus compares God seeking the lost sinner to a woman with a lost coin without implying that God is female, just as Paul compares himself to a nurse (I Thess. 2:7) or a woman in labor (Gal. 4:19) without implying that he is female.

---

[10]Krister Stendahl, *The Bible and the Role of Women: a Case Study in Hermeneutics* (Philadelphia: Fortress Press, 1966), p. 20.

[11]Joachim Jeremias, *Jerusalem in the Time of Jesus: an Investigation into Economic and Social Conditions during the New Testament Period* (Philadelphia: Fortress Press, 1969), p. 376.

[12]L. Swidler, p. 110.

What can we conclude about Jesus' behavior towards women? Women were active workers for his kingdom and valued disciples, but the specifics of their activity are not recorded in the Gospels. Nonetheless, there are two important conclusions we can reach. Jesus taught women about himself. Rabbis denied the need for teaching women God's law, and today that sentiment still exists. A corollary of knowing about the Lord is witnessing to him, as did Mary Magdalene and the woman with the flow of blood. This "right" needs defense against those who think that only men should do active witnessing to Christ, because it does not suit the meekness and nonassertiveness that Christian women should have. From Jesus' actions, we can conclude that women should be taught about the Bible and women should witness to their Lord. Before other conclusions can be drawn, it is necessary to consider the rest of the New Testament.

In the Early Church

As in the Gospels, the presence of women in the early church (in Acts and the salutations in the Epistles) is decided and important but the particulars are not described. Women were in the upper room praying when the Holy Spirit came upon the disciples and women spoke in tongues at Pentecost (Acts 1:14; 2:17–18). Both men and women believed in Christ, were baptized and were persecuted (Acts 5:14; 8:12; 9:2; 17:4, 12). According to the Jews, women did not count as part of the quota needed to have a synagogue; in contrast, Luke consistently noted that both sexes were involved in the growth of the church.

Lydia, the first convert in Europe, practiced hospitality (Acts 16:13ff.), and Tabitha is described as being full of good works and charity (Acts 9:36). Philip's four daughters were prophetesses (Acts 21:8), and Priscilla as well as Aquila explained the way of God more accurately to Apollos (Acts 18:26).

Paul greets many women in Romans 16: Phoebe is called "deacon" (servant) and "patronness"; Priscilla and Aquila are "fellow workers"; Mary worked hard among the congregation. In Philippians 4:2–3, Paul is concerned about two female fellow workers who rigorously labored beside him in the gospel. These are the only concrete examples of women's activity in the early church. It is clear that women participated in the spread of the gospel, and their role was not entirely limited to nonverbal help (Priscilla taught; Philip's daughters prophesied). But the exact nature of the work of the "patronness," "deacon" and "fellow workers" is not stated in the New Testament.

These passages illuminate the attitude of Paul, who is often accused of being a misogynist. ". . . this book [Acts] leaves little doubt that Paul was one of the best friends women had."[13] Paul could both limit the activity of women in the church and praise their valuable service without patronization or condescension.

Does the New Testament teach that the office of deacon was open to women? The biblical data are scanty and inconclusive, but seem to be better explained if female deacons existed.

One of the major objections to female deacons is that any officer in the church acts as Christ's representative and so possesses an authority that is forbidden to women. John Mitchell explains:

> These men [Eph. 4:11] given as gifts by Christ to his church are given to be representatives of the Head to the Body. Throughout the New Testament, those who were apostles, prophets, and the like, are spoken of as apostles *of Christ,* fellow laborers *with God,* ambassadors *for Christ.* What they do as apostles, prophets, teachers, pastors, or deacons, they do for the Lord, the King and Head of his church. . . .
>
> The Lord Jesus Christ is the *Head* of his body, the church. And the various church officers are Christ's gifts, his representatives to that body. But it is precisely because of Christ's headship, and the officers' character as Christ's representatives, that makes it appropriate for men only to be given to the church as officers.[14]

This sort of reasoning is extra-scriptural. Nowhere in Scripture is

---

[13]Culver, p. 55.
[14]John Mitchell, "Was Phoebe a Deacon . . . No?," *The Presbyterian Guardian,* 42 (November, 1975), 135.

there any statement that to represent Christ, one must be male. Both male and female were created in God's image and all believers are being conformed to Christ's image. In addition, with reference to the quotation above, there were prophetesses in the apostolic church. Women are forbidden to teach and exercise authority over men (I Tim. 2:11–12), and women should not hold any church office in which they would have to do these two things. The woman cannot be an elder because of these two requirements, not because acting as Christ's representative demands maleness. Authority is not attributed to the office of deacon; deacons, unlike elders, are not required to teach and rule. The deacon's primary duty is to serve. Therefore, it would seem that I Timothy 2:11–12 does not exclude women from the office of deacon.

In Romans 16:1, Phoebe is called διακονον (deacon), the common *masculine* form of the noun. This fact suggests that the office of deacon may be in view. However, διακονον is also a feminine noun and could simply indicate that Phoebe was an outstanding servant in the church. On the other hand, the official character of Phoebe's title may be supported by the use of the participle ουσαν (being) and the connection with the church—"Phoebe, being a διακονον of the church in Cenchreae." It reads like an official title.

In I Timothy 3, in the middle of the instructions to deacons, verse 11 is addressed to women. It is possible to understand this verse as addressed to the wives of deacons who would help them in their work. But the wives of elders have no requirements to meet. In addition, the qualifications for deacons' wives could be considered covered when deacons are told to have one wife and manage their households well (v. 12). The section in verse 11 begins with "likewise" as does the section addressed to deacons (v. 8). This fact implies that another similar, distinct group is considered—a group of female deacons.

Women's subordination in the church is not incompatible with the function of deacons—to do works of service. Female deacons would be needed in the early centuries when the sexes could not mingle freely. There were deaconesses in the early church; in the third and fourth centuries in the eastern church, the office of deaconess was clearly defined.[15]

Widows had a special place in the New Testament church. Certain qualifications had to be met for enrollment (I Tim. 5:9–10), which is usually thought to involve support; but whether or not specific duties were required of widows is unclear. If work was required, it was probably prayer (v. 5). An order of widows did develop in the early church, as indicated by church fathers (Ignatius and Polycarp); their duties were similar to those of female deacons (visiting the sick, caring for orphans).

As in the Gospels, omissions from the records of the New Testament church must be noted. There were no female apostles,[16] evangelists or elders.[17] There are no examples of women engaged in public teaching. The central figures for the initial spread of the gospel were men. It is inaccurate to assert that "From the beginning women participated fully and equally with men."[18]

It is difficult to know how much weight to give historical examples of women's church activity. Can we ignore the absence of women in leadership positions and reason that since there are no limitations or

---

[15]*The Deaconess: A Service of Women in the World Today* (Geneva: World Council of Churches, 1966), pp. 11, 14.

[16]There was some dispute over whether or not Junia (Rom. 16:7) was an apostle and whether Junia was a man or a woman. The name Junia was a common Roman name for a woman; however, all the nouns and pronouns in Romans 16:7 are masculine, and some scholars have suggested that Junia was a contraction of a man's name. More importantly, it is unlikely that Andronicus and Junia were apostles. "They are noted by the apostles" is a possible translation. The only apostles mentioned in the New Testament are the twelve, James (the brother of Christ and the head of the church at Jerusalem), Barnabas (Acts 14:14) and Paul. In Acts 1:20ff. the eleven chose one man to replace Judas as an apostle (v. 25). This action implies that those who met the qualifications in verses 21–22 were not necessarily considered apostles; only the chosen twelve were apostles. Because of this exclusiveness, Paul had great difficulty being accepted as an apostle. Time and again (I Cor. 15:9–11; II Cor. 12:11–13; Gal. 1:1, 11–2:10; Eph. 3:1–13), he was forced to give proof of his apostleship. Paul's call to the apostleship was a special case, the exception. If Junia and Andronicus were apostles, it would seem that more than an occasional reference would have been made to them in the New Testament.

[17]I Timothy 5:1–2 does not refer to the office of elder. Paul is telling Timothy how to behave towards all people, young and old, men and women. If $\pi\rho\epsilon\sigma\beta\upsilon\tau\epsilon\rho\omega$ and $\pi\rho\epsilon\sigma\beta\upsilon\tau\epsilon\rho\alpha\varsigma$ refer to an office, to what do "young men" and "young women" refer?

[18]Scanzoni and Hardesty, p. 60.

indications of subordinate status in Acts and in the greetings, women can do anything? How can we determine to what extent women are fellow workers?

Paul's Commands to Women

The key to the interpretation of the historical records concerning women both in the Gospels and Acts and the personal references in the letters is the specific directions in the Epistles and their theological foundation. This key does not eliminate all problems. Almost every passage that directly addresses women has a cryptic reference (such as "because of the angels" in I Cor. 11:10) or technical ambiguities (such as the referent of women in I Tim. 3:11). Another problem is alleged contradictions among these passages (I Cor. 11:5, 13 versus I Cor. 14:34-35; Gal. 3:28 versus I Tim. 2:11-15). Jewett (and others) explains the so-called contradictions by acknowledging that Paul was both a Jew and a Christian.[19]

> So far as he thought in terms of his Jewish background, he thought of the woman as subordinate to the man for whose sake she was created (I Cor. 11:9). But so far as he thought in terms of the new insight he had gained through the revelation of God in Christ, he thought of the woman as equal to the man in all things, the two having been made one in Christ, in whom there is neither male nor female (Gal. 3:28).
>
> Because these two perspectives—the Jewish and the Christian—are incompatible, there is no satisfying way to harmonize the Pauline argument for female subordination with the larger Christian vision of which the great apostle to the Gentiles was himself the primary architect.[20]

Scanzoni and Hardesty agree with Jewett:

---

[19]This Jewish/Christian explanation is essentially the same as that which attributes the subordination of women to Paul's concession to the cultural conditions of his day.

[20]Jewett, pp. 112-113.

> Many Christians thus speak of a wife's being equal to her husband in personhood, but subordinate in function. However, this is just playing word games and is a contradiction in terms. Equality and subordination are contradictions.[21]

The views which claim contradiction in Paul's thought fail to recognize three factors.

(1) Paul was intelligent. In several cases Paul allegedly contradicts himself in the same passage. In I Corinthians 11:3 he says the head of woman is the man and in 11:11 he points to mutuality by saying that neither men nor women are independent of each other.[22] The verses describing the wife's submission to her husband in Ephesians 5:22ff. are prefaced by the command, "Be subject to one another out of reverence for Christ" (v. 21); this verse indicates a mutual subjection among Christians, including husbands and wives. Peter, like Paul, includes both the element of subordination and equality in his directions to the married: women are to obey their husbands and yet are joint heirs of the grace of life with them (I Pet. 3:1, 7).

(2) The crucial difficulty with the contradictory theory is that Scripture is God's word and God does not contradict himself. All Scripture is inspired (that is, its authors did not write from their imaginations or even reasoning, but they were moved to write by the Holy Spirit) and all is profitable to the church (II Tim. 3:16–17).

(3) This view denies the possibility that the elements of submission and "equality" complement one another. It may not be immediately obvious to us how the two can be logically harmonized; they form an antinomy. But there is another case, which has not been deculturized, in which these two principles coexist. That case is Christ. In language that is difficult to understand logically but that is nonetheless true, Christ says, "I and the Father are one" (John 10:30) and "he who has seen me has seen the Father" (John 14:9);

---

[21]Scanzoni and Hardesty, p. 110.

[22]Jewett calls I Corinthians 11:11 possibly "the first expression of an uneasy conscience on the part of a Christian theologian who argues for the subordination of the female to the male by virtue of her derivation from the male" (p. 113).

and, on the other hand, "I can do nothing on my own authority; as I hear, I judge; and my judgment is just, because I seek not my own will but the will of him who sent me" (John 5:30) and "the Father is greater than I" (John 14:28). Christ is fully God (John 1:1; Col. 1:15–20) and yet God is his head (I Cor. 11:3; 15:27–28).

I Corinthians 11:2-16

There are so many different ideas in I Corinthians 11:2–16 that the main point of the passage is often missed. One suggests that Paul's real concern is the relationship of man and woman, "the *nature* of man and woman as such."[23] Another specifies that the subordination of the woman is in view. Others focus on the necessity of women's covering their heads.[24] None of these theories quite captures the main idea. *Paul's concern is that men and women (when they pray and prophesy) worship God in a way that is glorifying to him.* The glory of God is first in Paul's thoughts. Just before this section, Paul summarizes his instructions on eating food sacrificed to idols: "So, whether you eat or drink, or whatsoever you do, do all to the glory of God" (I Cor. 10:31). In addition, "glory" (who gets the glory?) in verse 7 is the determining factor in the matter of covering or not covering heads. The subordination of the woman is not the major consideration here; the relationship between man and woman is discussed because it determines how men and women are to participate in worship.

Many commentators[25] approach this passage with the assumption that Corinthian women had taken their freedom in Christ too far

[23]Hans Conzelmann, *I Corinthians* (Philadelphia: Fortress Press, 1975), p. 184.
[24]Alford says, "The law of subjection of the woman to the man (2–12), and natural decency itself (13–16), teach that women should be veiled in public religious assemblies," Henry Alford, *The Greek Testament, with a Critically Revised Text, a Digest of Various Readings, Marginal References to Verbal and Idiomatic Usage, Prolegomena, and a Critical and Exegetical Commentary* (Chicago: Moody Press, 1958), comment on I Corinthians 11:2–16.
[25]Alford, on I Corinthians 11:3; Conzelmann, p. 185; M. D. Hooker, "Authority on Her Head: an Examination of I Cor XI.10," *New Testament Studies,* 10 (1963–64), 410; Jewett, p. 52.

and had uncovered their heads. However, as Lenski points out, those who see a strong emancipation movement rely on their imaginations too much.[26] Paul *commends* the Corinthians in 11:2. In a parallel statement in verse 17, Paul begins his criticism of the Corinthian practice. So any wrongs in verses 3–16 could be hypothetical. The possibility that I Corinthians 11:2–16 was not intended to correct an actual wrong must be noted. Paul may be providing a theological foundation for what the Corinthians are already doing. If this is the case, the thrust of the passage need not be seen as putting women down. In addition, the cultural explanation for coverings may be weakened since the passage would not be viewed as righting a specific Corinthian practice.

Headship (v. 3) is a crucial concept for male/female relations. A current understanding is that "head" does not involve authority: the concept of the head's thinking and directing other parts of the body was not present in ancient psychology; man reasoned with his heart or diaphragm.[27] The meaning of "head" is said to be "source,"[28] a word that does not necessarily connote authority. However, the elimination of "authority" is not so simply done. In the Old Testament, "head" indicated highest, front, as well as first thing, beginning. The idea of height, elevation, and precedence led to its association with leadership (Exod. 18:25; Num. 1:16; 25:15). In Jewish Hellenism of the first century, the head was considered "the guiding organ of the human organism and the seat of his capacity for awareness. . . ."[29] Paul associates authority with the head; in Ephesians 5:21ff. the submission of the wife to her husband and of the church to Christ is seen as a consequence of headship. The

---

[26]R. C. H. Lenski, *The Interpretation of St. Paul's First and Second Epistles to the Corinthians* (Minneapolis: Augsburg, 1961), p. 430. See also William J. Martin, "I Corinthians 11:2–16; an Interpretation," in *Apostolic History and the Gospel; Biblical and Historical Essays Presented to F. F. Bruce on his 60th Birthday*, ed. by W. Ward Gasque and Ralph Martin (Grand Rapids: Eerdmans, 1970), p. 231.

[27]Stephen Bedale, "Notes and Studies; the Meaning of κεφαλή in the Pauline Epistles," *The Journal of Theological Studies*, new series, 5 (1954), 212.

[28]Calvin J. Roetzel, *The Letters of Paul; Conversations in Context* (Atlanta: John Knox Press, 1975), p. 2.

[29]A. van Roon, *The Authenticity of Ephesians* (Leiden: E. J. Brill, 1974), p. 275.

authority of headship is not unfounded; it points to a relationship of beginning, which determines the resulting authority/submission relationship. The concept of "source" is included. For example, Christ is the head of the church because he saves and preserves it; the church has its origin in him and depends on him for its continued existence.[30] Likewise, the woman had her source in the man (v. 8), a fact of creation, and so he is her head.

Headship does not involve superiority. The man is not the head because he is intrinsically better in any respect than the woman. This fact is proven by the inclusion of "the head of Christ is God."

"The head of woman is the man" is an ambiguous statement because the same Greek words are used for man and husband and for woman and wife. Does I Corinthians 11:3 teach the headship of all men over all women,[31] or does it refer to the husband's headship? I Corinthians 11:3 reads κεφαλη δε γυναικος ὁ ἀνηρ, and Ephesians 5:23 reads ἀνηρ ἐστιν κεφαλη της γυναικος. The same words are used (except for the articles, and the verb understood in I Corinthians 11:3 is expressed in Ephesians 5:23). This comparison suggests that I Corinthians 11:3 may refer to the headship of the husband. Because the Old Testament legislation teaches the submission of the wife to her husband,[32] it supports the husband-head theory. The use of the definite article before "man" may identify "man" as the husband, the absence of "every" before woman may suggest that every woman (i.e., the unmarried) does not have a man as her head directly. The headship of the man stems from the origin of the woman at creation (vv. 8–9). The ambiguity of verse 3 is present here too—Adam and Eve were the first man and woman

---

[30]Herman Ridderbos, *Paul, an Outline of His Theology* (Grand Rapids: Eerdmans, 1975), p. 381. Cf. Bedale, pp. 212–213.

[31]Many maintain the headship of the man is universal. Grosheide says, *"The man,* not the husband of a woman, but every man as man. Of every man it can be said that he is above the woman,"* F. W. Grosheide, *Commentary on the First Epistle to the Corinthians* (Grand Rapids: Eerdmans, 1953), p. 250.

[32]The exception in Old Testament law is the regulation of a daughter's vows by her father. Though sons were to obey parents, no parallel law exists for them. The laws regulating vows do not prove that all women were under the authority of a man because widows were free to make vows without answering to any man.

and the first husband and wife. However, in Genesis 2:18ff., when the woman was created, the whole narrative and especially verses 23–25 strongly suggest that the main relationship in view is marriage; Eve was taken from Adam's body so that he would love her as himself and so that there would be a foundation for the one-flesh principle in marriage.

Much evidence points to interpreting this verse in terms of marriage. If verse 3 does indicate a general headship of the man, it would be the only verse in Scripture to do so.

In spite of this evidence, there is a problem with this interpretation. If only wives have heads, then only wives should cover their heads when they pray and prophesy; however, verse 5, in which there seem to be no limits on which women should cover their heads, may indicate that all women should cover their heads.

A sort of combination may be the solution. Fritz Zerbst helpfully states that "to understand Paul we must bear in mind that the relationship between the sexes always has its center in marriage."[33] Marriage is the normal state; to be able to remain single is a special gift of God, which is intended to be used for greater service to God. Because marriage is the norm and because it is a possibility for any single person, the regulations based on the marriage relationship of the husband (head) and wife apply to all.

Perhaps there is a sense that the general statement, the head of woman is the man, could be true. The man could be spoken of as the head of woman because of the position to which he has been appointed by God in marriage and in the church (potentially). In its generalized form, the headship of the man would be something like an honorary title. The headship of the man would not be understood as placing every woman under the authority of a particular man, be it father, brother or pastor.

Whether or not this hiearchy is still valid today will be considered throughout this book. But in relation to I Corinthians 11:3, it should

[33]Fritz Zerbst, *The Office of Women in the Church* (St. Louis: Concordia Publ. House, 1955), pp. 33–34, cited in Prohl, p. 24.

be noted that the man/woman hierarchy is sandwiched between two unquestionably hierarchical relationships—Christ is the head of every man, and God is the head of Christ. Peter Brunner concludes:

> Even the relationship of Christ to God, the relationship of the Holy Spirit to Christ, the relationship of the church to Christ are determined by this fundamental principle of being set within and subject to an order that was instituted by God from the beginning.[34]

In the context of unchanging orders, it seems unlikely that the man/woman relationship has changed. This argument is not sufficient in and of itself, but it is also supported by the passages which will be considered later.

When is the woman to cover herself? Paul is explicit that the woman be covered when she prays and prophesies (vv. 4–5, 13). The woman is not told to cover herself at all times, not even in church unless she is going to pray or prophesy aloud, just as the man need not be uncovered all the time.

What do praying and prophesying refer to? First of all, prophesying must be distinguished from preaching; these gifts are distinguished by Paul in Ephesians 4:11. Preaching is a form of teaching, and as such was forbidden to women in I Timothy 2:11–15. Prophecy is different in that God puts the very words into the mouth of the prophet (II Pet. 1:21–22). Some take the coupling of prayer and prophecy as a description of officiating at public worship. Though it seems likely that public worship is the setting since prophecy is a gift for the edification of the church (I Cor. 14:3), there is no reason to suppose that leading the service is under consideration. The worship service at Corinth was more informal than the average service today—there was a sharing of gifts by many individuals (I Cor. 14:26).[35] Many members of the congregation prayed and

---

[34]Peter Brunner, *The Ministry and the Ministry of Women* (St. Louis: Concordia Publ. House, 1971), p. 25.

[35]Charles Hodge, *An Exposition of the First Epistle to the Corinthians* (Grand Rapids: Eerdmans, 1956), p. 207.

prophesied. The sharing as described in I Corinthians 14 is what is regulated by I Corinthians 11:2–16.

What does the woman cover? The "head" that is to be covered undoubtedly refers to the woman's own head, but it seems likely that it also refers to her figurative head, her husband. If "head" (vv. 3, 4–5) is a double entendre (literal and figurative senses), the covering should not be dismissed as a product of Paul's time. It is significant that Paul uses the same word in both senses. The woman must cover her head to prevent her head (husband) from receiving attention through her participation in worship. What the wife does reflects on her husband. In Proverbs 31:23 the husband is respected because of the good reputation of his wife. "A good wife is the crown of her husband, but she who brings shame is like rottenness in the bones" (Prov. 12:4). When the woman prays and prophesies with her head uncovered, her husband (her head) comes to the fore, because the woman is his glory. It is a shame for him to receive attention in worship. The covering covers her husband so that the woman's active worship glorifies God.

Perhaps the most debated question provoked by this passage is to what does the covering refer. There are three (at least) theories: veil, attitude, hair.

Most of those in favor of veils conclude that the covering is a cultural necessity, essential only to first century Christian women. Michael Bruce writes:

> Scholars tell us that it was unheard of, in respectable society, for a woman to appear uncovered in public, and that there was only one class of women who did so. . . . For St. Paul to take vigorous steps to prevent his converts, in the Corinth of the first century, from adopting an attitude towards the current conventions of dress, so lax that it would inevitably have led the outside world to have thought that Christians sat loosely to moral standards, is quite irrelevant to whether women and girls in the twentieth century should be compelled to wear hats in Church.[36]

---

[36]Michael Bruce, "Heresy, Equality and the Rights of Women," *The Churchman*, 85:4 (Winter, 1971), 279. See also Prohl, pp. 59–60.

It is uncertain whether or not the women of Corinth were veiled. Conzelmann states that the Jewess and the respectable Greek woman of Paul's day did not go out uncovered.[37] Ramsay cites Dion Chrysostom as indicating that veiling in Tarsus was an oriental, non-Greek custom.[38] *The Woman's Bible* provides this historical information: Corinth was leveled in 146 B.C. by the Romans who killed the men and carried the women and children away; it was then re-colonized as a Roman colony in 46 B.C., and Roman women did not veil themselves and mingled freely with the men.[39] Though times may have changed since the time of the patriarchs, Judah thought his daughter-in-law Tamar was a harlot *because* her face was covered (Gen. 38:15).

To add to the confusion, Greek men prayed with their heads uncovered and Jewish and Roman men with their heads covered.[40]

Brunner thinks that because Jewish men covered their heads and Corinthian women (priestesses active in the Aphrodite cult) uncovered and loosed their hair,

> When seen in relationship to their day, the New Testament injunctions against women taking an active role in the congregation represent exactly a rejection of those practices that were current in the social surroundings.[41]

Some scholars claim that Paul deferred to the customs of his culture, and others claim that he rejected precisely those customs. The facts of the Corinthian situation are uncertain. Consequently, it seems unprofitable to seek answers to the "covering" controversy in the customs of first century Corinth, until more conclusive data are discovered.

The traditional understanding of covering is some sort of shawl over the head. Note that it is the head, not the face, that is covered.

---

[37]Conzelmann, p. 185.
[38]W. M. Ramsay, *The Cities of St. Paul: Their Influence on His Life and Thought* (New York: A. C. Armstrong and Son, 1908), pp. 201–202.
[39]Stanton, part 2, p. 151.
[40]Lenski, *Corinthians,* pp. 434–435.
[41]Brunner, p. 23.

Some commentators (Grosheide) assume that the covering is a symbol of subordination. But is the symbol of subjection a veil (which covers the face) or a mantle (which covers the head)? Both men and women wore mantles sometimes. Verse 10 does not suggest that the covering signifies subjection. In any case, verse 15 provides a major objection to the covering-mantle theory. This verse states that the woman's hair is given to her *instead of* a mantle. "Instead of" (ἀντί) implies substitution or exchange.[42] Verse 15 is the only place where a mantle or shawl is particularly mentioned, and it indicates that the covering for the woman is not a mantle.

A second theory is the symbolic or figurative covering. The only explicit identification of what the woman has on her head is ἐξουσία (authority, power, or right) in verse 10. "Authority" is an intangible covering, which would be appropriate for a figurative head, her husband.

This theory has the same problem as the "mantle" theory. Verse 15 is not taken into account. Hair must be involved in the understanding of what the covering is.

If hair is involved, the regulations in I Corinthians 11:2–16 may pertain to hair length or hair style or both.

There are reasons for all this uncertainty regarding the covering of I Corinthians 11. There is technical difficulty with the translation of the phrase and the word usually translated "covered." The phrase in verse 4 is literally "having down from head"—a phrase whose object is missing; it could be understood as having hair hanging down from the head (or hair hanging loose)[43] as well as having the head covered. The other expression for "covered" or "uncovered" (vv.6–7, 13) is not the usual word for "cover." It is the root verb for "cover" or "conceal" with an unusual prefix κατα meaning down

---

[42]"There is conclusive proof now that the dominant meaning for αντί in the first century was instead of," H. E. Dana and Julius R. Mantey, *A Manual Grammar of the Greek New Testament* (New York: Macmillan Co., 1955), p. 100.

[43]James Bassett Hurley, *Man and Woman in I Corinthians: Some Exegetical Studies in Pauline Theology and Ethics*, a dissertation submitted to Cambridge University for the Degree of Doctor of Philosophy, 1973, pp. 46–54.

($\kappa\alpha\tau\alpha\kappa\alpha\lambda\upsilon\pi\tau\omega$). This word has been interpreted to mean long hair.[44]

If we look to the Old Testament for help, we find more confusion. Leviticus 10:6; 13:45; 21:10 and Numbers 5:18 give rules for the covering and uncovering of heads. The same expression is used in all: פָּרַע אֶת-רֹאשׁ, literally, something like setting the head free. The RSV consistently understands this expression to mean letting the hair hang down loose, but the KJV and the LXX understand it to mean baring or uncovering the head. It seems that Hebrew clause has the same ambiguity (to us) as the Greek expressions in I Corinthians 11:4–7. Possibly uncovering the head and loosing the hair are closely related; perhaps doing one involved doing the other.

The Hebrew clause (פָּרַע אֶת-רֹאשׁ) is probably best translated as loosing the hair. Lepers were to wear torn clothing and וְרֹאשׁוֹ יִהְיֶה פָרוּעַ. The purpose was to make them visible, easily recognizable as lepers. Loose and flowing hair would probably be more obvious and distinguishing than a bare head. פֶּרַע, the noun with the same radicals as "free" (פָּרַע) means hair, so that there is some connection between hair and the verb in this clause.

In Old Testament times, loose hair (or uncovered heads) and torn clothing were signs of mourning. Mourning also involved defilement (Lev. 21:1); those who go into the dead (mourn for them) are defiled. This idea is involved in the case of lepers as well; one is marked as defiled. In Leviticus 10:6, Aaron and his remaining sons are forbidden to mourn (tear their clothes and free their heads) for two of Aaron's sons who had sinned and died. Priests were forbidden to mourn for anyone but their closest relatives. In Leviticus 21:10, the high priest is forbidden to tear his clothes and free his head for anyone. Why? He is not to free his head because it is anointed with the consecrating oil, and he is not to tear his garments because he has been consecrated to wear them.

The ideas of mourning and defilement may be included in the case

---

[44]Stephen M. Reynolds, "Hair in Scripture, a Critique of Two Recent Studies and a Proposed Solution to the Problem," *The Reformation Review*, 21:21 (January, 1974), 68.

of the woman suspected of adultery (Num. 5:18); until her innocence is proved, her appearance reflects the possibility of being defiled (5:20). The loosing of her hair indicates she may have defiled herself. The loosing of her hair is not expressly related to her husband's headship. It has a more general significance. In other words, her unbound hair does not identify her as an adulteress automatically, or as one who has rejected her husband's authority, but rather as one defiled for whatever reason. This passage does not give us grounds for saying that the woman who prays uncovered identifies herself as an adulteress. (And there is no Old Testament background associating punishment for adultery with shaving the head.)

One major difference between Old Testament legislation and I Corinthians 11:2-16 is that rules concerning head covering do not seem to be made on the basis of sex in the Old Testament. The Old Testament regulations seem to be concerned only with the exceptional cases, with mourning, leprosy, and adultery.

The only Old Testament regulations for hair length are also exceptional cases. The Nazirite (Num. 6:1ff.) is not to cut his or her hair until the time his or her vow is completed; he is to let his hair grow long. (It is possible to have long hair and not wear it loose.) Why?—because his *head* is consecrated. He, like the high priest, is not to mourn for anyone. If he accidentally comes into contact with a corpse, he is to shave his head. Then he should let his hair grow until his vow is completed, at which time he is to shave it. The hair is then to be burned in the fire under the peace offering. (Paul may have been ending a Nazirite vow in Acts 18:18.)

In the vision of the new temple (Ezek. 44:20), the priests are neither to shave their heads nor let their hair grow long; they are to trim their hair (LXX has cover their heads). Though covering their heads is not mentioned in the Masoretic text, turbans are part of their priestly garb (44:18; Exod. 28:4, 37, 39-40).

It is tempting to associate the instructions to men in I Corinthians 11 with those to the priests of the new temple (Ezek. 44:20). Paul could be connecting the worship in the new temple with the worship of the church. There is one major objection to this theory. Though only men could be priests before Christ came, we still wonder why Paul would instruct *only* the men and *all* the men as priests; after Christ's coming, the official priesthood ended, and all believers, men and women, are priests in another sense. Ezekiel 44:20 may not be the source for Paul's instructions to men. Perhaps the only help we can get from the Old Testament background is the assurance that God is concerned with hair length and style.

Nonetheless, if we understand I Corinthians 11:4, 7 as forbidding the man to have long hair, as possibly suggested by Ezekiel 44:20, several problems are solved. I Corinthians 11:4, 7 would not disagree with the Old Testament commands for priests to wear turbans. The question of the Jewish tallith, which men, including Paul when he preached in the synagogue, were required to wear in the synagogues, would be irrelevant to Paul's idea of covering. If the covering for women is long hair, rather than a cloak, the command that women not have gold-braided hair in I Timothy 2:9 makes more sense. If the covering is long hair, verse 14[45] (in which long hair is said to be shameful to men) and verse 15 (in which it is stated that the woman's hair is given to her instead of a mantle) are taken into account.

As said before, Paul is not necessarily correcting an actual practice of the Corinthians. We do not need to suppose that Corinthian women were bobbing their hair or that Corinthian men wore long hair.

Verses 5–6 would have the following meaning: If the woman will not be covered with long hair, it is the same as being shaven. If she wears her hair short, she might as well shave her head. The disgrace in being shaven may only be a natural revulsion—natural in the sense that God intended that women wear long hair and all of humanity has some sense of God's law (see discussion of nature in v. 14, p. 115). Possibly very short hair on women should be as disagreeable to us as women with shaven heads. (It has been only in this century that women have bobbed their hair, and it caused a scandal at the time.)

---

[45]Verse 14 indicates that long hair rather than loose, flowing hair is forbidden to men.

One objection to this theory is that Paul says men should be "uncovered" and women should be "covered" *when* they pray and prophesy. If long hair is required, it would be involved during all activity, not just when praying and prophesying. Perhaps one answer to this objection is that one's appearance during worship determines one's appearance all the time.

James Hurley thinks that the expressions for cover in I Corinthians 11:3-16 also include their hair style; that is, women should have long hair and wear it in a bun or up when praying or prophesying. This conclusion is reached largely on the basis of the Old Testament passages dealing with lepers and the women suspected of adultery. If loose hair is a sign of defilement, it would be inappropriate during worship. But is there enough evidence to support this hypothesis?[46]

What the covering is remains a problem. This problem does not concern women only. It is as important for men to know what it means to be uncovered as it is for women to know what it means to be covered.

Does verse 7 exclude women from the image of God or imply that the divine image in woman is less than it is in man? Though the passage does not discuss of whom the woman is the image, many commentators answer the above question in the affirmative. Rousas J. Rushdoony is an example:

> Paul declares in Corinthians that even as man was created in the image of God, so woman was created in the image of man—so that the image of God in woman is a reflected image, a secondhand image, as it were.[47]

The above statement contradicts Genesis 1:26-27. A modification of this erroneous view specifies only one aspect of God's image that the man has and the woman does not have. Charles Hodge writes:

---

[46]Hurley (p. 49) bases much of his argument on a spurious reading of Leviticus 13:45, in which the word used in I Corinthians 11:5 ἀκατακάλυπτος appears, rather than the correct reading ἀκάλυπτος.

[47]Fellersen, p. 14.

> The only sense in which the man, in distinction from the woman, is the image of God, is that he represents the authority of God.[48]

However, it is questionable whether or not dominion is part of God's image in Man; in fact, it is very difficult to define what God's image is.[49] With reference to dominion, it seems probable that dominion is a result of Man's being in God's image. In Genesis 1:26, God says, "Let us make man in our image, after our likeness, and let *them* have dominion. . . ." In addition, authority over the earth is given to both man and woman, to humanity (Gen. 1:28).

Paul is careful in verse 7 *not* to say that the woman is man's image. The language of Genesis 1:26–27 is "image" ($\epsilon i \kappa \omega \nu$) and "likeness" ($\dot{o} \mu o \iota \omega \sigma \iota s$), not image and glory ($\delta o \xi \alpha$). Glory and likeness are not the same idea. Verse 15, which states that the woman's hair is her glory, makes this clear. Glory refers to rendering praise (or shame). "To be 'the glory of' someone is to manifest, reveal, or represent that person (see Ezek. 1:26–28; Exod. 33:18; Isa. 40:5; John 1:14–18)."[50] For example, Paul speaks of the Thessalonians as his glory, his crown of boasting; their faith brings honor to him (I Thess. 2:20).

As in verse 3 (which does not deny that Christ is also the head of the woman), Paul deals with the relation of man to God and the relation of the woman to the man because these relationships, the hierarchy of verse 3, determine their manner of participation in worship. Woman is in the divine image as is the man.

Verses 8–9 explain why the woman is the glory of man—because she was created from him and for him, not the reverse. These verses refer to Genesis 2, when God made the woman from Adam's rib to be a helper corresponding to him. The woman was not created for the man (v. 9) for him to do with as he pleases but for his sake, for his benefit, because he needed her help. This reference to creation is

---

[48]Hodge, *Corinthians*, p. 210.

[49]The only verses that suggest the content of "image" are Ephesians 4:24 (righteousness and holiness) and Colossians 3:10 (knowledge). Men and women have equal part in these virtues.

[50]Scanzoni and Hardesty, p. 28.

an appeal to the historical foundation of the order of man and woman. The man is the head of the woman and she is his glory because God established this order at creation. Therefore, this order cannot be explained away as culturally conditioned.

Because the woman is the glory of man, she is to have "authority" on her head because of the angels (v. 10). This verse is a puzzle to modern exegetes. Ἐξουσια in this context is surprising. It is usually interpreted as a symbol of the woman's subjection.[51] The veil is often considered the expression of that subjection, so the RSV translates ἐξουσια as veil, though the word does not have this meaning. "Authority" usually has an active sense indicating one's own power. The only reason for disregarding the natural meaning of "authority" and associating it with its opposite "subjection" is the context. But to do so is to misunderstand the context. The context does not mention subjection directly, nor is the subjection of the woman the primary interest; it is the glory of God through worship. Philologically, it is better to understand authority as belonging to the woman. It is the authority to participate in worship. "The head-covering which symbolizes the effacement of man's glory in the presence of God also serves as the sign of ἐξουσια which is given to the woman; with the glory of man hidden she, too, may reflect the glory of God,"[52] and glorify God through worship.

The reference to "angels" is equally cryptic. Several theories have been suggested. The angels might be guardian angels or ministers of the congregation. Women might need authority on their heads for protection against evil angels.[53] But "angel" never refers to bad angels in the New Testament, so it is almost sure that good angels are meant here. A common and probable theory for the mention of angels is that angels are concerned with proper order in the worship service.[54] Angels do observe the activity of the church (I Cor. 4:9;

---

[51]Church fathers are said to have identified ἐξουσια as a token of subjection by Alford, on I Corinthians 11:10.

[52]Hooker, pp. 415–416; cf. Leroy Birney, *The Role of Women in the New Testament Church* (Pinner [Middlesex]: Christian Brethren Research Fellowship, 1971), p. 9.

[53]Alford, on I Corinthians 11:10.

[54]Ibid.; John Calvin, *The First Epistle of Paul to the Corinthians* (Edinburgh: Oliver and

Eph. 3:10) and specifically obedience to God's commands (I Tim. 5:21).

We should observe that Paul says that the woman is not independent of the man before he says that the man is not independent of the woman. The conjunction beginning verse 11 means "even though," "but," "nevertheless," "besides." This contrasting conjunction between verse 10 and verse 11 *may* make more sense if "authority" is understood as belonging to the woman: even though the woman has authority on her head, she is not free from the man. Her relationship to man still matters. If the "authority" on the woman's head belonged to the man, it would seem more logical to state first that the man is not independent of the woman.

Verse 11, a verse not very different from Galatians 3:28, is described as a "pointer in the direction of equality"[55] between the sexes, and as a result, "some difficulty in his [Paul's] reasoning concerning the headship of the male"[56] is suggested. In other words, verse 3 and verse 11 are not in harmony. Such an interpretation misses Paul's thrust. The mutual dependence of the man and woman (the one cannot get along without the other) says nothing about equality or inequality. The executive needs the janitor and the janitor needs the executive, but whether or not they are "equal" is a different question. In addition, "equal" in terms of what must be determined. Paul's admonishment in verse 11 is intended to promote love and concern between the sexes; neither of them, because of their different advantages or position, should consider him- or herself better or treat the other with contempt or condescension. The phrase "in the Lord" suggests that Paul may be envisioning the body of Christ, in which men and women are members and if one suffers, both suffer together (I Cor. 12:25–26).

The mutual dependence of the man and woman is grounded in nature. The woman was originally created from the man, but now

---

Boyd, 1960), p. 233; Annie Jaubert, "Le Voile des Femmes (I Cor. XI.2–16)," *New Testament Studies*, 18 (1971–72), 427; Jewett, p. 57.

[55]Jewett, p. 113.
[56]Ibid., p. 114.

the man is born of the woman. Their interdependence is also grounded in God; all things are from God—another reason for humility in the relationship between men and women.

In verses 3–12 Paul has built an argument for the "covering" of women's heads and the "uncovering" of men's heads based on the order of creation established by God. Why does Paul now ask the Corinthians to judge for themselves (v. 13) and why does he appeal to nature (v. 14)? The Corinthians may be called upon to judge the question after heeding Paul's theological arguments. But to what does nature refer? Does the appeal to nature weaken Paul's argument? Some commentators have written that nature supports Paul's commands because women's hair naturally grows longer;[57] but men's hair does grow as long as women's, as recent hair styles have shown. Others conclude that the appeal to nature "is certainly an appeal to social custom since nature unprevented would veil a man's face and head in hair much more than a woman's."[58] Neither of these theories accords with Paul's usage of nature. Nature is not an objective principle or teacher, like "Mother Nature." Paul's point is that nature, since it reveals God's character (Ps. 19:1–4; Rom. 1:20), agrees with God's revelation of his will in his word. "Nature" in I Corinthians 11:14 includes both the sense of God's revelation of himself in the world and the knowledge of God's law placed in everyone's heart (Rom. 2:15), which is the conscience.[59] So the Corinthians can judge for themselves on the basis of Paul's arguments from the created relationship of man and woman, natural revelation and their own consciences; these three sources agree. Paul does not appeal to the customs of his day in this passage, though he adds extra support in verse 16 by referring to the custom of all the churches, the consensus of God's people.

Verses 13–15 apparently link the covering with long hair. It is proper for the woman to pray covered, and it is shameful for the

---

[57]Lenski, *Corinthians*, p. 450.

[58]Scanzoni and Hardesty, p. 67.

[59]C. H. Dodd, "Natural Law in the New Testament" in *New Testament Studies* (Manchester: Manchester University Press, 1953), p. 133.

man to have long hair (like a woman's). The woman's long hair is her glory. The most conclusive evidence that the woman's covering is her hair is verse 15b: God has given the woman hair *in place of a mantle*. The woman's hair brings glory to her because it fulfills a divinely appointed task—it covers her.

There are two possible interpretations of verse 16, but the thrust of both is that what Paul has said in the preceding verses stands. The question is to what does "practice" refer: to the practice of covering heads or the practice of being contentious. The former interpretation gives the added weight of universal observance by the churches of women's covering and men's uncovering their heads in prayer and prophecy. The latter, that the churches do not recognize the practice of disputing the word of the apostle Paul, is the more natural understanding of the Greek. In any case, the Corinthians should not contend about the matter of coverings but should obey Paul's instructions. That verse 16 does not relativize the issue is acknowledged even by Jewett, who, however, considers the entire passage a result of Paul's cultural conditioning for nonexegetical reasons.

> For him [Paul] these customs of wearing the hair long and of veiling the head express, as it were in symbol, the absolute will of God. Hence he is anything but indifferent to them. . . . Therefore the apostle's remark (v. 16) that the churches of God have no such "custom" (συνήθεια) of women unveiling themselves during public worship cannot mean that he regarded the whole matter as *mere* custom. Though one may argue that such indeed is the case, one cannot say that this is what the text means.[60]

The primary difficulty in understanding I Corinthians 11:3–16 is determining what the covering is. Most of the contextual evidence (vv. 13–15) points to associating long hair with the covering in the woman's case. If long hair is the answer, there are still other questions. How long is long enough? How short is short enough for the man? Does the hair style, rather than length, make the difference? It is hoped further study will give answers to these and other questions.

---

[60]Jewett, p. 118.

I Corinthians 11:2-16 and I Corinthians 14:34-35

I Corinthians 11:2-16 seems to allow women to pray and prophesy aloud, and I Corinthians 14:34-35 seems to command complete silence on the part of women in church. How can these two passages be reconciled?

One solution is to disregard one of the two passages; which one depends on one's bias. Some suggest that I Corinthians 14:34-35 is a secondary insertion, which was not written by Paul. (The question of whether or not it, as part of the canonical New Testament, would still be binding for the Christian is not considered.) The major reasons for rejecting I Corinthians 14:34-35 are that it interrupts the thought of chapter 14 (concerned with the exercise of spiritual gifts) and that it supposedly contradicts I Corinthians 11:2-16 "in which Paul clearly accepts without question the right of women to lead in worship."[61] However, the external evidence supporting the inclusion of I Corinthians 14:34-35 abounds. All of the major manuscripts include it.[62]

Those who affirm I Corinthians 14:34-35 at the expense of I Corinthians 11:2-16 do not disregard the entire passage. Their argument is exemplified by John Calvin:

> But it seems to be unnecessary for Paul to forbid a woman to prophesy bare-headed, since in I Tim. 2:12 he debars women from speaking in the church altogether. . . . For when he [Paul] takes them to task because they were prophesying bare-headed, he is not giving them permission, however, to prophesy in any other way whatever, but rather is delaying the censure of that fault to another passage (chapter 14.34ff).[63]

Georg Gunter Blum agrees:

---

[61]Robin Scroggs, "Paul: Chauvinist or Liberationist?," *Christian Century,* 89 (March 15, 1972), 307.

[62]ℵ, A, B, and D (which places vv. 34–35 after v. 40), p[46], dated in the 2nd–3rd centuries, also include I Corinthians 14:34-35. The text is rated B which means there is only a small degree of doubt as to its authenticity.

[63]Calvin, *I Corinthians,* p. 231.

> As St. Paul does not concern himself with this question [whether women may pray or prophesy] at all in I Cor. 11, we do not know whether, in this case, the praying and prophesying by women in church at Corinth is permitted or disapproved in principle. . . . But in I Cor. 14:33b–36, a thorough discussion and an enunciation of principle occur. . . . Whilst he merely puts glossolalia within proper bounds, St. Paul absolutely forbids women to speak at all.[64]

This line of reasoning misses the emphasis of I Corinthians 11:2–16, which is behavior when praying and prophesying. "It is quite lame to suggest that in chapter 11 Paul gives rules for a practice which he will subsequently condemn."[65]

A second explanation is that both the covering and the silence are cultural expressions which no longer apply. This theory fails to note the irrevocability of the bases of Paul's arguments. In I Corinthians 11:2–16, Paul cites the way in which God created man and woman as the basis for the order God established between them; this basis is an unchangeable and irreversible historical fact. In I Corinthians 14:34–35, the foundation of his argument is the law. Jewett supposes "that the apostle's remarks in I Corinthians 14:34–35 reflect the rabbinic tradition which imposed silence on the woman in the synagogue as a sign of her subjection."[66] Though Paul uses "law" in different senses, here he appeals to the law as that which would silence all objections. Such an authoritative usage implies that the Old Testament law is meant, as in I Corinthians 14:21. The reference in I Corinthians 14:34 is not to Genesis 3:16, which is not a prescription but a judgment; it refers to the whole body of Old Testament laws concerning women, which were intended to teach the submission of the wife to her husband. Paul's appeal to the law is authoritative for all times.

Another theory distinguishes between two types of Christian

---

[64]Georg Gunter Blum, "The Office of Woman in the New Testament," in *Why Not? Priesthood and the Ministry of Women* ed. by Michael Bruce and G. E. Duffield (Abingdon [Berkshire]: Marcham Manor Press, 1972), pp. 66–67.

[65]Noel Weeks, "Of Silence and Head Covering," *Westminster Theological Journal*, 35 (1972–73), 22.

[66]Jewett, p. 114.

meetings. I Corinthians 11:2–16 is said to describe a closed meeting, in which the Lord's Supper was served. Only baptized Christians were admitted, and women were allowed to participate. I Corinthians 14:34–35 regulates an open meeting where non-Christians, who might be offended by public activity of women, were present.[67] This hypothesis is ingenious, but there is insufficient evidence for it. It is clear that I Corinthians 14:34–35 describes a regular worship service (the ecclesia, the gathering of the congregation), where outsiders are present (vv. 22–25). However, no specific setting for I Corinthians 11:2–16 is stated. Whether or not the service was closed for the Lord's Supper (I Cor. 11:17ff.) is questionable, because the New Testament does not distinguish between private and public meetings. Both the meeting of the Lord's Supper (I Cor. 11:18, 20) and the "open" meeting (I Cor. 14:23, 26) are designated "ecclesia," when Christians "come together." In addition, there is no reason to assume I Corinthians 11:17ff. defines the setting of I Corinthians 11:2–16, "when praying and prophesying." Both of these activities were normal in the ecclesia gathering. Offending outsiders is an implausible motive for not allowing women to speak in public for two reasons. Women often led in the Aphrodite cult in Corinth; consequently, a woman's public speaking would not be shocking in Corinth. And women prophesied at Pentecost in public (Acts 2:17–18); concern for offending others did not hinder them.

The most reasonable theory is that the silence in I Corinthians 14:34–35 does not include praying and prophesying. The silence commanded of women is not absolute but qualified by the context.

On first reading, chapter 14, which deals with the use of gifts (speaking in tongues and prophesying in particular), seems to end with a repressive note to the women (vv. 34–35). Paul says, "Now I want you all to speak in tongues, but even more to prophesy" (v. 5). These gifts are to be used in the church (vv. 3, 4, 6). But the women are to be silent in church and not speak. Therefore, verses 1–33 should be marked, "For men only." Several commentators maintain this view vigorously.

---

[67]Prohl, p. 30.

Whether they have the gift of tongues or of prophecy makes no difference, in fact, Paul's prohibition is intended for just such. And this prohibition is general and complete.[68]

This command to be silent refers to all ecstatic and edifying speaking, in different possibilities having been enumerated in v. 26. . . . [λαλειν, to speak] embraces all kinds of charismatic utterance. . . . The special nuance of this word lies in its opposition to silence.[69]

If the silence is absolute, then women should not sing hymns, read responsive readings or pray the Lord's prayer in church.

A word study of "speak" does not solve the problems of these verses. Scanzoni and Hardesty emphatically state that "the word does *not* mean a formal lecture, exhortation, or teaching, but simply *talking,* idle talk or chatter."[70] Though "speak" does have these meanings, it can also mean a formal lecture. It has as wide a range of meanings as does the English "speak" or "talk," from just talking to making a talk. Only the context can determine the precise meaning of "speak," and there is nothing to suggest that idle talk or chatter is involved in I Corinthians 14:34–35.

However, "speak" may be qualified or limited by two factors: the law and asking questions (v. 35). Paul's appeal to the law is usually felt as a crushing, inhibiting force, but there is another way to look at Paul's appeal. The woman is to submit herself (the submission of the woman is voluntary and a recognition of her position as a woman, I Cor. 11:3) as the law says; that is, she is not to be subordinate in a way that the law does not demand. The Old Testament law permitted women to prophesy. For instance, Miriam led a group of women in prophecy before the assembled nation of Israel at the Red Sea. Therefore, I Corinthians 14:34 does not forbid prophecy to women.

It is usually assumed that chapters 12–14 form an indivisible unit and that the command to women in 14:34–35 should be understood

---

[68]Lenski, *Corinthians,* p. 615.
[69]Blum, p. 67.
[70]Scanzoni and Hardesty, p. 68.

in the context of charismatic gifts. Many have noticed a break in thought at this point, and some believe this section belongs after verse 40. Perhaps verses 34–35 should be considered a new section to be understood in the category of doing things decently and in order. In such a case, the definition of silence/not speaking would be found in verse 35, rather than in the preceding verses. Speaking would then refer to asking questions, instead of all forms of speaking mentioned in verse 26. Dialogue,[71] involving questions and answers, was a common method of instruction at this time. Women would not be allowed to participate in it, for to do so would be to teach. Paul's command to ask at home may be intended to give women an opportunity and encouragement to get answers to their questions. Verse 36 should not be included in the section addressed only to women. It is intended for the whole church at Corinth. The grammar supports this contention: "only ones" is masculine plural. It must refer to men or a mixed group.

---

[71]The sermons (the formal instruction) of the early church may have taken the form of a dialogue. There are few descriptions of worship services in the New Testament. Acts 20:7ff. is one of them; it takes place on the first day of the week and the group had gathered together to break bread. Paul conducts the teaching part of the meeting; he dialogues with (διαλεγεσθαι, which can mean converse or make a speech) the others. His talking is also described as τον λογον (the speech) and ὁμιλειν (confess or declare, from which homily is derived). In Acts 17:2, 17 διαλεγεσθαι denotes Paul's daily missionary activity in the synagogue and marketplace; it is coupled with συμβαλλω (discuss, dispute) in Acts 17:18. Paul was not allowed to speak unquestioned in either place; both Jews and Greeks argued with him. In Acts 24:25–26 διαλεγεσθαι and ὁμιλειν occur together again to indicate a two-sided discussion. In Luke 24:15, ὁμιλειν is joined with συζητειν, a term frequently used for conversations among rabbis or teachers on spiritual matters (Mark 1:27; 8:11; 12:28; Acts 6:9; 9:29). The method of instruction used by the rabbis was to set up questions and reply themselves or have their students reply. Dialogue was also used by the Greeks (Socrates) for instruction. So it is possible that διαλεγεσθαι and ὁμιλειν in Acts 20:7ff. refer to discussion and that the sermons in the early churches took the form of a dialogue between two or more teachers of the church who answered questions raised by one another or by other members of the congregation. If this be the case, Paul in I Corinthians 14:34–35 is prohibiting women from participating in the sermon, as he does in I Timothy 2:11–14. Women may have claimed the right to participate in the question-answer period because they could prophesy and pray aloud in the assembly. For a more complete discussion, see Nils Johansson, *Women and the Church's Ministry* (Uppsala: Pro Veritate, 1972?), pp. 59–80.

I Timothy 2:8-15

This passage begins with an exhortation to men everywhere concerning how to pray and then continues with a similar or parallel command to the women on how to dress. (Paul is not instructing women on how to pray publicly; the main verb missing from v. 9 is βουλομαι, "I want," in v. 8. Paul wants the men to pray [προσευχεσθαι] and the women to dress [κοσμειν].) In the case of the women, Paul, without indicating the reason, goes beyond the single command.

A current explanation for Paul's development in verses 11-14 is that "the primary concern here is not so much the role of women as the possibility of false teaching";[72] the application of these verses would then be: if women teach true doctrine and do not domineer, there are no restrictions on them. The basis for this assumption is the warnings against false teaching found in the letters to Timothy. The absence of any references to false teaching in I Timothy 2:9-15 is explained by identifying the cause of Adam's fall as false teaching by Eve. This theory is impossible for several reasons. The women in I Timothy 2:9-15 and the false teachers are approached differently. The false teachers are not believers, and they live in immorality (I Tim. 6:4-5; II Tim. 3:1-9; 4:3-4). Sound teaching and right living go together (I Tim. 1:9-10). The women mentioned in II Timothy 3:6 cannot be the same as those addressed in I Timothy 2:9-15, because the former "can never arrive at a knowledge of the truth" (II Tim. 3:6). Unlike the false teachers, the women of I Timothy 2:9-15 are believers who live in faith, love, holiness, and sobriety and who are urged to continue in those virtues.

In I Timothy 1:3-7, in which the false teachers could be believers, Paul urges Timothy to correct their wrong concerns. In

---

[72]Scanzoni and Hardesty, pp. 70-71; this theory is developed fully in Aida Dina Besançon Spencer, "Eve at Ephesus (Should Women Be Ordained as Pastors according to the First Letter to Timothy 2:11-15?)," *Journal of the Evangelical Theological Society*, 17:4 (Fall, 1974), 215-222.

contrast, there is no mention of false teaching, no word of correction in I Timothy 2:9–15. Paul says that women should not teach or exercise authority over men, period. There are no conditions attached which would allow exceptions to Paul's command.

Verse 14 is not a reference to false teaching in the Garden of Eden. Scripture does not state *how* Adam happened to eat the fruit. It is unfounded speculation to say that Eve persuaded or taught him. The fact that he was not deceived suggests that his fall was not the result of false teaching.

This false-teaching hypothesis does not take Adam's temporal priority (v. 13) into consideration. One of the reasons women are not to teach or exercise authority over men is that Adam was created first. This reason cannot be related in any way to false teaching.

The false-teaching theory intends to relativize I Timothy 2:11–15, as Scanzoni and Hardesty demonstrate:

> The passage seems directed at a particular situation rather than at stating a general principle. . . . In I Timothy the problem seems to be women who usurped authority from others, teaching when they had neither gift nor training. Perhaps one of the wealthier women thought her social position guaranteed her a leadership post. Or perhaps the church was even meeting in the home of a woman who was bossy and domineering. Maybe some women were putting their husbands down publicly. Whatever the local situation, we must be careful not to consider this passage the only and final word to women.[73]

It is very helpful to remember Paul is addressing specific problems; this fact probably accounts for what seem to be jumps in his thought (from v. 10 to v. 11). Nonetheless, speculation about concrete problems is still speculation; and this speculation, even if correct, does not (necessarily) relativize Paul's commands. In I Timothy 2:11–12, Paul does state a general principle. Because his commands are founded on unchanging historical facts that

---

[73]Scanzoni and Hardesty, p. 71

have specific theological significance (vv. 13–14), they are authoritative for all times and cultures.

What does Paul say to the women? Paul's concern for both men and women is not primarily for outward appearance, the posture of praying or the style of dress; but it is for the condition of the heart that produces external signs. Therefore, Paul's words to the women are not to be regarded as trivial or picky. According to Paul, women are to clothe themselves in appropriate (or dignified) apparel which is reverence and sobriety (or sound judgment). Their adornment should not be braids and gold or pearls or expensive clothing but good deeds. The point here is the same as that made by Peter in I Peter 3:3–4:

> Let not yours be the outward adorning with braiding of hair and decoration of gold or wearing of robes, but let it be the hidden person of the heart with the imperishable jewel of a gentle and quiet spirit, which in God's sight is very precious.

Paul does not so much forbid jewelry and expensive dress; rather he focuses on the internal condition. Paul tells the women to be concerned with righteousness, the fruit of the Spirit, not external beauty or adornment (Prov. 31:30).

When Paul writes, "Let a woman learn in silence . . . ," he is not limiting the way women may learn. Rather he is making an advance in women's education: do not forbid them to learn, *let* them learn. In Paul's day, Jewish women were not required to learn the law in spite of the Old Testament commands to teach them (Deut. 31:12; Josh. 8:35). Encouragement to let women learn was needed.

Learning in silence (or quietness) is not a negative thing; silence is the way to learn. "The words of the wise heard in quiet are better than the shouting of a ruler among fools" (Eccl. 9:17). Silence is a learning posture as opposed to one of teaching; this contrast is emphasized by the repetition of the need for silence in verse 12. Submissiveness, like silence, is in contrast to teaching and exercising authority over men. It is the same submission mentioned in I Corinthians 14:34. Both quietness and submissiveness are part of the attitude described in I Peter 3:3–4.

Even though the woman should learn, she is not to teach or exercise authority over men,[74] Paul says. Paul's permission is not to be disregarded; he has just mentioned the grounds for his authority in verse 7: he was appointed by God to be a preacher and apostle. The extent of what is forbidden to women has been debated. Some have extended it to include all forms of teaching and exercising authority, including teaching in public schools and having a job in which a woman has men under her authority. However, there is evidence that Paul's concern is limited by the worship/church situation. Most probably, public prayer that is regulated in verse 8 would occur during a worship service. "Likewise" in verse 9 indicates that the women's activity occurs in the same sphere. In I Timothy 3:14–15, Paul expresses the reason for his entire letter to Timothy:

> I hope to come to you soon, but I am writing these instructions to you so that, if I am delayed, you may know how one ought to behave in the household of God, which is the church of the living God, the pillar and bulwark of the truth.

If the context of verses 11ff. is worship, there are still two alternatives: women are prohibited from every form of teaching or public address; or women are prohibited from a certain type of teaching, that is, the office of teacher (held by elder or pastor). It is difficult to decide between the two. In any case, teaching[75] does not include praying and prophesying (I Cor. 11:2–16). The teaching forbidden to women is habitual teaching, as suggested by the infinitive in the present tense ($\delta\iota\delta\acute{\alpha}\sigma\kappa\epsilon\iota\nu$). Teaching and exercising authority over men may describe one function, that of an elder.

---

[74]Some (Scanzoni and Hardesty, Spencer) prefer the translation "usurp authority" or "domineer." If usurpation is connoted, the implication could be that women should not take the authority that rightfully belongs to men.

[75]Teaching in I Timothy 2:12 also does not include private instruction of men (Acts 18:26), women teaching other women (Titus 2:3–4) and women teaching children (II Tim. 1:5; 3:15; Prov. 1:8). Since the teaching of one's children in this society has been relegated to others better equipped, by extension, women may teach in the school systems.

Several commentators propose such an interpretation. Lenski defines teaching as the public teaching of Scripture with the capacity to rule and govern one's listeners with that word.[76] Paul's use of $\delta\iota\delta\alpha\sigma\kappa\omega$ (teach) gives some support to this claim (Col. 1:28; I Tim. 4:11; 6:2b; II Tim. 2:2). The qualifications for elders, one of which is aptness to teach, follow immediately in chapter 3. Paul may intend to eliminate women from consideration for the office of elder before listing the requirements for that office.

The verb $\alpha\dot{v}\theta\epsilon\nu\tau\epsilon\iota\nu$, to exercise authority over, occurs only here in the New Testament. Scanzoni and Hardesty give this background material on its meaning:

> Possible translations are "interrupt" (Dibelius), "dictate to" (Moffatt) or "domineer over" (NEB). In noun form, as used by the great Greek dramatists, it meant a "suicide" or a "family murderer." Later the noun came to mean "lord" or "autocrat." In the first century it was rather a slang word. . . . Because suicide involves deciding for oneself, taking one's life into one's own hands, to do so for others meant to become a "dictator." Thus the word came to mean "self-willed" or "arbitrary," interfering in what was not properly one's own domain, trespassing the socially proper limits.[77]

Scanzoni and Hardesty conclude that the women addressed in I Timothy 2:11ff. were doing something wrong—trying to teach without the necessary gifts, acting bossy or putting their husbands down in public. And therefore the statement in I Timothy 2:11 does not apply to us in its absolute sense. However, the translation of $\alpha\dot{v}\theta\epsilon\nu\tau\epsilon\iota\nu$ does not allow for such relativization. The self-will and interference in what is not one's own proper domain connoted by $\alpha\dot{v}\theta\epsilon\nu\tau\epsilon\iota\nu$ suits and supports the unconditional prohibition in I Timothy 2:11. A woman who teaches and exercises authority over men in the church is by definition an usurper, interfering in

---

[76]R. C. H. Lenski, *The Interpretation of St. Paul's Epistles to the Colossians, to the Thessalonians, to Timothy, to Titus, and to Philemon* (Minneapolis: Augsburg, 1937), p. 564; David P. Scaer, "May Women Be Ordained as Pastors," *The Springfielder*, 36:2 (September, 1972), 104.

[77]Scanzoni and Hardesty, p. 71.

an area forbidden to her. Paul does not say that a woman who usurps authority should not teach or exercise authority over men; he says that a woman should not teach or exercise (usurp) authority over men.

Paul states two reasons that women should not teach or exercise authority over men: Adam was created first,[78] and the woman was deceived, not the man. These are two historical events, which cannot be altered. We women cannot escape our history. The significance of Adam's prior creation is noted in I Corinthians 11:8; consequently, the man is the head of the woman, and women are to submit themselves to their husbands. Teaching and authority over men in the church are incompatible with the woman's relationship to the man established at creation. The second reason has produced much dangerous speculation. Many have assumed that this verse teaches that women are more susceptible to deception than men.[79] Paul "may have in mind the greater aptitude of the weaker sex to be led astray."[80] A variation of this inference is that women "are inferior in their gifts, so far as the teaching office is concerned."[81] However, the Bible does not say that women are more prone to error than men or that their teaching gifts are inferior (if they were, how could women be trusted to teach children?). Verse 14 is simply a statement of past fact (the tense is aorist, which indicates completed action). Paul speaks of the difference in the manner of sinning: the man was not deceived (implying that he knew what he was doing), but the woman was thoroughly deceived.

Paul's limitation of women's duties does not suggest that he would allow all men to teach and exercise authority over men. As Faith Martin perceptively points out:

---

[78]"First" is not an adverb but a predicate adjective; this indicates Adam's position as the head of the race, the first one (Lenski, *Colossians,* p. 565).

[79]Luther, *Genesis,* Vol. I, p. 68; Blum, p. 72.

[80]Donald Guthrie, *The Pastoral Epistles: an Introduction and Commentary* (Grand Rapids: Eerdmans, 1957), p. 77.

[81]Jewett, p. 60

Is there any scripture to support the notion that God has granted privileges to men solely on the basis of sex? Now there is no dispute that there are certain offices in the church to which only men may aspire. But that office is not automatically theirs if they claim it. . . .[82]

The office of elder has qualifications that must be met (I Tim. 3).

The last verse (v. 15) in this section is a puzzle and a sort of non sequitur. This verse has been linked with Genesis 3:16a, the curse of labor in child-bearing, and interpreted to mean that women will be kept safe through childbirth. However, this interpretation is not empirically true. Godly Christian women have died bearing children. Another suggestion is that women will be saved through the birth of the child Christ. But this interpretation forces an unnatural meaning on the Greek word "childbearing." In addition, if this is Paul's meaning, he has chosen an extremely obscure way of expressing it. If child-bearing does not refer to Christ's birth, "save" is not used to mean salvation from sin. Paul is not teaching salvation by good works, child-bearing or otherwise (cf. Titus 3:5).

Undoubtedly, Paul means to encourage the woman after he has limited some of her activities. He may be suggesting that bearing and raising children is not demeaning to a woman, that motherhood is an honorable and significant profession if she continues in her faith in Christ. Paul is in favor of motherhood, but to assume that Paul is restricting the woman to the home is to conclude too much from this verse.

Singlehood

Though Paul considers motherhood important and appropriate for Christian women, he did not believe a husband and family were necessary to fulfill everyone. In the Old Testament, marriage seemed to be the accepted lot of everyone and not much is said about

---

[82]Faith Martin, "God's Image in the Christian Woman," *Covenanter Witness*, 91:13 (June 18, 1975), 7.

singleness. Paul, on the other hand, legitimatizes, even exalts, the position of single *men and women* (I Cor. 7:25–38). In this respect, he is more progressive in his thinking than modern society, which still looks with pity and/or disdain on spinsters. Paul says that the unmarried can better serve Christ, and so he recommends staying single. The married have divided concerns, to please Christ and to please their spouses, so that singleness is an asset for service to the Lord.

Marriage

In Old Testament law, the relationship between husband and wife is portrayed and maintained, but an explicit description is not given. The New Testament fully develops this relationship in Ephesians 5:22ff.

Paul begins by exhorting all believers to be subject to one another for Christ's sake; this command for mutual submission forbids any pride or claim to superiority among Christians. The state of mind encouraged here is the same sort as in Philippians 2:3–4. As Calvin has said:

> But as nothing is more irksome to the mind of man than this mutual subjection, he directs us to *the fear of Christ,* who alone can subdue our fierceness, that we may not refuse the yoke, and can humble our pride, that we may not be ashamed of serving our neighbors.[83]

The specific commands, to wives and husbands, children and parents, slaves and masters, are based on verse 21. Paul does not speak of rights or privileges of any group but always of duties that demand self-sacrifice, that cannot be performed except by God's grace. This passage does not guarantee the husband the right to rule; it enjoins him to love to the uttermost—to the point of his own death (cf. I John 3:16).

---

[83]John Calvin, *Commentaries on the Epistles of Paul to the Galatians and Ephesians* (Grand Rapids: Eerdmans, 1948), p. 317.

The wife's duty is to submit herself to her husband, as to the Lord. "Be subordinate" or "be subject" conveys the wrong impression to the twentieth century reader. The idea conveyed in Colossians 3:18 (cf. Eph. 5:22–24) is not one of passivity but of voluntary action, of one equal to another. It has been argued that one cannot establish woman's subordination to the man "without the help of the traditional point—woman's *inferiority* to the man."[84] Ironically, in objecting to the analogy between husband/wife and God the Father/Christ, Jewett appropriately describes Christ's submission to the Father in terms that apply to the relationship of the husband and wife.

> . . . the subordination of the Son to the Father is not an ontological subordination in the eternal Godhead, but a voluntary act of self-humiliation on the part of the Son in the economy of redemption. As God, the Son is equal with his Father, though as Messiah he has assumed a servant role and become subordinate to his Father.[85]

The woman as Man is equal to the man, but she, as wife, submits herself to her husband as a voluntary act of obedience to God's command. The voluntary nature of her submission is supported by the corresponding command to her husband. He is not told to issue orders or to make his wife obey but to love her.

The wife's submission is not without reason or cause. She is to submit herself to her husband because he is her head. The wife's submission is not based on the husband's superiority or the wife's inferiority. As we have seen, the headship of the husband is based on creation (I Cor. 11:8–9). From the beginning, God has placed the husband in a position of authority over his wife; yet this authority is not to be exercised through force or any sort of manipulation but through self-sacrificing love.

The husband/wife relationship is compared to that of Christ and the church—a beautiful comparison that proves Paul's high view of marriage, but one that raises questions. Is the husband's authority

---

[84]Jewett, p. 84.
[85]Ibid., p. 133.

("as to the Lord," v. 22) equal to that of Christ? Is the wife's submission to her husband ("in everything," v. 24) as complete and as unquestioning as that of the church to Christ?

The phrase "as to the Lord" in verse 22 does not mean that the husband's authority is the same as Christ's but that "wives cannot obey Christ without yielding obedience to their husbands."[86] For the wife, to obey Christ is to submit oneself to one's husband. This submission as an example of obedience to the Lord is crucial to one's witness to the power of the gospel because through it, an unbelieving husband may be converted without a word (I Pet. 3:2). "In everything" (v. 24) refers to the extent—in all areas of life. It does not imply that the wife must respond "Yes, sir" to every request, decision, or opinion her husband has. The wife's attitude, what is called a gentle and quiet spirit in I Peter 3:4, is the key to understanding submission. The wife is to submit herself to her husband "as is fitting in the Lord" (Col. 3:18), in a way that is appropriate for a Christian. That the woman is not at the mercy of her husband is shown by Paul's instructions in I Corinthians 7:3-5, 33-34; there is mutuality in marriage that reflects the equal personhood of the partners but that does not annul the headship of the husband. According to Elisabeth Elliot,

> To say that submission is synonymous with the stunting of growth, with dullness and colorlessness, spiritlessness, passivity, immaturity, servility, or even the "suicide of personality," as one feminist who calls herself an evangelical has suggested, is totally to misconstrue the biblical doctrine of authority.[87]

What is the "authority" of the husband? In considering the comparison between the husband and Christ, some have questioned the phrase, "is himself its Savior" (v. 23). The husband is not the Savior of his wife, so how does this affect the comparison? Verse 24 begins with "but." The similarity between Christ and husband is not com-

---

[86]Calvin, *Galatians*, p. 317; cf. R. C. H. Lenski, *The Interpretation of St. Paul's Epistles to the Galatians, to the Ephesians, and to the Philippians* (Minneapolis: Augsburg, 1937), p. 625.

[87]Elisabeth Elliot, "Why I Oppose the Ordination of Women," *Christianity Today,* 19:18 (June 6, 1975), 14.

pletely perfect. Verse 24 conveys the idea that in spite of the unique fact that Christ saves the church, the headship of the husband is like that of Christ over the church.[88]

Paul goes into great detail to explain how Christ loves the church, and so husbands should love their wives. The husband's authority is to express itself in self-giving love so that the wife might benefit, might become holier. Though they deny the husband's authority, the biblical feminists capture the love required of the husband well. Scanzoni and Hardesty write:

> The husband who follows Christ's example will likewise do all in his power to help his wife in her spiritual and mental growth. He will encourage her to be a mature, fulfilled, fully developed personality. Such a husband will not force his wife into a mold that stifles her gifts, her spirit, her personhood.[89]

This special love of the husband for his wife and of Christ for the church has a reason: they are one body. In the case of Christ and the church, the church is Christ's body. In the case of husband and wife, they are one flesh. This unity is more than emotion or common interests. It also has its basis in creation—the woman was made from Adam's body (Gen. 2:21–24). So the man is to love his wife as his own body, which is to say as himself. This unity is initiated and then reenacted by sexual intercourse; intercourse is more than a biological function. It involves all aspects of the human being, not just the physical.

How this loving is to be done is elaborated in I Peter 3:7. The husband is to live with his wife according to knowledge and to treat her with honor, as a weaker vessel. The reason given for the husband's behavior is that both husband and wife are joint heirs of God's grace. "Joint heirs" implies that there is no difference in the benefits of salvation. The two problems in this verse are the meaning of "according to knowledge" and "weaker vessel." Calvin suggests that the knowledge is of the woman's weakness. ". . . just as we

---

[88]Lenski, *Galatians*, p. 627.
[89]Scanzoni and Hardesty, p. 105.

forgive children more easily, when they offend through inexperience of age, so the weakness of the female sex ought to make us not too rigid and severe towards our wives."[90] This interpretation misunderstands how husbands are to treat their wives; Calvin teaches condescension and patronization rather than the honor and respect the Scriptures command. Calvin also assumes that the weakness of the woman is inferiority of an intellectual or perhaps volitional sort. Consequently, his theory seems unlikely; Scripture does not teach the moral, spiritual, or intellectual inferiority of the woman. It seems more likely that the knowledge is the knowledge of Christ (II Pet. 1:5–6, 3:18). This knowledge includes an understanding of the husband's position as head and what his duties are (Eph. 5:25–31). Knowledge of Christ by definition produces moral living.

Modern commentators tend to understand "weaker vessel" as referring to physical weakness. There is some lexigraphical support for this explanation. Liddell and Scott define "vessel" as the body, the vessel of the soul (in the New Testament). I Corinthians 4:7 uses the phrase "earthen vessels" to describe frail human bodies. Even though in terms of tolerance of pain and endurance and even in terms of relative (to the size of the muscle) strength, women may surpass men, men on the whole have been and are stronger than women. Nonetheless, another interpretation is possible. The wife may be considered weak because of her role as wife. She, by marrying, has accepted a position where she submits herself to her husband. Such a position is vulnerable, open to exploitation. The husband is commanded not to take advantage of the woman's vows of submission. This interpretation may be preferable because Scripture does not speak of basic constitutional differences between men and women, and it does speak of the different roles men and women have in relation to one another. The husband, then, is to honor his wife, who has been placed in a position under his authority; he is to treat her as one better than himself. Such an attitude on the husband's part eliminates all the evils that are associated with

---

[90]John Calvin, *The Epistles of Paul the Apostle to the Hebrews and the First and Second Epistles of St. Peter* (Grand Rapids: Eerdmans, 1963), p. 283.

hierarchical marriage. According to Christ's teaching, the position of subordination is one of honor (Matt. 20:26–28).

The two becoming one is a great mystery. Paul understands Genesis 2:24 (v. 31) as referring to Christ and the church, but not necessarily exclusively (v. 32).

The relationship of Christ and the church is, for those who need proof, an actual case of the perfect merger of authority and loving service (a form of submission). Christ's authority over the church is not diminished by his self-sacrificing love for it. He serves the church but he does not submit to it in the same way that the church submits to him. This comparison of the marriage relation to Christ and the church points to the ultimacy of the authority structure in marriage (in this age). Husband and wife should always mirror the relation of Christ to the church.

In order to account for the analogy in Ephesians 5:23–24 and to defend her egalitarian model, Mollenkott adjusts her christology. She thereby illustrates how a faulty doctrine of Scripture affects the heart of the matter—what she thinks of Christ. She makes this astonishing statement:

> Had the Bible used the model of Christ's submission to the First Person as the model of woman's submission to her husband, we would have been faced with a clear model of the male as divine (therefore dominant) and the female as human (therefore submissive). Instead the model is that of Christ *in his human form* giving himself up for the church, and the church's submission in response to that self-sacrificial love. So instead of a dominance and submission model, we have a mutual submission model.[91]

Before we consider Mollenkott's christology, there are two other problems with her reasoning. The Bible does compare, if only indirectly, the God the Father/Christ relationship to the husband/wife relationship in I Corinthians 11:3; thus, it is appropriate to use the analogy. God the Father is Christ's head and the husband is his wife's head. Headship is the common element of comparison

---

[91]Mollenkott, *Women*, p. 124.

in I Corinthians 11:3 and in Ephesians 5:23–24. Headship and submission are correlative: if someone is your head, you submit to him. The model is not dominance and submission but loving headship (having God-given authority in the husband's case) and self-imposed submission.

The other problem is that Mollenkott carries the analogy too far. She says:

> To use the analogy that the wife is to the husband as Christ-on-earth is to the Father is to make the male the equivalent of the First Person of the Trinity—and then we are back into the idolatry of the masculine. . . .[92]

To interpret an analogy or comparison correctly, one must perceive what its terms are. The biblical analogy in I Corinthians 11:3 (and Ephesians 5:23–24) does not say without qualification that the husband is like God the Father (or Christ); it says the *headship* of the husband over his wife is like the *headship* of God the Father over the Son. (Even then, a comparison does not imply exact duplication but rather similarity.) It does not then follow that the husband is divine or even dominant (is "dominant" even an appropriate description of God?). To go that far is to carry the comparison further than it allows. Mollenkott's practical identification of divinity and dominance/authority is another way of undermining the husband's headship. She stacks the deck against the biblical teaching when she gives us a choice between the divinity/authority of the husband and an egalitarian marriage. If we reject the husband's divinity, we have to reject his authority according to Mollenkott's scheme. This is not a biblical choice. Headship is not the prerogative of gods only. God has given certain groups of people authority over other groups of people.

If one follows Mollenkott's reasoning, one would expect that the Christ/church analogy would be suspect to the feminist, because Christ is God and the church is human. In the God the Father/Christ analogy, both are God. However, as we have seen, Mollenkott

---

overlooks I Corinthians 11:3; and so the Christ/church analogy, which does occur more frequently in Scripture, attracts feminist attention. It must be explained. It stands in the way of their egalitarian model for marriage, because Christ is able to love the church in a self-sacrificing way while he possesses absolute authority over it. The relationship of Christ to the church is an eloquent and eternal illustration that love (including service) and authority (hierarchy) are compatible.

To explain away this aspect of the Christ/church model, Mollenkott commits a christological error.

> Those who are disturbed that the husband is compared to Christ while the wife is compared only to the human church are, I think, forgetting that the analogy is not to Christ-as-divine but to Christ-as-self-emptied, Christ-as-flesh, Christ-giving-himself-up. Unlike the extra-biblical [sic] metaphor of wifely submission as Christ submited to the First Person, this metaphor does not picture woman as human and man as divine. The emphasis is on the human nature of Christ, the self-sacrifice of Christ, which in turn calls forth submission from the church.[93]

Again she says, Christ chose "to empty himself of the divine nature in order to become human. . . ."[94] Mollenkott apparently holds to the kenotic theory[95] of the incarnation, which states that in the

---

[93]Ibid., pp. 124–125.

[94]Ibid., p. 123.

[95]This theory in its classic form dates back only as far as the mid-nineteenth century (Thomasius of Erlangen). It is based on the misunderstanding of Philippians 2:6–8. The verb in 2:7 (ἐκένωσεν), from which "kenotic" is derived, is usually translated "emptied himself." This verb occurs only 4 other times in the New Testament (Rom. 4:14; I Cor. 1:17; 9:15; II Cor. 9:3); in all of these it is used figuratively. If a figurative sense is understood in Philippians 2:7, the idea is that Christ made himself of no account, that is, he humbled himself. This interpretation fits with the best understanding of verse 6, that Christ did not consider equality with God a thing of which to take advantage. The incarnate Christ remains in the form of God; the verb ὑπάρχων, present participle, has the force of being and continuing to be. Christ, being in the form of God, did not take advantage of his equality with God. Instead, he humbled himself. The rest of verse 7 and verse 8 tell *how* he humbled himself. (Even if the idea of "emptying" is retained, the passage does not say of what he emptied himself; it tells how he did it.) He took on the form of a servant, being born in the likeness of humans. No mention is made of the abandonment of the Godhead, equality with God, or any divine attributes. Still in the form of God, Christ humbled himself (or emptied himself) by taking on the form of humanity. Integrally related to the kenosis of Christ is his

incarnation Christ gave up his divine attributes. It means that when Christ became human, he ceased to be God. Therefore, reasons Mollenkott, when the husband is compared to Christ in Ephesians 5:23–24, he is compared to a human.

In contrast, the Scriptures present the incarnate Christ as fully human (but without sin) and fully God in one person. John 1:14 affirms this: "And the Word became flesh and dwelt among us, full of grace and truth; we have beheld his glory, glory as of the only Son from the Father" (cf. Col. 2:9; I John 1:2). The incarnate Christ was *God made manifest* on earth. Jesus said, "He who has seen me has seen the Father . . ." (John 14:9). The two natures, divine and human, are inseparable; what can be said of either nature can be said of the person (hypostatic union).[96] (The author of Hebrews illustrates this in Hebrews 1:1–3.) So it is Christ the God-man who is head of his church and gave himself up for it. The incarnation is a great mystery (I Tim. 3:16) requiring faith, faith that believes everything the Bible says about Jesus Christ.

Mollenkott separates Christ's natures; she must speak of him as human only to forestall a comparison of the husband to one with unquestionable authority. An error in one area of the faith produces other errors. Hence we find a cluster of incorrect doctrines in Mollenkott: a doctrine of Scripture that mixes divine and human ideas and commands; a denial of the husband's headship in marriage; and a misunderstanding of the divine-human person of Christ.

To try to support the egalitarian model with Ephesians 5:23–24, one's conception of Christ must be seriously damaged. The relationship between Christ and his church must be understood as an hierarchy; if it is not, Christ as the unique God-man is lost.

---

death (v. 8). This passage can be considered an exposition of Isaiah 53:12: "he poured out his soul to death." Paul uses a verb with the literal meaning "to pour out, to empty" to recall this Old Testament passage.

For the theological problems implied in the kenotic theory, such as the mutability of God, see L. Berkhof, *Systematic Theology* (Grand Rapids: Eerdmans, c1941), pp. 328–329.

[96]Westminster Confession, VIII, ii: "So that two whole, perfect, and distinct natures, the Godhead and the manhood, were inseparably joined together in one person, without conversion, composition, or confusion." The church universal holds this view (Charles Hodge, *Systematic Theology,* Vol. II [Grand Rapids: Eerdmans, 1968], p. 388).

In the summary of marital duties (Eph. 5:33), nothing new is mentioned for husbands. But a new thought is introduced with reference to wives: they should fear their husbands. Some translations (RSV) tone this concept down to "respect" but respect does not convey the awe and reverence to be given the husband. A substitute for "fear" is sought because fear and love are usually considered incompatible. However, the Christian is both to love and fear God (Ps. 34:8-9; Prov. 1:7; 31:30; Deut. 11:1), and the Christian wife is both to love and fear her husband. This fear is not cringing before a hand that is quick to strike or a tongue quick to lash. "Fear" for the wife involves valuing the authority or headship of her husband. This attitude is necessary for proper submission.

Christians in favor of egalitarian marriage offer two major objections to the husband/wife relation as described in Ephesians 5:22ff. and I Peter 3:1-7 (also Col. 3:18-19). The foundation of both objections is the claim that Paul (and Peter) were influenced by their culture when they taught the submission of wives.

(1) The headship of the husband is unacceptable because it violates the law to love one's neighbor. Scanzoni and Hardesty explain:

> The pattern, if allowed to work itself out over history, with mutual love and delight and self-sacrifice on the part of both husband and wife, could not help but move in the direction of egalitarianism and democracy in the home. . . .
>
> . . . Once Christian husbands would see that they were called to emulate Christ in his love for the church, an atmosphere would be created for raising the position of women in marriage instead of "keeping them in their place." If a wife is an equal heir of grace, she is surely not intended to be treated as a servant without any rights except to fulfill her husband's demands and wishes.[97]

The biblical concept of marriage, which includes the headship of the husband, does not include a license for husbands to suppress their wives or slavery for wives. From the preceding discussion of the

---

[97]Scanzoni and Hardesty, pp. 106-107.

husband's attitude towards his wife, it should be obvious that self-sacrificing love is the primary duty of the husband. Because of this, the headship of the husband and the submission of the wife do not contradict "the reciprocity of mutual respect, self-sacrificing concern, and deep affection,"[98] advocated by marriage-egalitarians. Both hierarchy and mutuality are required in the Christian marriage.

In addition, there is no exegetical evidence for a self-destruct mechanism in the husband's headship or the wife's submission. Exegetically, the command in Ephesians 5:22-23 still stands.

(2) Jewett and Stendahl state the second reason respectively:

> Now if one were to press the subjection of the wife to the husband in the home because of Ephesians 5:22, then he should, by parity of reasoning, press the subjection of the slave to his master because of Ephesians 6:5f.[99]

> It is our contention that all three pairs [in Gal. 3:28] have the same potential for implementation in the life of the church, and that we cannot dispose of the third by confining it to the realm *coram deo*.[100]

Both Ephesians 5:22 and I Peter 3:1-7 are in contexts where corresponding instructions are given to slaves (and masters in Eph.); Galatians 3:28 mentions slave and free. Because there are historical limitations in the commands to slaves, some conclude that the marriage relation must be similarly conditioned. However, such reasoning jeopardizes the parent/child relation (Eph. 6:1-4), an authority/obedience relationship that is still valid. The answer to this dilemma is that each pair in Ephesians 5:22-6:9 should be considered in terms of itself. In chapter 2 (p. 31ff.), we have disputed the "cultural conditioning" of Paul's commands to slaves. But however slavery is viewed, the cessation of the master/slave relationship does not automatically mean the end of the husband's headship and the wife's submission.

---

[98]Ibid., p. 101.
[99]Jewett, pp. 137-138.
[100]Stendahl, *Bible*, p. 34.

Galatians 3:28

These arguments for complete equality between the sexes are based on Galatians 3:28, the cornerstone text for women's liberation. If there is no difference between the husband and wife, if Galatians 3:28 establishes the complete equality between man and woman, there are contradictions in Scripture (between Gal. 3:28 and the passages that teach the headship of the husband and the submission of the wife). The biblical feminists conclude that those passages that teach differences between men and women must be culturally conditioned and therefore nonauthoritative. This explanation is questionable because of its attitude towards Scripture. All Scripture is inspired by God (II Tim. 3:16–17), and therefore Paul's instructions concerning women cannot be understood as a mere product of Paul's rabbinic training or cultural conditioning.

In addition, the case for cultural conditioning has no support in the texts themselves. It is based on a misunderstanding of Galatians 3:28; this misunderstanding creates the contradiction between Galatians 3:28 and Ephesians 5:22–23, etc. A correct interpretation of Galatians 3:28 vanquishes this alleged contradiction.

The context of Galatians 3:28 is faith in contrast to law as the means of salvation. Paul's point is that without respect to nationality, social status or sex, all are justified by faith (v. 24), all are children of God (v. 26), all have put on Christ (v. 27), all are heirs according to the promise (v. 29). From these verses, it is clear that the emphasis is *coram deo,* the Christian's relation to God; men and women have the same relation to God through Christ. Nonetheless, there are consequences for human relations, but not those advocated by the biblical feminists. The point of Galatians 3:28 is not equality in Christ, but oneness in Christ. The practical applications of oneness are explained by Paul in I Corinthians 12. Hostilities, jealousies, and resentments between believers are to be put aside (this does not mean that the immediate causes or circumstances, such as the headship of the husband, are necessarily bad and to be removed). Oneness means that what benefits one believer benefits all, that there should be mutual caring and help. I Corinthians 12 describes both oneness (v. 13) and hierarchy (v. 28). So, oneness and hierarchical relations are not contradictory in the body of Christ. Oneness, being part of one another, enables hierarchy to exist without questions of superiority or inferiority (I Corinthians 12:15–26). Similarly, the relationship of husband and wife is based on their oneness (Eph. 5:22ff.), and questions of superiority and inferiority should be irrelevant.

Galatians 3:28 was true when Paul wrote it, even though slavery existed and even though civil laws and customs may have placed wives at the mercy of their husbands. As Mollenkott points out, believers have already been united with Christ and clothed with Christ; because of what has already happened, there is (present tense) oneness in Christ. The fulfillment of Galatians 3:28 is not in the dim, distant future, when all distinctions between Jew/Gentile, slave/free, and male/female can be obliterated. The realization of Galatians 3:28 need not wait even for that far distant twentieth century with its cry for equal rights. Galatians 3:28 was true in the first century A.D. The implementation of Galatians 3:28 does not depend on the existence or nonexistence of any social institution.

One note of warning must be sounded against the social implementations of Galatians 3:28. The biblical feminists affirm that Galatians 3:28 does not intend to remove biological distinctives between male and female. That may seem like an obvious point. However, there are trends in society moving in the direction of unisex. The visibility of homosexuals and their campaign to legitimize homosexuality is one step towards removing biological differences (by removing the significance of biological differences) between male and female. This trend is contrary to the plain command of Scripture (I Cor. 6:9–10; I Tim. 1:9–11; Jude 5, 7; Rom. 1:24–27). We should also note that some gays use the biblical feminists' hermeneutic and claim that Paul was culturally conditioned when he prohibited homosexuality. With the "advances" in medicine, the removal of biological differences may be surgically possible in the future. Consequently, we must be careful when we hear cries to remove all distinctions in the name of Galatians 3:28.

The social implementations for the three categories in Galatians

3:28 are not the same because the categories differ in nature. Slavery is a social institution created by sinful men; as a purely human invention, it can be obliterated. Because the relationship can be erased, the commands could be considered conditional or obsolete. Nonetheless, insofar as the categories master and slave exist, the commands to them still apply. For instance, these commands still apply to the employer/employee relationship. Jew/Gentile distinctions cannot be completely erased. The biblical word on this relationship is that the two racial groups be reconciled (Eph. 2:14–16); and this exhortation remains valid. The man/woman relationship, unlike the other two, was established at creation; it cannot be removed. The categories of husband and wife remain, so Paul's commands to them still apply. Each of these pairs must be understood in terms of itself, in the way that Scripture understands them.

Galatians 3:28 does not annul the passages that teach the submission of women in the church or of wives to their husbands. Elements of hierarchy and equality occur side by side in the New Testament passages (I Cor. 11:2–16; I Pet. 3:1–7; I Cor. 12:13, 28); the co-existence of the two concepts is explained, at least in part, by the idea of oneness—between husband and wife and between Christ and believers.

Christ gave the reason for his coming:

> The Spirit of the Lord is upon me,
> because he has anointed me to preach good news to the poor.
> He has sent me to proclaim release to the captives
> and recovering of sight to the blind,
> to set at liberty those who are oppressed,
> to proclaim the acceptable year of the Lord (Luke 4:18).

Are women among the oppressed to be freed? Both men and women are freed from the shackles of sin through faith in Christ. Both men and women who believe in Christ become children of God and heirs with Christ. This is the crucial difference Christ's coming makes in the lives of women. But the freedom Christ gives is not freedom from God's law (Rom. 6:15ff.) but freedom to obey the law (Gal. 5:13–14).

The law regarding women involves an element of subordination (I Cor. 14:34). But this submission does not reduce the woman to a secondary, auxilliary status in God's kingdom, nor are her gifts to be wasted. What women's submission means is that women cannot perform certain duties in the congregation and that women are to submit themselves to their husbands. The Old and New Testaments are consistent on these points. The same three principles concerning men and women in the Old Testament are expressed more clearly in the New Testament. (1) Men and women, both in God's image, have the same relationship to God through Christ (Gal. 3:28; I Pet. 3:7). (2) Women have a role different from men in the church and in the family; it is one of submission (I Cor. 11:3; 14:34; I Tim. 2:11). (3) In church and family, a union established by God harmonizes the first two principles. The union of believers in Christ and of husband and wife are founded on love (I Cor. 12–14, especially chapter 13; Eph. 5:25–31).

FIVE

GOD AS MALE AND FEMALE

IS God male or female? Perhaps to eliminate the biological-sexual aspect, we should ask: Is God masculine or feminine? With the rise of the feminist movement and the consequent "raised consciousnesses" of women, this question is inevitably asked of the Christian religion, which teaches that God is Father, Son, and Holy Ghost. When Christians witness to Jesus Christ, they encounter objections from women who say they cannot believe in a religion that oppresses, discriminates, or ignores half of humanity. Must Christians apologize for the maleness of Jesus Christ?

Responses from Christian feminists vary. It is appropriate to begin with an early (1895) and honest feminist response, from Stanton:

> The first step in the elevation of woman to her true position as an equal factor in human progress, is the cultivation of the religious sentiment in regard to her dignity and equality, the recognition by the rising generation of an ideal Heavenly Mother, to whom their prayers should be addressed, as well as to a Father.[1]

Some feminists blatantly disregard God's self-revelation in the

---

[1]Stanton, part 1, p. 14.

Bible. Consider the authority the following author, A. Durwood Foster, gives to Eastern thought, which is alien to and contrary to the inspired Scriptures; he proposes Eastern thought as a corrective to the biblical concept of God.

> We are also freed in principle from a conceptual literalism with respect to the masculinity of biblical-traditional God symbols. This opens the door for, even if it does not yet amount to anything approaching an adequate thematization of God's femaleness, God as the ground of the female as much as the ground of the male. Tillich's proposal of the "ground of being" as not lacking in female affinity is a pertinent thought toward such thematization, as is dipolar conceptuality in general. Much help in this might come from the profoundly rich sensibility of the East—for instance, from the mood and intuition of Sri Aurobindo Ghose in his meditation on God as the Mother. It is still an open question too whether the figure of Mary may not have a more exalted role in the Christian vision—not only as co-redemptrix but as co-creatrix.[2]

This unjustifiable, unbiblical exaltation of Mary to the point of deity (co-redemptrix or co-creatrix) is developed further by Mary Daly. The title of her book, *Beyond God the Father*, reveals her purpose. She suggests that Mary's virginity symbolizes the woman's autonomy, her completeness and integrity without the man. The idea of female (or male) autonomy contradicts I Corinthians 11:11–12. Daly carries her feminist reasoning even further and rejects Jesus in favor of Mary as the redemptive symbol for women. Mary as a replacement for Jesus as redeemer obviously has no scriptural warrant (Acts 4:7–12). Jesus is the only Savior. In raising Mary's position, Daly actually lowers Christ's.

> As the idolatry and the dehumanizing effects of . . . limiting "God" become more manifest in women's expanded consciousness, it will become less plausible to think of Jesus as the "Second Person of the Trinity" who "assumed" a human nature in a unique "hypostatic union." Indeed it is logical that the prevalent emphasis upon the total uniqueness and supereminence of Jesus will become less meaningful.[3]

---

[2]A. Durwood Foster, "God and Woman: Some Theses on Theology, Ethics, and Women's Lib," *Religion in Life*, 42 (1973), 55–56.

[3]Daly, pp. 69–70.

Mary Daly's desire to represent women fully and equally in Christianity, to move beyond God the Father and also God the Son, has led her to the denial of the deity of Christ, which is heresy. Christ's incarnation as a man is a problem for those who wish to do away with exclusively masculine language, and Daly's solution is to do away with Christ's deity and to offer a female counterpart in Mary. (Since Mary was not God, and Daly cannot make her God, Daly must cut Christ down to Mary's level.)

Daly sees the women's movement as a rival to Christ.

> In its depth, because it contains a dynamic that drives beyond Christolatry, the women's movement *does* point to, seek, and constitute the primordial, always present, and future Antichrist.[4]

And so, she indicates that the religion she has proposed is not Christianity.

Daly's feminism is radical, and yet, it is a consistent development of sexual equality, "freed" from biblical norms. To carry sexual equality to its logical conclusion is to create a new religion, to humanize Christ and to erect a female counterpart.

Daly and Foster have criticized the "masculinity" of God because it excluded women. Dorothee Soelle and Rosemary Ruether criticize it because they think it is used as an excuse for domination. Ruether writes:

> Traditional theological images of God as father have been the sanctification of sexism and hierarchicalism precisely by defining this relationship of God as father to humanity in a domination-subordination model and by allowing ruling-class males to identify themselves with this divine fatherhood in such a way as to establish themselves in the same kind of hierarchical relationship to women and lower classes. Jesus, however, refers to God as father in such a way as to overthrow this hierarchical relationship of the rulers over the ruled.[5]

---

[4]Ibid., p. 96.
[5]Rosemary Radford Ruether, *New Woman/New Earth: Sexist Ideologies and Human Liberation* (New York: Seabury Press, 1975), p. 65.

Soelle writes:

> . . . It is important to recognize under which god one has been socialized. The 'male God' is a fundamental part of our culture. He is a being whose most important activity is rulership. Theologically, power becomes omnipotence, and rulership becomes world domination—total control and determination of all things, as at Auschwitz. The male God is the ruler of the universe, he has created the universe and has the power to intervene in it at any time. He is autonomous, totally independent of his creation. His rule is overall and he himself needs no one. This ruler derives neither stature nor happiness from having created any of us. He is, in theological terms, *aseity* (self-derived existence) raised to infinite power.
>
> One must ask why people speak and think of God in terms of such *aseity* and omnipotence. In order to answer this question we may use the method developed by Ludwig Feuerbach. He holds that this God corresponds to a deep-seated fantasy of mankind. Men, too, wish to be self-sufficient, autonomous, dependent on no one. They too would like to be omnipotent rulers. Probably all of us, even women, have dreams of omnipotence, but these dreams find their verbal expression in the religion fabricated by men in the interest of men. The highest satisfaction men can imagine is to be autonomous and independent.
>
> Actually, *Christian* faith can arise only if we dismiss this God once and for all. For if anything can be said with assurance about Christ—in contrast to this male God who is of course adored equally by many women—it is that Christ had no special prerogatives or privileges. Privileges are an integral part of the omnipotent male God; they are his essence. Christ, however, did not want any privileges; he abandoned them. In mythological language he left heaven, assumed servant's clothes, became vulnerable, hungry, thirsty, and mortal. . . . When will we rid ourselves of the male God and reach that point in faith where we can radically turn to Christ, without fear and without desire for special privilege? When will we be emancipated?[6]

The Fatherhood of God is not the only aspect of God's being that is at stake; his dominion and authority are also suspect. Soelle's

---

[6]Dorothee Soelle, "The Emancipation That Never Happened," in *Women in a Strange Land: Search for a New Image*, ed. by Clare Benedicks Fischer, Betsy Brenneman, and Anne McGrew Bunnett (Philadelphia: Fortress Press, 1975), pp. 84–85.

theology is another attempt by sinful humanity to bring God down to our level.

Whereas dominion and authority describe God's omnipotence and aseity, domination, with its connotations of corrupted power and oppression, cannot be used with reference to God. Nor should anyone imagine that oppression or misused power can be justified by an appeal to God's power and authority. God has *revealed* himself as autonomous, independent of his creation, and all-powerful (Eph. 1:11; Rom. 11:34–35; Isa. 40:22–23; Dan. 4:35); these attributes are not human fantasies à la Feuerbach, as Soelle says. Soelle also neglects to mention God's righteousness, mercy and love; God always exercises his power rightly, justly. Without aseity and omnipotence, God would not be God; he would not be able to save us. It was God's "special privilege" to send his only Son to die for his people (Rom. 5:8); Christ's coming demonstrates God's love for us, but our salvation was accomplished by God's power.

God has established hierarchical relationships in which authority is given to one party. For instance, God has made the husband head of his wife; and in accord with his character, God has commanded that the husband love and honor his wife in order to exercise his authority properly. God has also given the elder in the church authority over the congregation, and the elder is not to domineer but to lead by example (I Pet. 5:2–5). Humility is to characterize both the elders' leading and the congregation's submission.

The problem of misuse of power by governments is too complicated a question to tackle in a book about women, though it is related to our subject. There are two pertinent principles concerning the Christian's relationship to governments: "Let every person be subject to the governing authorities . . ." (Rom. 13:1); and "We must obey God rather than men" (Acts 5:29).

Both Ruether and Soelle reflect the current cultural inclination away from authority, whether God's over humanity, man's over woman or government's over people, towards complete equality, extending even to equality between God and human beings. Though their concern about oppression and corrupted power is not to be belittled or neglected, they fail to understand that in God, power, holiness, and mercy meet and that he has commanded those to whom he has given power and authority to exercise it with love, humility, and justice. This "masculine" image of God does not have to be thrown out in order for Christianity to exist, for Christians to be truly emancipated.

The authors cited above (Stanton, Foster, Daly, Ruether, and Soelle) have not seriously concerned themselves with understanding the scriptural material regarding God's gender. They began with the presupposition that the Bible is an important but not the final authority and that women must be made equal to men in every respect, no matter what. This last presupposition led Mary Daly to posit a female redeemer for women.

The biblical feminists react more responsibly with the Scriptures. Three of the most important figures (Letha Scanzoni, Nancy Hardesty, and Paul K. Jewett) in this category agree that sexuality should not be attributed to God. Scanzoni and Hardesty write:

> In essence, however, God is neither masculine or feminine. As Jesus told the Samaritan woman at the well, "God is spirit, and those who worship him must worship in spirit and truth" (John 4:24). . . .
>
> The adjectives we use of God are not intended to indicate sexuality but generic personhood. . . . God is neither and both. He contains all personhood; we are all made in his image, male and female. In thinking of God we should use neither "he" nor "she" but "Thou" in whose presence we stand at all times.[7]

Jewett says that there is no "sexual distinction in God."[8] Virginia Mollenkott asserts, "Whatever else this [Gen. 1:27] may mean, it certainly must mean that there is a feminine aspect as well as a masculine aspect in the nature of God."[9] Later she essentially agrees with the others that God is not "to be limited by sexual dichotomies."[10]

---

[7]Scanzoni and Hardesty, p. 21.
[8]Jewett, p. 165.
[9]Mollenkott, "Challenge," p. 23.
[10]Ibid.

It is true that God is spirit and that "he" is invisible (I Tim. 1:17; Deut. 4:15), and as such, he is not characterized by sex. But how are we to address and talk about God? And are we to ignore the entire biblical witness to the fatherhood of God? And what about the incarnation of Christ as a man?

The Father

Concerning fatherhood, Scanzoni and Hardesty, Jewett, and Mollenkott appeal to a few Old Testament passages in which God is pictured in maternal terms (Deut. 32:18; Isa. 42:14; 46:3; 49:15; 66:13; Ps. 131:2). But what do they hope to prove by an appeal to these passages? Evidently, Scanzoni and Hardesty only intend to demonstrate that God is neither masculine nor feminine or that he is both; and they seem to sympathize with Helen Reddy who accepted her Grammy Award with these words, "I'd like to thank God because She made everything possible," and with the pastor who prays "Our Mother, who art in heaven. . . ."[11] Mollenkott wants to show that there are masculine and feminine elements in the Godhead. Jewett refers to these passages to destroy an argument against the ordination of women based on the masculinity of God; his purpose, too, is to show that "God is no more (or less) 'he' specifically than 'she,' no more (or less) like the male than like the female."[12] Though none of these go so far as to say that we can address God as Mother, that step seems to be a logical conclusion from their use of these Old Testament passages.

We have already established that God is neither masculine nor feminine; God is spirit. The problem before us is whether or not it is appropriate to address God as Father and/or Mother or Parent. Is there nothing essential to the concept of God that requires the use of masculine language?

Jewett combats the abundance of masculine imagery by appealing

to the analogical nature of language about God. All language about
God is metaphorical in that the infinite must be expressed to finite
minds in finite words and concepts. Jewett says:

> The fact that God likens himself to a Father much more frequently
> than to a Mother does not alter the analogical character of the
> paternal, as well as the maternal, language of such Scriptures.[13]

However, there are different degrees of comparison; and the difference in comparison between paternal and maternal imagery is the
difference between saying "God is our Father" (describing the
person of God) and "God comforts his people as a mother comforts
her child" (describing an action of God). In the former, God is
identified ("is") by a noun, "our Father." In the latter, an action of
God is compared to ("as") an action performed by mothers.

Let us consider the Old Testament passages with maternal
imagery.

> For a long time I have held my peace,
>   I have kept still and restrained myself;
> now I will cry out like a woman in travail,
>   I will gasp and pant (Isa. 42:14).

The Lord has been silent for a long time while his people were in
captivity. But now is the time for him to deliver them. The point of
comparison is that God will cry out with intensity, with the earnest
and determined desire to do that which he has purposed to do, as a
woman in labor would do. In the previous verse, the Lord likens
himself to a mighty warrior who also cries out. The common
element in these comparisons is the crying out, and the result of
God's crying out is wasted mountains, dried up vegetation and pools,
and the deliverance of his people.

> Hearken to me, O house of Jacob,
>   all the remnant of the house of Israel,
> who have been borne by me from your birth,
>   carried from the womb . . . (Isa. 46:3).

It is doubtful that this verse is a reference to God's maternity. The

---

[13]Ibid., p. 167.

Hebrew words for "borne" (הָעֲמֻסִים) and "carried" (הַנְּשֻׂאִים) do not refer to birth; they mean to bear or carry a burden. The sense of the verse is that God has carried his people from their very beginning, from their birth, and he will continue to bear them up through their old age. God has made them, carried them, and will save them. God plainly states, I am "he" (הוּא, masculine pronoun) who has done these things.

> "Can a woman forget her sucking child,
>> that she should have no compassion on the son of her womb?"
> Even these may forget,
>> yet I will not forget you (Isa. 49:15).

> But I have calmed and quieted my soul,
>> like a child quieted at its mother's breast;
>> like a child that is quieted is my soul (Ps. 131:2).

The emphasis in these two verses is on the comforting. The Lord comforts as a mother comforts. Once again, the comparison is in terms of the action (comforting, remembering, crying out) rather than the person of the mother.

The above maternal analogies are in the same category as those used by Moses, who compared himself to a woman who conceives and a nurse carrying a sucking child (Num. 11:12), and by Paul, who compared himself to a nurse (I Thess. 2:7) and a woman in labor (Gal. 4:19). No one would suggest that it is proper or enlightening to refer to Paul or Moses as "Mother" or "Nanny" or in feminine terms. It is possible for a man to describe himself with a feminine comparison without losing his masculinity. So it is possible for God to use this particular kind of analogy (action compared to action) to reveal himself without sanctioning the use of feminine terminology, without intending to teach anything about his person or "sexuality."

One last parental passage may put the parenthood of God in proper perspective.

> You were unmindful of the Rock that begot you,
> and you forgot the God who gave you birth (Deut. 32:18).

The last verb (translated "gave birth," הֻגֵל) is undoubtedly maternal. In this verse, the maternal and paternal responsibility for Israel's birth is said to be God's. The point is that God alone is their progenitor. At first glance, this verse seems to be ideal for those who advocate the Motherhood of God. However, the maternal verb is a *masculine* singular participle; all adjectives, verb forms and pronouns that refer to God in the Old Testament are masculine. The fatherhood analogy is definitely and overwhelmingly the controlling analogy. The more direct type of analogy used for the Fatherhood of God can be found in Deuteronomy 32:6; Psalm 89:26; Isaiah 9:6; 63:16; 64:8; Jeremiah 31:9.

In addition, Jesus always referred to God as Father and taught his disciples to address God as their Father (Matt. 6:9). Jesus' parable in Luke 15:8ff., in which the woman with the lost coin represents God, is not an exception. The point of the parable concerns God's relationship to the lost sinner, not the gender of God (see p. 93).

To repeat, the difference between paternal and maternal references to God is the difference between God's saying, "I am a father to Israel" (Jer. 31:9) or Christ's saying, "you have one Father, who is in heaven" (Matt. 23:9), and God's saying, "I will cry out like a woman in travail" (Isa. 42:14). God is neither masculine nor feminine; he created the two sexes, he created gender. God existed before such distinctions. Yet, God has revealed himself in his word as Father. Christ has told us to pray, "Our Father. . . ."

For the fatherhood of God to be significant, there must be a difference between fatherhood and motherhood. There are significant similarities, such as the compassion a parent has for his/her child (Isa. 49:15; Ps. 103:13). The only difference to be seen in Scripture between the two is their relationship to one another. The father is the head of the household; consequently, his wife must submit herself to him and reverence him (Eph. 5:22–24, 33). It is the husband's headship and the wife's submission that makes it necessary to address God as Father, not Mother. If one erases the biblical distinction between husband and wife, as Scanzoni and Hardesty, Jewett, and Mollenkott have done, then the reason for maintaining God's fatherhood disappears. The feminists then remove the fatherhood of God as a cultural vestige of a patriarchal era.[14] However, the fatherhood of God is part of God's self-revelation in the Bible, apart from which we, because of sin in us, cannot know him. We, because our reason is finite and fallen, cannot reason that God is something other than who he has revealed himself to be.

The Son

God is neither male nor female; however, Jesus Christ was a man. Why did God become a man rather than a woman? First of all, biblical feminists have brought out an important truth that may have been slighted in the past: "Jesus came to earth not primarily as a male but as a person."[15] As Scanzoni and Hardesty point out, the New Testament writers, when discussing the incarnation (Phil. 2:7; Rom. 5:12, 15), use ἄνθρωπος (Man, human being)[16] as distinguished from ἄνηρ (man). As a person, Christ is able to represent men and women. There is no need, as Mary Daly has done, to introduce a redemptrix (Mary) to save women.

Despite this healthy emphasis on the personhood of Christ, some feel the necessity of seeking feminine attributes in Jesus, just so women will not feel left out. Jewett, as observed in chapter 3, is anxious to show that "Man is like God as male *and* female."[17] As an example of this and in an effort to balance the requirement of male animals for the Passover sacrifice, Jewett cites Matthew 23:37 in which Christ likens himself to a hen who gathers her chicks under her wings. The consistent, carefully developed (and observed) sacrificial system and the poignant but incidental comparison to the hen can hardly be put in the same category. In addition, the sex of the sacrifice is specified; it is significant. Christ's desire to protect and

---

[14]"When our spiritual ancestors first put their faith in Him as Jahweh the God of battles who rescued them from Egypt and fought for them against the Amorites and Moabites and others, they naturally thought of Him as He, and went on to look up to Him as their Father in heaven and the Husband of His chosen people": Margaret Sittler Ermarth, *Adam's Fractured Rib* (Philadelphia: Fortress Press, 1970), pp. 126–127.

[15]Scanzoni and Hardesty, p. 56.

[16]Ἄνθρωπος can describe a male (John 1:6; 3:1).

[17]Jewett, p. 168.

his concern are the point of the hen simile, not the sex of the
chicken. This simile is in the same category as those Old Testament
maternal analogies.

Mollenkott writes:

> The Son is pictured not only in the stereotypically feminine aspects
> of submission to the will of the First Person, but also in the stereo-
> typically masculine roles of the powerful generator, upholder, and
> judge of the universe (Colossians 1:16, 2 Thessalonians 1:7-8). . . .
> As the Logos Christ is associated with the Old Testament figure of
> wisdom, always personified as feminine . . . (Proverbs 4:4-7).[18]

Mollenkott admits that the roles of submitting and ruling are only
stereotypically feminine and masculine; such stereotyping is a
misrepresentation, and so her argument is self-defeating. Submission is to be the characteristic of every Christian, and most Christians
at some time have authority over someone (i.e., the mother has
authority over her child). An appeal to such a misunderstanding of
the nature of submission cannot justify the attribution of feminine
elements in Christ, nor should Christ's submission be placed on the
feminine side of the balance sheet. Submission and authority are not
sex specific characteristics; they are related to sex only in two
particular relationships; marriage and church government.

The use of the feminine figure for wisdom in Proverbs 8:22-31,
which has been understood as a representation of the preexistent
Christ, bears closer examination. A strong case can be made against
an *identification* of wisdom and the preexistent Christ. The verb
קנה[19] (translated "create" in RSV) in verse 22 suggests the idea of
possession: God produced wisdom in order to possess it. קנה occurs
in Proverbs 4:5, 7 with the sense of acquisition: "*get* wisdom, *get*
insight." God does not "get" wisdom from without as people do.
Wisdom is "brought forth" (חול), a concept repeated in this passage;
wisdom is brought forth in the sense of exposed, revealed, or
demonstrated.[20] Wisdom as an attribute of God is eternal; but his

---

[18]Mollenkott, "Challenge," p. 23.
[19]קנה does not convey the idea of creation out of nothing as does ברא (Gen. 1:1).
[20]C. F. Keil and F. Delitzsch, *Commentary on the Old Testament in Ten Volumes,* Vol. VI
(Grand Rapids: Eerdmans, n.d.), p. 184.

wisdom is shown in creation because he brings it forth to participate in creation (see Prov. 3:19–20). Wisdom is a possession of God; it is not God (nor is it Christ).

Wisdom is clearly portrayed as a possession of Christ (Luke 2:40, 52). "And the Spirit of the Lord shall rest upon him [the Messiah], the spirit of wisdom and understanding . . ." (Isa. 11:2). Christ is the one "in whom are hid all the treasures of wisdom and knowledge" (Col. 2:3). "Worthy is the Lamb who was slain, to receive power and wealth and wisdom and might and honor and glory and blessing!" (Rev. 5:12).

Wisdom in Proverbs 8:22–31 is better understood as an attribute of God personified rather than the second person of the Trinity. It is too simplistic to say with the biblical feminists, "In the New Testament Wisdom (feminine) becomes Word [a masculine noun in Greek] (cf. Proverbs 8 and John 1:1–18)."[21] Christ is not God's wisdom; the triune God possesses wisdom.

The *New Bible Dictionary* gives this explanation:

> The purpose of wisdom's recitation of her credentials is to attract men to pay her rightful heed, as viii. 32–36 indicates. Therefore, caution must be exercised in reading into this passage a view of hypostatization, *i.e.* that wisdom is depicted as having an independent existence. The Hebrews' characteristic resistance to speculation and abstraction frequently led their poets to deal with inanimate objects or ideals as though they had personality.[22]

Christ himself speaks of wisdom as a person. "Yet wisdom is justified by all her children" (Luke 7:35; Matt. 11:19). "Therefore also the Wisdom of God said, 'I will send them prophets and apostles, some of whom they will kill and persecute . . .'" (Luke 11:49). Christ does not identify himself with wisdom.

But why is wisdom personified as a woman? J. Edgar Bruns suggests that there is something in the nature of wisdom that associates itself with woman.

---

[21]Scanzoni and Hardesty, p. 21.
[22]J. D. Douglas, ed., *New Bible Dictionary* (Grand Rapids: Eerdmans, c1962), p. 1333.

Are we confronted here, then, in these texts from the Old Testament with a further instance of the concept that knowledge is a feminine gift? Our earlier study showed that the desire for knowledge was—in the biblical narrative—a feminine trait (Eve's), but also it was represented there as evil. These later passages [such as Prov. 8] seem to reflect a stage in the evolution of Israelite religion when patriarchy was established firmly enough to allow for the reappearance of the very ancient conviction that wisdom and woman were inseparable, and that, furthermore, wisdom was not inimical to man but, on the contrary, his guarantee of "the good life" whether in the judgment of God or in that of his fellow human beings.[23]

He concludes that because the Hebrew words for spirit (רוּחַ) and wisdom (חָכְמָה) are feminine, there is "ample justification, if we choose, to speak of God as a woman as well as a man."[24] Surely, this sort of thinking puts too much emphasis on the gender of words (all Hebrew nouns are either masculine or feminine), especially when in Greek, spirit (πνευμα) loses its femininity and becomes neuter.

Why a noun, such as wisdom in Hebrew, is feminine would be extremely difficult, if not impossible, to determine with certainty. However, the fact that the noun wisdom is feminine probably accounts for its personification as a woman. Those who want to absolutize wisdom-woman association should remember that wisdom's antagonist folly is also represented as a woman.

Proverbs 1–9 is a unit that contrasts wisdom and folly, both of which are represented as women (for the clearest juxtaposition, see Prov. 9).[25] These personifications should be viewed as a poetic device depicting the competition of wisdom and folly to win souls, so to speak. Even if one is convinced of the identity of wisdom and Christ, the poetic nature of this section should deter one from

---

[23]J. Edgar Bruns, *God as Woman, Woman as God* (New York: Paulist Press, 1973), p. 38.
[24]Ibid., p. 40.
[25]This contrast also appears as fidelity to the wife of one's youth, an example of wisdom, versus succumbing to the enticements of a loose woman, the epitome of folly (Prov. 5). The harlot seems to become Folly, and the wife, though not identical with wisdom, is clearly associated with it (compare 8:11 and 31:10). The woman of Proverbs 31 is an example of wisdom.

making too much of the personification of a feminine noun as a woman.

In spite of the feminists' efforts to provide a feminine element in Jesus, the incontrovertible and outstanding fact remains that he lived on earth as a *man*. To account for this, they argue, "Given the setting of patriarchal Judaism, Jesus had to be male."[26] Scanzoni and Hardesty list symbolic reasons (Christ "came as the Messiah, the heir to David's throne, our great high priest, and a lamb without spot or blemish to be an offering for our sin"[27]), and practical reasons ("Jewish women were kept in subjection and sometimes even seclusion";[28] they would have had little scriptural knowledge, could not have taught publicly and would have been ritually unclean for a fourth of the time). Jewett concisely summarizes: "the Incarnation in the form of male humanity, though historically and culturally necessary, was not *theologically* necessary."[29]

On the contrary, we maintain that God had a theological reason for sending Christ as a man and that historical and cultural necessity, though existent, are subservient to God's plan and intention. In short, God as Lord of history and culture, is not conditioned by them. Just as God freely chose to create two sexes, to create Adam the man first and so establish him as head of the race and the man as head of his wife, and to reveal himself in masculine pronouns, adjectives, and verb forms, God chose to be incarnate as a man.

Those who deny the theological necessity of God incarnate as a man also reject those passages which teach any differences between men and women as culturally determined. As in the case of the fatherhood of God, these theologians first eliminate the distinctions Scripture makes between men and women; then they say there is no ultimate reason Christ came to earth as a male. If one believes, "I permit no woman to teach or to have authority over men; she is to

---

[26]Scanzoni and Hardesty, p. 55.
[27]Ibid.
[28]Ibid.
[29]Jewett, p. 168.

keep silent" and its theological justification, "For Adam was formed first, then Eve; and Adam was not deceived, but the woman was deceived and became a transgressor" (I Tim. 2:12–14), to be true, then there is one obvious reason why Christ could not have been a woman.

God has forbidden the teaching and ruling offices in the church to women, and he has appointed the husband the head of his wife. These facts would be enough reason for the maleness of Christ. However, God has given the reasons for these commands: Adam was created first, the woman was created for the man's sake and from him, and the woman, not the man, was deceived. A consideration of the first of these reasons is most helpful in understanding the theological necessity for Christ's maleness. Adam was the first person, and all other persons came from him; he is the source of the whole human race. As such, he is our representative, and so he appears in Romans 5:12–21 and I Corinthians 15:45–49.

> For as by one man's disobedience many were made sinners, so by one man's obedience many will be made righteous (Rom. 5:19).

> Just as we have borne the image of the man of dust, we shall also bear the image of the man of heaven (I Cor. 15:49).

By creating the man first, God established him as the head of the human race. There is a sense in which the woman is included in the man, is represented by him, but the reverse is not true. (And so in the one-flesh union, the husband is the head; the male elders in the church can represent the whole congregation—men and women.) The male is representative by God's appointment or decision, not because men are valued more or are superior in being. Since God has given this representative ability to the male, Christ, as the head, source, and representative of the church, had to become incarnate as a man.

Adam, because he represents the whole of humanity, is the first *type* of "him who was to come" (Rom. 5:14). Scanzoni and Hardesty reverse the reasoning when they suggest that Christ had to be male because of the culturally determined male symbols of Christ. All of the types and symbols pointing ahead to Christ are male (from

Adam to Isaac to Moses to David); God set up the sacrificial system and chose the types in order to prepare the way for his Son. The sex of the types did not determine the incarnate Christ's sex, but God determined both.

Why did God choose the man and not the woman to be head of the race? Why did God choose to reveal himself in masculine imagery? Unfortunately, the answers to these questions are not given in Scripture. The answer is no easier for those who assume that the man's headship is based on his superiority. The question then is: why did God make man superior? Perhaps the only answer we can expect at this point is:

> But who are you, a Man [$\dot{\alpha}\nu\theta\rho\omega\pi\epsilon$], to answer back to God? Will what is molded say to its molder, "Why have you made me thus?" (Rom. 9:20).

This answer may not be satisfying, but God is under no obligation to explain everything to us. And we are perhaps unable (because we are finite) to understand all things. We are to live and walk by faith in God who loved us so much that he sent his Son to die for us, not by sight.

The Holy Spirit

The Holy Spirit is the most gender-less person of the Godhead. The first two persons of the Trinity have revealed themselves as "Father" and "Son," distinctly masculine designations, but the name "Holy Spirit" has no connotations of gender. In addition, descriptions of the Holy Spirit are not anthropomorphic. Because of the elusiveness of the Spirit, some have doubted his personality and considered him an "it," an influence or force. This view is unbiblical, but it illustrates the elusiveness of the Spirit.

Our concern is not so much to defend the use of masculine imagery with reference to the Spirit, as it was in the cases of Father and Son, but to show the lack of gendered references to the Spirit and to disprove the idea of a feminine or androgynous Spirit.

According to Mollenkott, the Spirit in Genesis 1:2 is "femininely brooding over the face of the waters like a hen on her nest."[30] But Genesis 1:2 does not justify this female conception of the Spirit. The factor that lends femininity to this image is simply the gender of the Hebrew רוּחַ (Spirit), a feminine noun. The root of the participle מְרַחֶפֶת (piel), sometimes translated brooding, means to loose or slack. In the piel, it is applied to birds in the sense of loosening their wings or hovering;[31] and it does not describe the actions of the female exclusively. In Deuteronomy 32:11, the same verb (יְרַחֵף) describes the actions of the parent eagle when the young are forced to leave the nest: the parent eagle hovers with outstretched wings to catch them in case they fall. According to the *Encyclopedia Americana,* both eagle parents perform this function. Also the Hebrew noun for eagle is masculine, and the verb agrees in gender. The translation "brooding" is inaccurate; and if one considers upon what the Spirit is supposed to be brooding, water (an unlikely "nest"), the inappropriateness of that translation is underlined. The Holy Spirit in Genesis 1:2 is not pictured as a female bird hatching her eggs.

The Old Testament references to the Holy Spirit do not personify or anthropomorphize him (Num. 11:29; I Sam. 11:6; 16:13; Ps. 51:11; 104:30; 139:7; Isa. 11:2–3; 61:1; 63:10–11; Hag. 2:5) and, consequently, have little bearing on a consideration of the Spirit's gender, except to suggest the lack thereof.

The Holy Spirit is symbolized by water, wind, breath, fire, oil, a dove, a down-payment, and a seal, all nonpersonal imagery. Gender is irrelevant to them. Some have suggested that the dove is an androgynous image, because "Throughout mythology,"[32] the dove

---

[30]Mollenkott, "Challenge," p. 23.

[31]Edward J. Young, *Studies in Genesis One* (Philadelphia: Presbyterian and Reformed Publ. Co., 1964), p. 36. The Ugaritic supports the meaning of "hover." Young cites this example:

the eagles hovered over him, the flock of hawks looked down, and Anat hovered among the eagles (Aqhat i:30, 32).

Here the eagles hover above their prey, ready to pounce upon it. So מרחפת does not necessarily describe the activity of a female bird. Young eliminates "brooding" as a possible translation.

[32]Mollenkott, "Challenge," p. 23.

has been considered androgynous. But the meaning of a dove in pagan mythology does not determine its significance in Scripture. In the Bible, the dove is the messenger that shows Noah that the flood waters had receded. As a result of this role, the dove is considered a messenger of peace. Why the dove as opposed to some other bird is chosen by Noah is not said. One answer may be that the dove will return to its home (cf. Isa. 60:8). Noah first sent a raven, but the raven flew to and fro over the waters until they receded (Gen. 8:7) so that Noah was unable to know. The dove returned to the ark two times. Noah knew that when the dove did not return, the waters had receded. Perhaps in the case of Christ's baptism, the Spirit's descent on Christ marked the Spirit's return home.

Matthew 10:16 provides another clue as to why the dove represents the Holy Spirit in Matthew 3:16. Jesus characterizes the dove as pure. Associations of purity and peace explain the dove as a representation of the Holy Spirit. Masculinity, femininity, and androgyny have nothing to do with this symbol.

Because of the lack of personification of the Spirit, most discussions of him include a defense of his personality. In Greek, the noun for spirit is neuter, and grammar requires that pronouns agree in gender with their antecedents. So in Greek when pronouns are used to refer to the Spirit, they would normally be neuter, as is the case in John 14:17. However, because the Spirit is a person and it was unnatural to call him "it," the grammatical rule is broken in several places (John 14:26; 15:26; 16:13–14) and masculine pronouns are used. These exceptions "prove" the Spirit is personal, and they indicate that as a person, the Holy Spirit should be referred to with masculine pronouns.

We have noted the lack of gendered images of the Spirit. But this absence does not allow us to conceive of the Holy Spirit in any way we want. For example, Elizabeth Cady Stanton thought a "Heavenly Father, Mother, and Son would seem more rational."[33] And in a spurious work, the "Gospel according to the Hebrews," Jesus

---

[33]Stanton, part 1, p. 14.

supposedly says, "Even now did my mother the Holy Spirit take me by one of my hairs and carry me away to the great mountain Thabor."[34] It is natural for one to look at the human family and project it onto one's gods (as in most pagan mythology) or God. But God has not revealed himself as such; God has revealed himself as Father, Son, and Holy Spirit, and Mary is the only mother Christ had. We must conceive of the Holy Spirit as he has been revealed by himself in the Scriptures. Most importantly, he is a person, and we know persons as "he" or "she." Christ, as reported by John, breaks the rules of grammar to refer to the Spirit as "he." And we are not at liberty to change to "she." But it is the personhood, not the gender of the Holy Spirit, that must be emphasized.

Summary

God is spirit and, as such, is beyond the categories male and female. He created those categories and existed before they did. Nonetheless, he has consistently revealed himself as Father in the God-breathed Scriptures. God became incarnate as a man. Even the elusive Holy Spirit is referred to in masculine terms, when spoken of personally. The masculine terminology has significance because God has given the man authority in the family (husband) and in the church (elder), rather than the woman. Therefore, if Christians are to be obedient to God's will, expressed in the Bible, they must continue to address God as he has taught them—as Father, Son, and Holy Spirit.

---

[34]Bruns, p. 40.

SIX

THE METAPHYSICS OF SEX

IN the last chapter, we concluded that God, though neither male nor female, has revealed himself in masculine terms, which are significant, and that Christ's incarnation as a man has theological significance. We think that these conclusions are based on God's word and that God's word does not need to be deculturized in terms of what we women think is fair to us. But the question still remains: How does the woman relate to a male Savior, to her God who has revealed himself as Father rather than as Mother or Parent? Though this question, which perhaps is the wrong question to ask, cannot be answered simply and directly (nor to everyone's satisfaction), a consideration of what are the differences between women and men may give some insight into the problem along these lines: if men and women are alike, are fundamentally persons, then the answer to our question is that women are to relate to God as persons.

Are women different from men? The answer seems so obvious to some that they laugh and add, "Vive la différence!" Of course, there are biological differences, but the question that concerns us is one of psychology or personality. Did God create us with masculine and feminine souls and minds as well as bodies?

In our society, the majority will probably say yes. Scanzoni and Hardesty summarize some of the distinctions our society makes:

Strength, action, sound reason, decisiveness, aggressiveness, ambition, energy, drive, courage, inventiveness are thought to characterize "masculine nature." The male biological symbol is that used in astronomy for Mars, god of war, and represents his shield and spear: ♂. The mirror of Venus, ♀, goddess of love and beauty, is the female symbol because "feminine nature" is thought to be narcissistic, subjective, dependent, passive, intuitive, tender, fragile, irrational, frivolous.[1]

The "mentally healthy male," according to a 1968 survey of mental health professionals by Donald and Inge Broverman, is aggressive, independent, unemotional, logical, direct, adventurous, self-confident, ambitious. The "mentally healthy female" is passive, emotional, dependent, less competitive, nonobjective, submissive, vain, easily influenced, religious and in need of security. . . .

Male personality traits and behavior are defined as "adult" and "healthy" while those defined as "female" by society are still regarded as childish and even neurotic. The Brovermans discovered this by asking psychologists to list traits of a "mentally healthy adult." It conformed exactly to the list previously drawn for a male but contrasted sharply with that for a female. A woman who exhibits "male" traits of aggressiveness and rationality is labeled "masculine," "neurotic," even "lesbian." If she conforms to female stereotypes, she is not a healthy adult; if she does not conform, she is sick. It is a no-win option.[2]

The church reenforces these stereotypes. The man is the head of the home (a fact we do not dispute) because "the heart of a woman is more easily discouraged and dejected. God made her that way."[3] The Bible does not suggest this reason for the husband's headship, nor does it distinguish between the hearts of men and the hearts of women. One seminarian, who, I am sure, is not alone in his thinking, reasons from I Peter 3:7 ("weaker sex") that all women are inferior to all men in every way.

Adherence to sexual stereotypes need not take such a negative

---

[1]Scanzoni and Hardesty, p. 73.
[2]Ibid., p. 81.
[3]Larry Christenson, *The Christian Family* (Minneapolis: Bethany Fellowship, 1974), p. 128.

turn. For instance, men are said to be assertive, analytic, manipulative (not manipulating), thing-oriented, whereas women are inter-
dependent, contextual (aware of the whole situation), adjustive,
responsive, people-oriented. The woman tends to be verbal and
qualitative specific; the man tends to be numerical and quantitative
specific.[4] In other words, men and women are different, but one is
not better than the other and both types of thinking are needed.

Another variation of sexual stereotyping is to say that personality
traits are not sex specific; however, they have manly and womanly
forms.[5] Perhaps this reasoning lies behind the RSV's translation of
σωφροσυνη. The word means reasonableness, rationality, mental
soundness, good judgment, moderation, and self-control. As a
feminine virtue, it is translated "decency" (Arndt and Gingrich) or
chastity. In the RSV, it is translated "modesty" in I Timothy 2:15
with respect to women and "sensible" (adjectival form) in I Timothy
3:2 with respect to elders. A man and a woman may do the same
thing, but the man will do it in a masculine way and the woman in a
feminine way. Metaphysically, man is always purely masculine and
woman purely feminine. Sexuality affects everything we do. This
theory tries to eliminate all of the negative connotations associated
with the feminine, but it still emphasizes basic differences between
men and women.

Because of his view that man as male and female expresses God's
image in Man, Paul Jewett, unlike Scanzoni and Hardesty and
Mollenkott, underlines the differences between men and women,
though he cannot say what the differences are. They are as mysterious as they are obvious, he says. He avoids trying to make
distinctions because of his sensitivity towards cultural influence. Yet
he intimates that sexual duality has ultimate significance.

On what grounds is the difference(s) between men and women
based? The common argument for all those who maintain a metaphysical difference between the sexes is observation and experience

---

[4]Eric Mount, "The Feminine Factor," *Soundings*, 53:4 (Winter, 1970), 382, 384.

[5]Derrick Sherwin Bailey, *Sexual Relation in Christian Thought* (New York: Harper &
Brothers, 1959), p. 291.

(in Jewett's case, theological consistency may be his ultimate reason). The feminine mystique and the concept of the woman as "the other" pervade Western culture. If one surveys a segment of the population concerning their concepts of man and woman, one will find distinctions made between the sexes along the lines Scanzoni and Hardesty describe. Furthermore, observation of men's and women's behavior will most likely support the stereotypes. But what does observation prove? Nothing, unless it can be isolated from culturization or linked indisputably to biology. It is highly unlikely (and also unethical) that children could be raised in complete isolation from their culture in an experiment to discover if clusters of personality traits are determined by sex. It is impossible to separate what is cultural conditioning or socialization from heredity. Culturization occurs from birth, from the color-coded bracelets for newborns to the responses evoked by parents and relatives. In a study by Jeffrey Rubin, Frank Provenzano and Zella Luria (Tufts University), 30 mothers and fathers were asked to describe their newborn babies after their first glimpses. Though diapered newborns look alike, the parents of daughters described them as tiny, soft, fine-featured, delicate; sons were described as strong, alert, well-coordinated.[6] Sexual stereotyping begins early.

No discussion of the relationship of innate differences between the sexes and cultural conditioning is complete without a reference to Margaret Mead's study of primitive tribes, *Sex and Temperament in Three Primitive Societies*. In two of the tribes, there were no personality differences between men and women. In the third tribe the women were dominant, impersonal, and unadorned, and the men were less responsible, emotionally dependent, gossips, and concerned with their appearance. Mead's findings indicate the important role socialization plays in the determination of what behavior is thought to be masculine and what behavior is thought to be feminine.

Another avenue of appeal is biology. Elisabeth Elliot writes:

---

[6]Alice Lake, "Are We Born into Our Sex Roles or Programmed into Them?" *Woman's Day* (January, 1976), p. 24.

> There are strong biological reasons (a matter of hormones) why the male has always dominated and will continue to dominate in every society.[7]

> Recent scientific research is illuminating, and as has happened before, corroborates ancient truth which mankind has always recognized. God created male and female, the male to call forth, to lead, initiate and rule, and the female to respond, follow, adapt, submit. Even if we held to a different theory of origin the physical structure of the female would tell us that woman was made to receive, to bear, to be acted upon, to complement, to nourish.[8]

In short, anatomy is destiny. Eric Mount explains his theory:

> By somatic design the woman harbors an inner space which destines her to bear offspring and commits her biologically, psychologically, and ethically to caring for human infancy, although a woman can reject this destiny and be at odds with her womanhood.[9]

Women's Lib responds to such reasoning. In Kate Millett's words:

> But biology is a word to conjure by, particularly in the social sciences; a vague reference to the male's larger musculature is expected to silence criticism. It is also expected that, even though it is intellectually understood that (beyond breast-feeding) the assignment of child care is cultural rather than biological, middle-class Americans will let that slip by and infer that childbirth must mean child care, the two together again constituting "biology."[10]

Scanzoni and Hardesty, biblical feminists, report:

> Hormonally the sexes are not antithetical in their makeup. Rather the spectrum is more like a continuum with most people having a preponderance of either androgen (male) or estrogen (female).[11]

This author does not have the expertise to evaluate scientific data concerning hormonally determined "personality" differences between men and women, and this author has read only one book that

---

[7]Elisabeth Elliot, *Let Me Be a Woman: Notes on Womanhood for Valerie* (Wheaton: Tyndale House, 1976), p. 58.

[8]Ibid., p. 59.

[9]Mount, p. 381.

[10]Kate Millett, *Sexual Politics* (Garden City: Doubleday & Co., 1970), p. 225.

[11]Scanzoni and Hardesty, pp. 74–75.

advances biological "data" to support hormonally caused differences in behavior between the sexes, that is, *The Inevitability of Patriarchy* by Steven Goldberg,[12] a sociologist. Though Dr. Goldberg believes

---

[12]Steven Goldberg, *The Inevitability of Patriarchy* (New York: William Morrow & Co., 1973/74). Dr. Goldberg's theory relating biology to the inevitability of patriarchy has been embraced by some Christians. However, it should raise several objections and questions for the Christian. Most importantly, the Christian has an alternate explanation that accounts for the universality of patriarchy and male dominance and that also explains why the real power (not authority) in dyadic and familial relationships often belongs to the woman (Goldberg, p. 67). The biblical explanation is that God has established the headship of the husband. This fact explains why both men and women recognize that the man (in marriage) has authority; God's law is written on their hearts (Rom. 2:15). The fall and the results of sin explain why the woman does not honor her husband's God-given authority and why she maneuvers to usurp control of the family. Goldberg's opinion of an explanation based on God's intentions should make the Christian cautious about accepting Goldberg's theory wholeheartedly: Goldberg thinks an explanation based on God's intent is "intellectually worse than worthless" (p. 77).

Whether or not God's law written on human hearts is written via hormones is debatable. In any case, Dr. Goldberg's biological evidence seems less convincing to the Christian. All experiments specifically relating testosterone to aggression were performed on rats, mice, and other nonhuman mammals. (The evidence of the human hermaphrodites does not prove that hormones cause aggressive behavior. The hermaphrodites were genetically male but lacked male genitalia. The male hormones in question were absent both fetally and in puberty. The hermaphrodites were successfully socialized as females. What these causes prove is that *male genes alone do not determine* "aggressive" or "masculine" behavior. It does not prove that male hormones produce aggressive behavior or that their absence produces less aggressive (female) behavior. The latter is not proven because no attempt was made to socialize the hermaphrodites as males.) For the scientist who believes in evolution and who would therefore expect to find continuity and correlations among the species and for the non-Christian who does not recognize the uniqueness of Man created in the image of God as distinct from the animals, the significance of such biological data is greater. The Christian, who believes that man was created separately from the dust and given life by the breath of God, does not view a necessary correlation between rat physiology and behavior and human physiology and behavior. There are other factors at work in Man's behavior: self-transcendence, rationality, and an ethical sense.

These elements unique to Man lead to another question concerning Dr. Goldberg's theory. Is "aggressive" behavior as he defines it acceptable to God? Certainly, "propensity for fighting, and willingness to fight" (as aggression is partially defined for rats, p. 87) is not. Although singlemindedness of purpose, endurance, and willingness to sacrifice pleasure and affection, when properly directed (i.e., for God's glory), could be acceptable and expected behavior for the Christian, male or female (cf. Matt. 10:21–22, 37). Some aspects of "aggression," as defined by Dr. Goldberg on pages 257–258, are sinful behavior, according to God's standards. For instance, the tendency to assert one's ego contradicts Matthew 16:24–25. Even the "tendency to dominate in relationships with the other sex" does not meet God's requirement that the husband *love* his wife or that the Christian count others better than himself. The man does not have the right to pursue suprafamilial goals "aggressively" to the neglect of his family; God commands that the man love his wife in a self-sacrificing way and that he teach and discipline his children.

that there are cognitive differences between men and women (men have an aptitude for dealing with logical abstractions necessary for achievement in mathematics, musical composition, philosophy, and theorizing), his central and best developed thesis is that patriarchy (men holding positions of status and authority in society) and male dominance (men possessing authority in dyadic and familial relationships) are inevitable. They are inevitable, he argues, because they are hormonally conditioned; that is:

> . . . the male hormonal system engenders a greater male "aggression"[13] that results in a male superiority at attaining roles and positions given high status (except when men are biologically incapable of playing a role) so that it is inevitable that positions and roles of leadership and status will be attained by men. . . .[14]

The universality and inevitability of patriarchy and male dominance, whatever the cause, are irrelevant to this chapter's argument, which concerns "personality" or psychological differences between men and women. In spite of his belief that "men and women are different from each other from the gene to the thought to the act . . . ,"[15] Goldberg himself notes that "all questions of gender identity are irrelevant to this theory,"[16] the inevitability of patriarchy. In addition, Goldberg admits that the evidence for cognitive differences between the sexes is less conclusive than for the inevitability of patriarchy because there is no extensive cross-cultural evidence or direct biological evidence.[17] Consequently, "scientific research"

---

[13]Dr. Goldberg defines "aggression" as: "1. a tendency to compete in any environmental situation that lends itself to competition; 2. a singlemindedness of purpose and an endurance that attaches itself to any (non-child-related) pursuit; 3. a willingness to sacrifice the pleasure and affection offered by many sources for the possibility of control and suprafamilial power in one area; 4. an unusually great tendency to ('need for') assertion of the ego; 5. a general tendency to impose will on environment (whether for the purpose of controlling individuals, attaining honors, or 'conquering mountains'); 6. a relatively great resistance to doing what one has been told (has been socialized) to do (which at its extreme results in behavior that society finds intolerable—i.e., crime); 7. a tendency to dominate in relationships with the other sex (though not necessarily to maintain a real power advantage . . .); 8. and all the tendencies, emotions, and actions that represent these factors" (pp. 257–258).

[14]Ibid., p. 92.

[15]Ibid., p. 228.

[16]Ibid., p. 80.

[17]Ibid., p. 188.

cannot be conclusively invoked to end all arguments concerning psychological differences between men and women.

With a question of metaphysics, the only appropriate place to find an answer is the Bible, which tells us who we are, why we exist, our relation to the universe, how we and the world came into existence and what our future is. The Bible does not tell us expressly who man is and who woman is, but we can consider what is said about them and to them. What sorts of distinctions does the Bible make between men and women?

As stated elsewhere, most of the major figures mentioned in biblical history are men. However, comparatively few commands are addressed specifically to men or women as groups. In the Old Testament, most of the commands distinguishing between men and women fall into two categories—they are either ceremonial or concerned with marriage. The ceremonial laws differentiating between men and women involved biological functions, such as menstruation and childbirth, which are obviously different for men and women. As suggested in chapter 3, the laws seeming to favor husbands, such as the law regulating women's vows, were probably intended to undergird and to concretize the husband's headship. In the New Testament, many of the commands directed to men or women as groups concern the headship of the husband. Another group of commands addressed to women are those regarding behavior in the ecclesia. Both groups of instructions are based on facts of creation and of the fall (the man was created first, the woman was created for and from the man, and the woman was deceived) and not on differences in being or character; and both sets of commands regulate functions or roles without mentioning personality differences. The man receives his place as head of his wife and the possibility of becoming an elder in the church by God's appointment or decision. God created the man first and intended the man to be the head of his wife and men to be rulers of the church; these two facts are coordinated. The distinctions between men and women made in the Bible have been summarized as an equality in being and a difference in function (economic subordination of the woman). The difference in function refers to the husband's role as

head and the wife's role as helper and to the exclusion of women
from the opportunity to become teachers or elders in the church.
(We maintain that this functional difference is the only distinction
Scripture makes between men and women.) What does equality in
being mean? Doesn't it suggest that men and women are basically
alike? Doesn't it suggest that personality traits are not sex
specific?

The first statement the Bible makes about men and women
indicates similarity.

> So God created Man in his own image, in the image of God he created
> him; male and female he created them (Gen. 1:27).

We have attempted to show that "male and female" does not define
the image of God in Man (chapter 3), but the phrase states the
extent of the image. In short, individuals are in God's image. Since
both men and women are in God's image, in that respect they are
alike. This likeness is expressed in Genesis 2:23. When he sees the
woman, Adam does not consider her "other"; his delighted response
to her recognizes their similarity, their unity. Man and woman are of
the same substance. God formed the man's body from the ground
and breathed life into him; God then took the man's rib and formed
it into woman. No separate infusion of the breath of life into the
woman is recorded. This fact suggests that man and woman are also
of the same spirit.

The Hebrew words for man and woman (איש and אשה) are said to
denote respectively "the strong one" and "the delicate one"; this
interpretation is congruous with the prevalent concept of woman
and implies a basic difference between man and woman. However,
the biblical narrative indicates a different etymology: Adam calls her
"woman" because she is taken from the man. They are alike.

The fact that the majority of the commands are addressed to both
men and women supports the contention that men and women are
basically alike. Those who would deny that men and women are
equal as sinners in need of God's grace in Christ or as recipients of
that grace are few, at least today. But are personality traits included
in that basic similarity between men and women? Does the Bible

have different character goals for men and women? Aren't Christian *women* to be characterized by submissiveness and meekness?

One way to answer these questions is to investigate what is commanded for men and women and for Christians in general. Here is a list of some of the characteristics Christian women are to have:

I Timothy 2:9–15

καταστολη κοσμιω	orderly or appropriate clothing. Elders are to be κοσμιον (I Tim. 3:2) or "orderly"; RSV translates it as "dignified."
αἰδους	reverence. Required of all Christians (Heb. 12:28).
σωφροσυνης	sensibility. Required of elders (I Tim. 3:2), older men (Titus 2:2), and young men (Titus 2:6).
ἐργων ἀγαθων	good works. Required of all Christians (Eph. 2:10; II Tim. 3:17).
πιστει	faith
ἀγαπη	love
ἀγιασμω	holiness/sanctification. Required of all Christians (Heb. 12:14).

I Timothy 3:11 (women deacons)

σεμνας	grave. Required of male deacons (I Tim. 3:8) and older men (Titus 2:2).
νηφαλιους	sober. Required of older men (Titus 2:2) and all Christians (I Pet. 5:8).
πιστας ἐν πασιν	faithful in all things.

Titus 2:3–5

καταστηματι ἱεροπρεπεις	reverent demeanor.
καλοδιδασκαλους	teachers of what is good
φιλανδρους	lovers of husbands
φιλοτεκνους	lovers of children.
σωφρονας	sensible, cf. I Tim. 2:9–15 above.
ἀγνας	pure. Required of all Christians (I John 3:3).
οἰκουργους	home workers.[18]

---

[18]There is one quality mentioned in Titus 2:5 that may cause some distress. It is often translated "domestic," a word that spells confinement to the home or the cultivation of joy in cooking, sewing, and cleaning. Perhaps the word, which occurs only here in the New

ἀγαθας	good.
ὑποτασσομενας τοις ἰδιοις ἀνδρασιν	submissive to own husband.

I Peter 3:1–6

ὑποτασσομεναι τοις ἰδιοις ἀνδρασιν	submitting yourselves to own husband.
ἀγνην ἀναστροφην	pure conduct, cf. Titus 2:5 above.
πραεος και ἡσυχιου πνευματοις	meek and quiet spirit. Meekness is a fruit of the Spirit (Gal. 5:23), and quietness is the way Christians are to work (II Thess. 3:12).
ἀγαθοποιουσαι	doing good.
μη φοβουμενοι μηδεμιαν πτοησιν	not fearing any terror. Required of all Christians (Heb. 13:6).

The qualities that characterize Christian women, for the most part, are not confined to women alone. All Christians are shown to be characterized as the following:

Ephesians 4:31–32	kind
	tenderhearted
	forgiving
Ephesians 5:21	submitting to one another
Colossians 3:12	compassion
	kindness
	humility
	meekness
	longsuffering
I Peter 3:8	sympathetic
	loving to the brethren
	compassionate
	humble-minded
Galatians 5:22–23	love
	joy
	peace
	longsuffering
	kindness
	goodness
	faithfulness
	meekness
	self-control

Testament, should be translated home-workers. It is a combination of οἰκος (household) and ἐργον (work). Rather than implying keepers *at* home, it implies keepers *of* the home. For an illustration of what the word means, we have only to turn to Proverbs 31:10ff.

A comparison of the list of general Christian virtues and the personality traits of a healthy adult male or female according to psychological studies reveals little similarity. One difference is that qualities desired in Christians are clearly virtues; the traits describing healthy adults are not clearly virtues. A distinction should be made between what traits are virtues, which are commanded of every Christian, and personality differences. God does not order that all Christians should have the same personality; where conduct and characteristics are not regulated in Scripture, there is room for diversity among Christian people as individuals. There are no biblical indications that personality should be or is sex-related.

The most significant difference for our study between the psychologists' list of healthy adult traits and the Bible's commands to Christians is that the Bible does not define Christian men and Christian women but Christian persons. The goal for Christians, men and women, is conformity to the image of Christ (Eph. 4:13), which is not sex-specific; and both men and women can be equally conformed to Christ's image.

After attempting to find support for masculine and feminine traits in each person of the Godhead, Mollenkott tries to explain what bisexuality means for psychology. She maintains:

> Damage is done to the human spirit when these characteristics are assigned to only one sex exclusively—that is, when men are taught to be exclusively and stereotypically "masculine," and women are taught to be exclusively and stereotypically "feminine."[19]

Mollenkott advocates that each person become "a unique and unstereotyped harmony of male and female components."[20] Though Mollenkott may be conceding to the cultural understanding of human nature in her designation, "male and female components" (for Mollenkott, are there such ontological realities as "male and female components"?), it would be more accurate, if we believe that men and women are basically persons, to cease thinking of certain traits

---

[19]Mollenkott, "Challenge," p. 23.
[20]Ibid., p. 24.

as being masculine or feminine and to advocate that each person develop into a *godly* individual.

In addition, an argument that seeks to prove that the members of the Godhead have both masculine and feminine traits by demonstrating that each member has what our culture has defined as masculine and feminine traits proves nothing. Who is to say that what our culture defines as masculine or feminine is ultimately or metaphysically masculine or feminine? Perhaps it only proves that our culture's (or any culture's) conception of what is masculine and what is feminine is provincial.

We cannot prove conclusively that all psychological (personality) differences between men and women are either physiological or culturally conditioned. However, the Bible does not even hint at any mysterious, metaphysical differences between men and women; God's word is mainly concerned with persons.

Several important conclusions can be drawn from the biblical emphasis on personhood.

(1) The myth of the feminine mystique, of woman as "the other" is a *myth*. One of the functions of this myth is to separate men and women, to put up a barrier between them. Even wise Christians, such as Elisabeth Elliot, have accepted this myth. She writes to her daughter:

> He's a man. You're a woman. There are some areas in which ne'er the twain shall meet and we should be glad of that.[21]

> It is probably not only a safer course but much wiser not to tell a man everything that is on your mind, not to press him with hard questions. Leave room for mystery.[22]

In short, she accepts and promotes the idea that men and women cannot understand one another. She suggests that open communication is not the best way to have a good marriage. Undoubtedly, there are certain thoughts any individual should not share with spouse or

---

[21]Elliot, *Let Me Be,* p. 84.
[22]Ibid., p. 86.

with friend or with anyone. However, the biblical rules for communication, which are not restricted to any one relationship, are to speak the truth in love (Eph. 4:15) and "let no evil talk come out of your mouth, but only such as is good for edifying, as fits the occasion, that it may impart grace to those who hear" (Eph. 4:29).

To realize that men and women are basically persons opens the lines of communication. The difficulties in communication are those between persons and can be worked out because there are no mysterious or metaphysical differences between masculine and feminine natures to block it.

The myth of the feminine mystique is a result of sin, one weapon in the battle of the sexes begun at the fall.

(2) To understand men and women as persons removes the need to try to find so-called feminine attributes or aspects in the Godhead, and it even removes (or should remove) any slight or offense women might feel because of God's Fatherhood or Christ's incarnation as a man. Since men and women are fundamentally persons and, as Christian feminists have pointed out, the main thrust of Christ's incarnation is that he became Man (a person), women are unquestionably in the image of God just as men are and, if believers, will be fully conformed to Christ's image just as Christian men will be.

This emphasis on the similarity between men and women and on personhood does not contradict or lessen the one distinction the Bible does make between men and women: in terms of function in marriage and in the church. Biblical feminists carry the idea of personhood beyond God's word when they eliminate distinctions in marriage and in the church. The other extreme is the idea that if there is a functional difference, God must have made women different from men, God must have given woman a subservient mentality and/or not given her any talents for ruling or teaching. Neither is correct. The Bible maintains this functional difference between men and women (there is no chance for unisex). Certain socialization or "Christianization" for these different roles is desirable as in Titus 2:3–5. But the Bible allows freedom for personality development within the framework of a Christian character (which is neither male nor female), without stifling sexual stereotyping. In the distribution of spiritual gifts, including ruling and teaching, the Bible makes no distinctions (I Cor. 12:11). The woman may be given gifts for ruling or teaching, but she may not use them as an elder in the church.

One more question must be answered or at least asked: what is the purpose of sexual duality if men and women are basically persons, if there are no metaphysical differences, if they are truly equal in being? The difficulty in answering such a question is that we must go into an area of speculation, we must try to guess the motivations of our creator. And as he said, "Where were you when I laid the foundation of the earth?" (Job 38:4). Our question cannot be definitively answered, but certain hints and guesses can be made.

One answer is to regard sex as merely a means of reproduction, which humanity has in common with the animals. But this view does not account for the "sacredness" of sex in the marriage relationship, with all of the regulations to maintain it; nor does it account for the indissolubility of the one-flesh relationship resulting from sexual intercourse, nor for the beauty and delight depicted in the Song of Solomon.

Hints as to the significance of sexual duality can be found in these objections to a purely reproductive biological explanation and in the only distinction the Bible makes between men and women—the functional (head/helper). This functional distinction is most obvious in marriage. God created the two sexes for marriage, to give it a physical basis for union in sexual intercourse and to give enjoyment (Prov. 5:18–19).

The next question is: why did God create the marriage relationship? The clearest clue we have is Ephesians 5:25–27, 32, in which Paul compares marriage to the relationship between Christ and the church. Perhaps God established marriage as a union (one-flesh) with the husband as head and the wife to submit herself in order to show what the relationship God has with his people is like. This metaphor occurs in the Old Testament prophets, especially Hosea, and in Revelation. The church is to submit itself to its head, but also the church is the object of the constant, self-sacrificing love of its head, Jesus Christ, and the two are one. After Christ came and expressed this love absolutely, the analogy is reversed, because of the clarity of Christ's example. Christ's love for the church teaches husbands how to love their wives. Possibly God created the roles of husband and wife to illustrate, to help us understand, how he relates to us and we to him. The analogy is not perfect because husband and wife are both creatures, whereas God is our creator, perfect and holy in all respects. But both relationships are covenants, both require faithfulness, love and union; and there is an authority structure in both.

Another purpose of sexuality is that it teaches mutual dependence (I Cor. 11:11–12), which points to dependence on God.

God could have created man and woman simultaneously or he could have created Man in one sex with some other means of reproduction, but God chose to create the man first to establish his headship and then create his wife. He created the woman from the man and designed them so that the one-flesh relationship between them (in marriage) would have a basis in creation and would continually be acted out through sexual intercourse.

The New Heavens and the New Earth

A consideration of the metaphysics of human sexuality raises the question of sexuality's ultimate meaning. Will we retain our sexuality in the new heavens and the new earth? Will we exist as men and women?

The biblical feminists differ on this question. Scanzoni and Hardesty write, "we seek a city in which we have been told that sexual polarities will be irrelevant."[23] Jewett, as stated earlier, thinks sexual distinctions will exist in eternity; to be theologically consistent, he must maintain the continuance of sexuality because of his

---

[23]Scanzoni and Hardesty, p. 85.

understanding of the image of God: in order to be in the image of God, Man would have to continue as male and female, because the image of God in Man and Man's existence in two sexes are so closely related. Jewett also considers the man/woman (rather than husband/wife) relationship to be the most basic form of human fellowship.[24] This opinion contributes to his belief in the eternal existence of Man as male and female. If the husband/wife relationship is considered most fundamental, there is no reason to maintain that the sexes are eternal: Mark 12:25 states that there will be no marriage after the resurrection of the dead.

What conclusions can be drawn from Mark 12:25? The only certainty is that there will be no marriage in the new heavens and new earth. The resurrected believers are like the angels *in this respect,* not necessarily in other respects. Most probably Mark 12:25 means that earthly marriages do not continue. The end of marriages means the end of the woman's subordination to her husband. And without marriage, there can be no sexual intercourse. The purposes of marriage and sexual intercourse will have ceased. There is no need for reproduction (eternal life), and the believers' relationship with the Lord God will supercede all others. The fulfillment and union once experienced in marriage is replaced by what it pointed to, what it was a shadow of, what it was intended to teach about—its eternal counterpart—the believer's relationship with God. In the new earth, the church is "married" to her God (Rev. 21:2).

Because of the end of marriage and sexual function, many students of the Bible have concluded that sexual differences also end, that believers will not be raised as men and women. (What they mean, says Jewett, is that all believers will be raised as men.[25]) This

---

[24]Jewett, pp. 34, 36. This view leads to the conclusion that all women are to be submissive to all men (pp. 71, 131), an unscriptural idea. Jewett rightly rejects this conclusion, but he also rejects all passages teaching the woman's subordination to her husband and in the church, because he sees these particular instances of subordination as based on the fundamental form of human fellowship, between men and women. The basic relationship is between men and women, Jewett postulates. Then if it is a hierarchy, all women are subordinated to all men. That is not scriptural. If it is an equal partnership, all male-female relationships derived from it (marriage, etc.) should reflect that partnership.

[25]Ibid., p. 40.

conclusion is not inevitable. It is possible that resurrected believers will be identifiable as men and women. This possibility is suggested by the continuity between the mortal body and the immortal body (cf. I Cor. 15:36–37). We bear the image of the man of dust as men and women; it is possible that we shall bear the image of the man of heaven as men and women. We keep our identity (we are recognizable) in the resurrection; such a notion also indicates the retention of our sex.

Galatians 3:28 is irrelevant to the question of the eternity of the sexes. Galatians 3:28 deals with present reality, with the consequences of being clothed with Christ. All who have faith in Christ *are* one in him. They share the same benefits of salvation. Nonetheless, this oneness and this sharing do not obliterate all distinctions in the body of believers. The union of believers will be perfect in the new earth, but perfect union does not necessarily imply the removal of all differences.

The scriptural teaching is not clear on the sexuality or asexuality of the resurrected body, and the question may be delving into areas not open to mortals. The Corinthians evidently asked a similar question. "How are the dead raised? With what kind of body do they come?" (I Cor. 15:35). Paul answered that the resurrected body is imperishable, immortal, spiritual, in the image of Christ, not flesh and blood. John writes, "We are God's children now; it does not yet appear what we shall be, but we know that when he appears we shall be like him, for we shall see him as he is" (I John 3:2). That is all believers need to know. We are God's children *now,* and we shall be completely conformed to Christ's image, including the glorification of our bodies, when Christ comes again. Whether or not we exist as men and women in the new earth, we know that all sin and sorrow will be destroyed and that we shall see our Lord as he truly is, face to face.

SEVEN

MARRIAGE: SUBMISSION AND LOVE

IN the beginning marriage was perfect.

But ever since the fall, theories of the perfect marriage have abounded; and recently, hosts of marriage manuals, how-to books, and how-to-solve-your-problems or how-to-save-your-marriage books have been written. This chapter purports to be none of the above. In chapters 3 and 4, we have established three biblical principles: the equality in being between man and woman; a difference in function in marriage and the church; and the oneness of husband and wife. In this chapter we will consider in greater detail how these principles apply to marriage.

Christianity is a religion of balance; it contains antinomies, ideas that are in tension with one another (for example, Christ is God and Christ is man). If the balance is tipped one way or the other, serious errors in doctrine and life will result. The biblical idea of marriage contains this tension and needs this balance: wives are told to submit themselves to their husbands, and husbands are told to love their wives. These are not the two commands a human would issue. To remove the tension, to make things more logical and orderly, a human would say either wives, submit yourselves to your husbands and husbands, rule your wives; or, wives and husbands, love each other. Too often we are forced to choose between these two humanized versions of marriage, between dictatorship and democracy. This is the choice presented to the Christian by the biblical feminists. Listen to Scanzoni and Hardesty:

> "But why is it so wrong for persons to stand on equal footing in a relationship of love?" some are wondering. "Why must there be a hierarchy of superior inferior, a dictatorship instead of a democracy, an insistence that one person must lead in all practical and spiritual matters—regardless of abilities—simply because of having been born a member of a certain sex?" The answer they usually hear is that God has simply designed things that way, that woman was created to meet man's needs, and that to complain that it's an unfair setup is to rebel against God himself.
>
> A traditional view of marriage stressed such matters as respect, duty, authority, obedience, and role differentiation. Today another ideology emphasizes the importance of companionship, affection, self-actualization, growth and equalitarianism.[1]

Each alternative has some biblical elements, but neither expresses the biblical ideal, which has room for both respect, duty, authority and obedience and companionship, affection, self-actualization (if that means development and use of God-given gifts and talents) and growth. Marriage, according to the Bible, has an irreversible authority structure, which requires different duties or different modes of acting from the husband and the wife but yet creates no dictatorship. It is Christian love, a love that is founded on God's love for us and produced by the Holy Spirit, that makes this relationship possible. The oneness in marriage, founded in creation and enacted by sexual intercourse, provides the basis for love in Christian marriage.

What Submission Is Not

In the past, the imbalance has been weighed on the side of the wife's submission; the wife's submission and the corresponding headship of the husband have been emphasized at the expense of understanding what the command to the husband to love his wife means. This

---

[1]Scanzoni and Hardesty, pp. 88–89.

myopic concentration on the wife's submission has produced a misunderstanding of what that submission means. Some Christian women have been told they should obey their husbands even if that means to sin. (Some add that God will not put you in a situation in which you will have to choose obedience to God or obedience to husband—a hope that is not supported by the facts, even in Christian marriages.) A favorite example is: if your husband does not want you to go to church, you should not go. Some Christian women are told that they should not criticize their husbands under any circumstances; they should make no demands (such as to take out the trash or to wipe mud off their feet before coming in the house). Some Christian women are told to knock themselves out looking for ways to show their submission to their husbands. Wives exist solely for the pleasure and service of their husbands. And some Christian men are taught to expect, if not demand, this unthinking, unquestioning obedience and service from their wives.

This concept of submission misses the biblical mark. The analogy of faith helps us understand submission. The principle that we owe obedience to God first and foremost applies to Christian wives, too. Though Christians are to submit themselves to the governing authorities (Rom. 13:1; I Pet. 2:13), if there must be a choice between obedience to God and obedience to men in authority, God is to be obeyed (Acts 5:29). Likewise, wives should obey God, for instance, by attending worship services regularly (Heb. 10:24–25), even if their husbands disapprove. Primary obedience to God is implied in I Peter 3:2 when Peter says that the unbelieving husband may be won to Christ by the pure and reverent behavior of his wife. God's word is the only standard of pure conduct, so the wife's behavior should conform to God's commands, even if it means disobedience to her husband. I Peter 3:6 supports this idea: "And you are now her children if you *do right* and let nothing terrify you." This qualification of the "traditional" concept of wifely submission does not mean that the wife has an excuse to follow her "better judgment" when she disagrees with her husband. The wife's submission to her husband is qualified by God's commands, not her own preferences, opinions, or even expertise.

For the Christian wife, "doing right" does involve submission to her husband. How do disobedience for Christ's sake and submission for Christ's sake square with one another? Perhaps submission and obedience are not completely synonymous. It would be possible for the Christian wife to disobey with submission. Submission in I Peter 3:3–4 is an attitude, a quiet and gentle spirit; and it is one that calls her husband lord, one that regards him with a godly fear as a divinely appointed authority. If a wife must disobey her husband for Christ's sake, she can do it with submission.

The concept of submission as an attitude frees wives from a constant drive to find active, concrete ways to show their husbands submission. It enables the Christian wife to keep her own personality and to be able to say what she thinks. It also enables married couples to work out their own patterns of submission. Submission no longer is defined as a prescribed set of actions, such as a wife is not submissive unless she never asks her husband to help with housework or unless she always has dinner on the table when he gets home from work. The Bible does not give a detailed, play-by-play description of what should go on in a marriage; it does not say who should change the diapers or make the bed. By omitting the details, God recognizes and allows individuality (and cultural changes). Each marriage is different, and the wife's submission (and the husband's love) expresses itself in different actions. In such a light, the example of Sarah as the biblical model for wives makes more sense. Christian wives are to emulate Sarah's attitude toward Abraham, rather than her specific actions, as we read about them in Genesis 12:10–20; 20:1–18. It is her submissive attitude that causes her to call her husband "lord."

All of the commands to Christians in general apply to the Christian wife. Keeping this in mind protects us from many misunderstandings of the Christian wife's role. Every Christian is told what his or her goal is:

> And his gifts were that some should be apostles, some prophets, some evangelists, some pastors and teachers, for the equipment of the saints, for the work of ministry, for building up the body of Christ, until we all attain to the unity of the faith and of the

knowledge of the Son of God, to mature manhood, to the measure of the stature of the fulness of Christ; so that we may no longer be children tossed to and fro and carried about with every wind of doctrine, by the cunning of men, by their craftiness in deceitful wiles. Rather, speaking the truth in love, we are to grow up in every way into him who is the head, into Christ, from whom the whole body, joined and knit together by every joint with which it is supplied, when each part is working properly, makes bodily growth and upbuilds itself in love (Eph. 4:11–16).

The Christian wife has the responsibility to grow in Christ, to know doctrine, to be able to speak the truth in love. That is, she is not to be ignorant, nor to rely on her husband's knowledge and/or participation as a substitute for her own. In addition, she is not to be silent when her husband sins (Matt. 18:15), but she is to teach and admonish him (Col.3:16). However, she is to do all these things with a submissive heart. Her submission manifests itself in lowliness, meekness, patience, forbearance in love, and eagerness to maintain the unity of the Spirit in the bond of peace (Eph. 4:2–3) but also in reverence for her husband as her head. The Christian wife is neither passive nor mindless. She does not have to pretend her husband is always right or hide her own talents of intelligence. She is to use her gifts for the upbuilding of the body of Christ, which includes her husband.

The submission of the wife to her husband is not that of an inferior to a superior. The woman is joint heir (with the man) of God's promises; she, like the man, bears the image of God and as a Christian will be conformed to Christ's image. The different roles husband and wife have are by God's appointment and design. That the woman and man are equal in being is reenforced by the command to wives. Wives are to *submit themselves* (reflexive); their submission is voluntary, self-imposed. It is part of their obedience to the Lord; the Lord is the one who commands it, not the husband.

Another misconception of submission involves confining the wife the home and to children. C. Harinck writes:

> The first field in which a woman is allowed to speak about God and His deeds is in her family. . . . According to these verses [I Tim.

2:15; 5:10] and many others, children are to be the special domain of women; they are to be their special concern. Of course, the fathers are also involved in the bringing up of their children, but the Bible shows us that here the women have a special place above the men.

. . . When the Lord appeared to Abraham at Mamre and asked where Sarah was, he replied, "She is in the tent." That is the special domain of women. Therefore, mothers, I beseech you, do not neglect your special domain. Your place is in the family and the children are your preeminent task.[2]

Scanzoni and Hardesty object to this sort of identification of the submissive wife and the homemaker. They refer to it as role differentiation, role stereotyping and "a functional arrangement with rigid roles and fixed duties assigned on the basis of sex."[3] They object to the mind-set that says women cannot repair cars or build furniture and men cannot sew, needlepoint, or cook (at home), that says the woman's place is in the home and the man must be the breadwinner.

Is this role differentiation (woman = homemaker and man = breadwinner) really the biblical teaching, as so many Christians assume? First of all, the wife's submission and the husband's headship are not intertwined with their stereotyped roles as homemaker and breadwinner. The headship of the husband exists no matter what his occupation is, because God has established it. The wife's attitude may be submissive no matter what her occupation is. She may be a submissive wife as a doctor whose salary pays the bills, while her husband, whose talent is writing, works at home and earns little if any money for his articles and books.

There are two commands addressed to both man and woman (husband and wife) at creation; both commands involve both people. They are to be fruitful and multiply and to subdue the earth. However, these are the two areas usually divided between women

---

[2]C. Harinck, "The Biblical View of Women in the Church," *The Banner of Truth*, 39:5 (May, 1973), 16.

[3]Scanzoni and Hardesty, p. 106.

(multiplying or child-raising, at home) and men (subduing or labor). Why?

In Genesis 3, the woman is punished in terms of child-bearing and the man in terms of labor. Genesis 3 is judgment and does not state what should be; it cannot be considered justification for division of labor on the basis of sex. We can wonder why God divides the punishments, the results of sin, as he does; but an answer is not forthcoming. Possibly, the present state of affairs, the division of labor on the basis of sex, stems from the judgments; that is, perhaps because the woman suffers in the area of child-bearing, that area has become her main identity; and because the man suffers particularly in labor, that area has become his chief identity. The consequences of sin (Gen. 3:15–19) may produce and contribute to these stereotypical roles of men and women.

In the New Testament, there is no evidence for a sex-based division of labor. Commands concerning child-rearing and work are still addressed to both men and women. "If any one will not work, let him not eat" (II Thess. 3:10, cf. 11–12). All Christians are expected to work, and there are examples of women with "careers," such as Priscilla, a tent-maker, and Lydia, a seller of dyes. Fathers are told, "do not provoke your children to anger, but bring them up in the discipline and instruction of the Lord" (Eph. 6:4). In Scripture, both fathers and mothers have the responsibility to raise their children.

Many evangelical Christians assume that all women are better with children, that children are the woman's or mother's special domain. One such author, Wayne Mack, bases the idea that children are the woman's special domain on I Timothy 2:15; 5:10 and 5:14. The latter two verses deal with widows. I Timothy 5:10 gives requirements for enrolling widows; bringing up children is listed as one of their good deeds. In I Timothy 5:14, Paul says that he would rather young widows remarry, bear children, rule their households, and live model lives. Undoubtedly, raising children is a praiseworthy occupation for women. But it is not women's special province. Mack belies his own idea when he explains what "bringing up" children involves. He quotes a verse addressed to *fathers,* Ephesians 6:4.[4] Unlike I Timothy 5:10, 14, which are concerned with a special case (widows), Ephesians 6:4 directly addresses fathers and is explicit as to the father's involvement with his children. According to the Scriptures, both parents are to bring up their children (Prov. 1:8; 6:20; 10:1; 15:20; 17:25; 23:22). The Bible emphasizes the father's involvement with his child in discipline and instruction (Prov. 3:12; 15:5; Eph. 6:4; Col. 3:21; I Tim. 3:4, 12; Heb. 12:9).

Our culture works against these scriptural injunctions, because the father is often absent from the home: he may leave early and come home late on commuter trains or hold down two jobs to make ends meet. He may wish to could spend more time with his children; but because of economic pressures and the structure of modern society, he cannot. In ages past, before the day of factories and mass production, most businesses were run from or near the home, and so the father was not separated from his children. In fact, the father included the children in his work so that they might learn a trade. In our society it is too easy for the father never to know his children. As President Carter admonished his staff: Those of you who don't know your children's names, get reaquainted. When the biblical commands are ignored, when child care falls solely on the mother's shoulders, all suffer—fathers, mothers, children. What is the answer? We cannot return to a pre-manufacturing, pre-technological society in which all business is done from the home—though that may be the answer for some families who move from the cities to the country. Setting priorities can help to solve the problem. What do you value more—$30,000 a year, two cars and three TVs and a home in the suburbs, or God's word and your responsibilities to your children and wife? Perhaps giving up overtime or the moonlighting, or even getting a new job or moving closer to work can be a step toward a solution. You may be able to involve your children in your work through part-time or

---

[4]Wayne Mack, *The Role of Women in the Church* (Cherry Hill, N.J.: Mack Publishing Co., c1972), p. 66.

summer jobs. But it is most important that the father acknowledge and accept his part in the rearing of his children with love.

The father has the responsibility to instruct and discipline his children. But does the mother or wife have the option to work outside the home? There are two verses that have bearing on this question: I Timothy 2:15 and Titus 2:4–5. I Timothy 2:15 has been quoted to support the idea that the woman's job is child-bearing; her primary purpose is to bear and raise children. I Timothy 2:15 is difficult to interpret (p. 128) so that it is impossible to draw dogmatic conclusions from it. This verse relates to the curse in Genesis 3:16 and presents child-bearing as a necessary and worthwhile function; however, it does not define women purely in terms of motherhood, nor does it indicate that the woman's place is in the home. Faith, love, and holiness with sound judgment are the crucial factors.

Titus 2:4–5 lists some requirements for wives. Among them is οἰκουργούς or literally home-workers. By some this word is taken to be confirmation that the woman's work should be confined to the home. It is sometimes translated "domestic," a word that conjures up a woman whose delight is baking homemade bread, sewing all her family's clothes and making her pots and pans shine and whose dress is incomplete without an apron. Because of these connotations, "domestic" is a misleading translation. The verb form of οἰκουργούς is translated by Arndt and Gingrich as "to fulfill one's household duties." The Christian wife should fulfill her household duties; she should not avoid working at home. This understanding of the word is helpful in that it does not limit the woman to working only at home. The virtuous wife of Proverbs 31 illustrates the meaning of "home-worker." Her activities include travel, commerce, agriculture and charity, but she does not neglect her household. She sees that the needs of her husband and children are met. A test for whether or not a wife and mother should take a job is whether it helps or hinders the family.

The exclusion of women from the labor force and the housewife syndrome of *The Feminine Mystique* are recent developments. Sociologist Alice S. Rossi writes:

... For the first time in the history of any known society, motherhood has become a full-time occupation for adult women. In the past, whether a woman lived on a farm, a Dutch city in the seventeenth century, or a colonial town in the eighteenth century, women in all strata of society except the very top were never able to be full-time mothers as the twentieth century middle class American woman has become. These women were productive members of farm and craft teams. . . .[5]

On the other hand, οἰκουργούς implies that women *do* have duties in the home. These duties may not demand full-time attention, but they are not to be neglected. What these duties are and how they are to be executed are not spelled out. If your husband enjoys cooking, there is no reason for you to insist that you be the sole cook because that is one of your God-ordained tasks. Being a "home-worker" does not mean that the wife must personally perform every job in the home. Fulfilling her household duties could mean having a maid come in once a week (the woman of Prov. 31 had servants).

I Timothy 5:14 supports the woman's responsibility for home *management* when Paul says he would have younger widows marry, bear children and *rule their households* (οἰκοδεσποτειν). Christ refers to himself with this word (Matt. 10:25) along with teacher and master. It does not suggest a menial job. Women are to manage or rule their homes. Though women are not confined to the house, the New Testament does (as well as the example of Prov. 31) give the wife responsibility for running the household.

What then is the husband's relationship to the home? Is he relieved of all responsibility for home maintenance? One of the requirements for elders and deacons is that they rule or manage their households well (τον ἰδιου οἰκου καλως προιστᾰμενον, in I Tim. 3:4–5, 12). Consequently, it is not to be supposed that either the wife has absolute dominion in household affairs (she is to submit herself to her husband in this area also) or the husband can

---

[5]Alice S. Rossi quoted by A. Swidler, p. 92; cf. Scanzoni and Hardesty, p. 184.

be aloof from household responsibilities. It seems that both husband and wife are responsible for the management of their home.

In Titus 2:3–5 and I Timothy 5:14, women are instructed to be home-workers and rule their households so that the word of God would not be discredited. The word of God and the reputation of Christ are at stake. Scanzoni and Hardesty want to place these verses "in context."

> Women in the situations described, lacking in educational opportunities and often emerging from paganism, needed to be taught what it meant to be Christian wives and mothers. They were told to center their interests in building Christian homes so that criticism by enemies of the faith could be avoided and "the word of God may not be discredited" (Titus 2:5). In other words, the sanctity of marriage must be upheld in the midst of charges that Christianity was a sect that would undermine the home.[6]

Their point is that women are not to be confined to the home or to center their interests on the home *for all time,* and they suggest that our different cultural situation makes these instructions less applicable to us. (Scanzoni and Hardesty would surely say that Christian women no longer need to be taught to be submissive to their husbands.) However, the need to be taught what it means to be Christian wives and mothers still exists and will continue to exist. In writing to Titus, Paul gives varying instructions for older men, older women, younger women, and younger men; Paul writes to correct actual sinful behavior of these various groups (Titus 2:2–6). His main concern here is not the Christian family; it is all wrong action that would discredit Christianity. He addresses sins characteristic of the various groups. Paul is not telling young Christian women to focus their interests on the home; he is telling them to do what is right according to God's requirements for young Christian women. As married women, they are to love their husbands and children and submit themselves to their husbands; they are also to be sensible, chaste, home-workers, and kind.

---

[6]Scanzoni and Hardesty, pp. 109–110.

Today's Christian women may not lack educational opportunities, but it is difficult to obtain instruction based on sound biblical principles. We may not be emerging from paganism, but most of us have emerged from secularism and all of us are bombarded with secular values through the mass media. Even if the world can no longer charge Christianity with undermining the family (possibly because our culture no longer values the family), the value of the family has not ceased to be an important teaching in Christianity. The sanctity of marriage needs to be proclaimed in a world that says marriage is outdated. The maintenance of the family structured by biblical principles continues to be a powerful and needed witness to the world. The Christian family is a demonstration of Christian love, and Christian marriage is a picture of Christ and the church. Christian wives still need to be taught to love their husbands and children and to be sensible, chaste, home-workers, kind and submissive to their husbands.

The Total Woman Way

In reaction to the feminist movement, many women have headed in the opposite direction, toward greater femininity. Marabel Morgan's *The Total Woman* exemplifies this trend. This book has produced staunch disciples (because "it works") and out-spoken, offended critics. Much of the criticism has been based on a misrepresentation of the book. People who have not even read it ridicule it because of the costumes Mrs. Morgan suggests. Everyone knows about the pink baby doll pajamas and white boots and wonders where one puts her children if she wants to meet her husband at the door in the nude. However, too much attention has been given to such details; they are not the message of the book. One can become a Total Woman without ever wearing a costume to the front door.

Should the Christian woman want to become a Total Woman? The Total Woman comes across as being a "yes woman," a doormat, one who is always giving in, subservient, mindless, self-less—all undesirable qualities in a person of worth. Mrs. Morgan writes:

> It is only when a woman surrenders her life to her husband, reveres
> and worships him, and is willing to serve him, that she becomes
> really beautiful to him.[7]

She also appears to be manipulative. She *acts* in the prescribed way
to get her husband to adore her; she *acts* in a submissive manner to
get what she wants.

> I do believe it is possible, however, for almost any wife to have her
> husband absolutely adore her in just a few weeks' time. She can
> revive romance, reestablish communication, break down barriers,
> and put sizzle back into her marriage. It is really up to her. She has
> the power.[8]

Women inclined towards feminist persuasions react on two
accounts. It is demeaning to play up to your husband, to do
everything his way. It amounts to man-worship, which is idolatrous;
it is bad for him (inflates his ego) and for the woman (destroys her
self). It is also deceptive and manipulative. It is pretending to be
selfless to get your own way.

The latter criticism (manipulation) is one Mrs. Morgan
recognizes as an abuse, a misuse of her philosophy. She responds:

> Some people have thought of Total Woman as just a manipulative
> tool. It depends upon your motive. Two women can do the same
> thing, like making lovely meals for their husbands, for vastly
> different reasons. One woman is thinking, I'll make him a nice
> fried-chicken dinner because I'm going to ask him for fifty dollars
> tonight. It's all wrong, and chances are he will see that as soon as she
> asks him. If you've giving to get, that's manipulation, and it won't
> work. But in Total Woman, I point out that you must give with no
> thought that you're going to get in return. It just means giving
> because you love the guy.[9]

The real goals of Total Woman are to save marriages and to make
marriage pleasant and full of love, not to get presents, etc. These

---

[7]Marabel Morgan, *The Total Woman* (Old Tappan, N.J.: Fleming H. Revell, 1973), p. 71.
[8]Ibid., p. 27.
[9]"Marabel Morgan: 'Preferring One Another'; an Interview," *Christianity Today*, 20:24
(September 10, 1976), 15.

goals may be selfish in the sense that they benefit the woman, but they also benefit the husband (he responds in love to his wife's loving him and that is why the Total Woman gets so many presents, etc.). The goals, including the wife's receiving her husband's love, and the basic premise, that the husband is the head of his wife and she is to submit herself to him, of Total Woman are also God's will. That is why Mrs. Morgan's plan works in so many marriages. If we look beyond the specific applications and suggestions that may seem silly, superfluous, and just not our style, if we look behind the hyperbolic language and overstatements ("worship" your husband), there are biblical principles in *The Total Woman*. As we have said before, the Bible does not fill in details for us (Mrs. Morgan has filled in one set of details). We must obey the biblical principles, and details may vary.

If Mrs. Morgan had been addressing only a Christian audience, perhaps she could have begun with the idea of obedience to God as the incentive or primary aim. Since she is addressing non-Christians, she begins with the aim of making one's marriage work.

The four A's (accept your husband, admire him, adapt to him, and appreciate him) and the corresponding self-lessness demanded of the Total Woman offend many women. "But why shouldn't husbands do some of the adjusting?"[10] ask Scanzoni and Hardesty. Why should the woman subordinate her interests and needs to her husband's?

Why do we react negatively to Mrs. Morgan's four A's? Why do we want the right to have our way some of the time, to have others, especially our husbands, adjust to us? Isn't it only fair and just? The answer is quite simple—it is ego or pride, putting oneself first, before others and before God, that makes us react to the four A's. The requirements Mrs. Morgan makes for wives are really no different from those required for all Christians. But sometimes it is easier to practice outdoing one another in showing honor (Rom.

---

[10]Scanzoni and Hardesty, p. 103.

12:10) or in humility counting others better than yourself (Phil. 2:3) with reference to anyone other than your own spouse. The submission required of all Christians is required particularly of the wife to her husband. It is true that in a marriage where both husband and wife are seeking to obey the Lord, both will adjust to the other; both will try to help and please the other. It is when disagreements occur that the husband's headship comes to the fore.

When reminded that Paul's instructions to wives in Ephesians 5:22 are prefaced by "Be subject to one another in the Lord," Mrs. Morgan replies:

> You're right. But I know how a woman reacts. If I had said, "Be subject one to another," she would have said, "Got that, Harry?" It wouldn't have worked. She would have missed it, and she would have put it right back on his back.[11]

It is our natural (sinful) tendency to demand our own rights, to apply biblical principles to anyone but ourselves. Because of God's judgment in Genesis 3:16, the woman is particularly susceptible to sin against her husband in this way; because of sin, she rebels against her husband's headship. "Why shouldn't my husband have to give in to me sometimes?" The Christian who loves does not demand his or her own way. Look at I Corinthians 13 again. It is most frequently read at weddings, even though the context concerns the relationship of the believer to the body of Christ and the love among Christian brothers and sisters. Unfortunately, its appropriateness for marriage does not last any longer than the honeymoon, unless it applies to one's spouse. It is lost in the shuffle for *my* rights, for justice for *me*. Or maybe it suffers from the trailing "but's"; "love does not insist on its own way," but my husband never takes me out to dinner. . . . God's rules for marriage do not include rights, only duties. And the fulfillment of the wife's duty to submit herself to her husband does not depend on his fulfillment of his duty.

---

[11]"Marabel Morgan . . . ," p. 14.

The Total Woman way is not *the* answer for Christian women. But it does contain, along with Mrs. Morgan's personal embellishments, the formula for a successful marriage, God's formula, which is: the husband is the head of his wife, and she must submit herself to him. *The Total Woman* is not the clearest statement of this principle nor the best exposition of it. It is one-sided; it is addressed only to wives and is concerned only with the wife's obligations in marriage. That is why the husband's corresponding duty to love his wife is not developed.

What Is Submission?

We have said a lot about what the wife's submission is not: it does not require the wife to obey her husband if that means disobedience to God; she is not confined to the home and to children nor solely responsible for it and them; she is not to acquiesce silently to all her husband's decisions and actions but to point out his sin when he disobeys God's word and to give her opinion or information to help him in decision-making, submissively. The wife's submission to her husband is not that of an inferior to a superior; rather it is voluntary, self-imposed submission. She is to submit herself.

We have emphasized that submission is an attitude and that the wife's submission to her husband is similar to Christian submission in general (Eph. 5:21). But more must be said about what the wife's submission involves.

Because the wife's submission to her husband is an expression of the mutual submission of all Christians to one another, it is easy not to distinguish it from the command to the husband to love his wife, which is also an expression of mutual submission. In practice the two duties resemble each other. James H. Olthuis writes:

> To conclude from these texts [Eph. 5:21ff.; Col. 3:18] that women do not have to love their husband is as preposterous as to claim that husbands do not have to submit to their wives. Paul is calling both husbands and wives to obedience to the norm of marriage. This involves mutual love and mutual submission. The mutuality is

heightened even more when we recall that in Christ's life "submission" and "love" were synonymous. To love is to serve. Christ emphasized the service concept of office in direct contrast to any of the other concepts in existence at that time. Six times in the synoptic Gospels we read that the greatest must be the servant of all (Matt. 20:26–28, 23:11; Mark 9:35, 10:43–45; Luke 9:48, 22:26–27). Naturally, then, Christ requires that husband and wife submit to each other in love and thus obey the will of God.[12]

Though, in a sense, both husband and wife are to love and to submit to one another, to make this idea preeminent in Ephesians 5:21ff. is to obscure what Paul is saying about the distinctive nature of the wife's submission and the husband's love. Paul has reasons for telling the wife to submit and the husband to love. Here is where balance is badly needed but difficult to maintain. The apostle Paul, being inspired by God, is able to maintain this balance in a succinct paragraph; whereas, those of us who are not inspired by God have extreme difficulty in keeping balance though we write page after page. When Paul speaks of the wife's submission and the husband's love, he refers to irreversible modes of relating. The wife's submission is more than that of one believer to another because her submission is based on an additional fact, the headship of the husband established at creation.

Ephesians 5:22–23 says that the wife is to submit herself to her husband *because* he is her head. The husband's headship is grounded in creation; the woman was created from him and for his sake. She was created to be a helper to him. The purpose for the woman's creation was to help the man; to be obedient to God, she must fulfill this purpose. Being a helper to her husband has several implications that are contrary to feminist goals but express the wife's distinctive submission to her husband. Biblical feminists are eager to point out that the Hebrew word "helper" does not imply an inferior. That is true, but it does not change the fact that the mode of and the purpose for the woman's creation are the foundation of the husband's

[12]James H. Olthuis, *I Pledge You My Troth: a Christian View of Marriage, Family, Friendship* (New York: Harper & Row, 1975), p. 145.

headship and consequently her submission. Both men and women are to subdue the earth—with the husband as the head and the woman as his helper (king and queen or president and executive vice-president are common illustrations of this relationship). As a result, the wife is to put her husband's interests first and help him achieve his goals. He is the one who ultimately makes the decisions and sets the goals.

Once again, this principle may have been easier to see and to implement in the days before the Industrial Revolution. Husband and wife may have run a business from their home. The wife actually helped her husband in the work. Priscilla and Aquila are a biblical example; both were tentmakers. It is harder for the wife of the executive or truck driver to help him tangibly and directly. The executive's wife may give dinner parties, and the truck driver's wife may refrain from complaining about his overnight absences; but it is a less direct type of help. In a way, modern society has become more specialized in family life. The idea that the woman can best help her husband by creating a retreat, a comforting home for him is popular. Its counterpart is the idea that the husband can best cherish and nourish his wife by freeing her from the work world and enabling her to stay at home.

This role differentiation is not wrong in and of itself, but it should not be held up as the biblical norm. In addition, it creates problems that the Priscilla-Aquila type of marriage did not have. In it the wife may be expected to help her husband while in complete ignorance of what he does on the job and what his aspirations are. She has no idea how he operates at work or how it makes him feel. Even if her husband tells her about his work, there are still things she will never know about it because she has never experienced it. It may be hard for her to have enough interest in his work to help him as a wife should. As a result, she may develop her own interests, separate from and sometimes competing with his. This is not to say that a wife should not have her own interests, but she has a responsibility to help her husband in his; her interests should not prevent her from doing that. In a role-differentiated marriage, husband and wife may operate in their own private spheres seldom if ever touching the other's. Is it then desirable for husband and wife to share the same professional interests? If your husband is a tentmaker, do you have to become one? No, but wives do have the obligation to help their husbands, and this means that wives cannot ignore their husbands' professions and professional needs. To help their husbands, wives must know and share their goals in life. How wives help will vary.

Wives of policemen suffer from the problem, described above, of not understanding their husband's work and thus not being able to help them. As a result, serious marriage problems abound in policemen's home lives. Some police departments, to combat marriage difficulties, have begun a program in which the policemen's wives were allowed to be at work with them during the day. The wives said this program has helped them understand their husbands. Perhaps such a policy would help husbands and wives in other professions.

The woman as her husband's helper is to submit to him in a way that he does not submit to her. The requirement for the wife is characterized by submission; for the husband, it is characterized by love. The requirements are not the same. The difference is made sure in Ephesians 5:31. The woman should fear ($\phi o \beta \epsilon \omega$) or reverence her husband, and he is to love her. The reverse cannot be said. In addition, the comparison with Christ and the church cannot be reversed. Christ serves the church and the church serves Christ, just as there is mutual service between husband and wife. Yet, Christ's authority over the church is in no way undermined by his self-giving love. Likewise, for all the mutuality between husband and wife, he remains her head and has authority over her.

Problems with the hierarchical model for marriage arise only when husband and/or wife are disobeying God's word. The husband is commanded to nourish and cherish his wife, and so his decisions should be qualified by concern for his wife's best interests. When the husband obeys God's commands, the wife suffers no hardship through her submission to him. In addition, the submissiveness of the wife frequently evokes the love response in her husband. By obeying God first and submitting herself to her husband, the wife makes it easier for the husband to obey God, to love his wife as Christ loves the church. (The reverse is also true; if the husband loves his wife, it is easier for her to submit herself to him.) If the husband does not respond in love, his wife is not excused from obedience (cf. I Pet. 3:1ff.); but her submission does not go unrewarded because it is obedience to Christ and for his sake.

The biblical concept of the wife's submission is as revolutionary as the loving headship of the husband. It is foolish to suppose that the women of the first century were more willing to accept a subordinate position than women today, though they may have had less opportunity to rebel. It was news to hear that wives should willingly, voluntarily submit themselves to their husbands, regardless of what their husbands were like.

In view of the pervasiveness (even in evangelical Christianity) of the secular spirit of feminism, the young Christian women of today desperately need to be taught to submit themselves to their husbands as Titus 2:4–5 indicates. They should be told before they marry what a Christian marriage means for a wife. They should be instructed to include on their list of what they want in a husband: will I be able to submit myself to him and accept him as my head?

Submission goes against the grain, because it is a denial of self. It, like Jesus' teaching on the indissolubility of marriage, may make us say: "If such is the case of a man with his wife, it is not expedient to marry" (Matt. 19:10). If a Christian woman cannot submit herself to a man, she should remain single and serve her Lord with a single-minded devotion.

For Husbands

The husband's chief duty is to love his wife as Christ loved the church. The most common description of Christ's love in this context is "self-sacrificing." Christ's love for the church is self-sacrificing, but it is self-sacrificing with a purpose—to sanctify and to present her to himself in splendor, without blemish. And so the husband is to nourish and cherish his wife. He is to do for his wife what he would do for himself. He is to encourage her growth into the image of Christ and to help her develop and use her gifts. But how does one do that? Christ knows his bride's needs and how to meet them; he knows what her goal is and how to reach it. How can the husband know what is best for his wife? Part of the difficulty in the husband's task is *how* to love his wife, what to do for her.

As in the case of wives helping their husbands, communication is necessary. To love their wives in a way that will develop their growth, husbands must know their wives' interests, abilities, personalities, and thoughts. Though the wife's duty is to help her husband in his interests, her interests will not be lost because her husband's job is to nourish her. This Christlike love prevents the wife from becoming a victim of vicarious living, a slave, an immature child, or a clinging vine. This sort of love means that the husband will see that his wife's gifts are used in the management of the home; he will delegate authority to her. For example, very few husbands interfere in grocery shopping or meal planning. True, this example is "domestic," woman's work. But the principles of delegated authority can be applied to other areas. It is conceivable that if one's wife had more marketable job skills (such as those of a lawyer), she could become the primary breadwinner. There is no one pattern for husbands to follow. A husband cannot think he has nourished his wife if he puts the finances of the home in her hands and gives her authority in that area; her interests and talents may not be in money matters. Wives are individuals and so each husband must tailor his loving to his own wife's needs.

The Christian wife's talents may not be used in the way the world expects. In the use of talents, the "fulfillment" of the wife is not the aim. The goal is the glory of God and the furtherance of his kingdom. To help her use her talents in her best interests, the Christian husband directs her to use her abilities for Christ.

Larry Christenson's concept of cherishing is that of complete role differentiation. He writes: "God's intention is that a husband should stand between his wife and the world, absorbing many of the physical, emotional and spiritual pressures which would come against her"[13] because "the heart of a woman is more easily discouraged and dejected. God made her that way."[14] This type of protection would be called overprotection or smothering if applied to children, and it is not part of the love that Paul commands. Cherishing and nourishing one's wife involve encouragement and making it possible for her to grow and mature. It is like the love Christ has for the church—to present the church pure and blameless. Christ does not protect the church from suffering or temptations. To mature, the church must suffer and overcome temptations. So it is not for the husband to shield his wife; to do so would be to stunt her growth. The church is to be in the world, with all of its evils, its attractions, its pain, but not of the world. As a member of Christ's body, the woman is also to be in the world, not buffered by her husband on all sides.

Husbands sometimes feel threatened by their wives' abilities. Just as women should consider if they can submit to a prospective husband, men should consider if they can encourage their prospective wives' gifts and talents.

The husband's love for his wife must include appreciation. He should praise her, verbally express both admiration and gratitude for her abilities. A man's compliments to his sweetheart should not end as soon as the honeymoon is over. How do we know that a husband should praise his wife? Intelligent appreciation is a part of encouragement, nourishing, and cherishing. In addition, "A good wife who can find? She is far more precious than jewels" (Prov. 31:10). The husband of the superwoman of Proverbs 31:10ff. was full of praise for her: "Many women have done excellently, but you surpass them all" (v. 29). The apostle Peter, a married man, tells husbands specifically to *honor* their wives (I Pet. 3:7). Honor not only includes praise and appreciation; it means respect. This command to honor one's wife excludes a patronizing or condescending attitude on the part of the husband. The husband who belittles or demeans his wife sins against God.

---

[13]Christenson, p. 37.
[14]Ibid., p. 128.

Husbands are to honor their wives as weaker vessels. Such a statement is paradoxical. It is more natural to honor what is stronger or better. Christianity reverses that "natural" inclination with commands such as "Clothe yourselves, all of you, with humility toward one another, for 'God opposes the proud, but gives grace to the humble'" (I Pet. 5:5). Is that attitude all that is involved for the husband in I Peter 3:7? In chapter 4, we suggested that the wife's weakness was her position of subordination. She is weaker because she has placed herself in a vulnerable position—in submission to someone else. Peter's command to husbands is that they should not take advantage of their wives' subordination. As head, it would be easy to abuse one's wife and to be harsh (cf. Col. 3:19). Instead, husbands are to honor their wives for taking the place of submission.

The self-sacrificing nature of the husband's love is extreme. The husband must be willing to die for his wife. The Greek word *agapē* is the highest form of love, love that is defined as self-sacrifice (I John 3:16). As biblical feminists have pointed out, men are not often called upon to die for their wives, but to wash dishes for their wives is another matter. The husband who, knowing that such a situation is unlikely, loudly professes a willingness to die for his wife may never lift one finger to promote her spiritual maturity or to help her with the grocery shopping. Such a man does not understand the meaning of self-sacrificing love. We have said that the wife must give priority to her husband's occupation. This means that she should be willing to give up a job she enjoys, if her husband's work requires a move. However, the husband's love for his wife may cause him to give up a promotion involving a move to another town so that his wife can keep her job. This decision would depend on how important the wife's job is to her, how important the promotion is, do they need the money, how strong the family's ties are in the present community, etc. Husband and wife should discuss the choice. The husband could make the sacrifice for his wife's sake, but the decision is ultimately his, as head of his wife.

Women are instructed by the world with its wide array of cosmetics and by some Christian leaders to make themselves lovable and attractive, as in the Total Woman course. Scanzoni and Hardesty quote one such Christian leader, James Montgomery Boice:

> Do not forget that your husband spends the better part of his day with people who are not only interested in his work but who are often well-informed and stimulating. Furthermore, women he meets and works with in the business world make a consistent effort to be neat and attractive. How then is he to be excited about loving you as Christ loves the Church if he comes home to find you with your hair in curlers and so taken up with the household affairs that the most interesting part of your conversation has to do with enzyme active detergents or baby food?[15]

Scanzoni and Hardesty rightly criticize Boice for shifting the responsibility of the husband to love his wife from him to her. She must earn his love. If she is not lovable, how can she expect him to love her? The answer is that God has commanded him to love her as Christ loves the church. Christ's love is unconditional; it does not depend on the loveliness of the church. In fact, he loved us when we were most unlovely to him (Rom. 5:8); and Christ is responsible for our adornment and our splendor as his bride (Eph. 5:27). The husband has the obligation to love his wife unconditionally and to love her in such a way as to make her lovely, to cultivate that internal beauty of I Peter 3:5. No one wants to say one should not try to be attractive for one's spouse, but that is not the important thing. The Bible never encourages outward adornment, and to do so is to pander to the spirit of the world. "Charm is deceitful, and beauty is vain, but a woman who fears the Lord is to be praised" (Prov. 31:30).

The husband must love his wife even if he does not *feel* like it. Hollywood has given us a distorted picture of love; on TV love is uncontrollable; it comes and goes at its leisure and so do relationships. It is romance, passion, hearing music, feeling dizzy. This is not the love demanded of the Christian husband. Agape-love, as we have said, is defined in terms of self-sacrifice. It expresses itself in action. Agape-love is commanded; that means that it is

---

[15]Scanzoni and Hardesty, p. 101.

subject to the will. One can will to love and act in love, even if he does not *feel* like it. The verb in Ephesians 5:25 ($\alpha\gamma\alpha\pi\alpha\tau\epsilon$) is the present imperative, which implies continuing actions. Husbands should keep on loving their wives.

The reason given for the husband's love is not his headship, though many associate the two. Some put it this way: it is the husband's duty as head of his wife to love, nourish and cherish her. The wife as subordinate submits; the husband as head loves. Nevertheless, the headship of the husband is not the basis of his love. Paul grounds the command to the husband on the one-flesh relationship in marriage. The husband is to love his wife as himself, as his own body, because they are one flesh (Eph. 5:31). Christ cherishes the church because we are members of his body (Eph. 5:30). The oneness of husband and wife is a sounder basis for love, because, as Paul points out, no one ever hates his own body (Eph. 5:29). By doing what is best for his wife, the husband helps himself because husband and wife are one.

The husband's headship is not forgotten in the section addressed to husbands, but it is not the main idea. Headship is implied in the analogy comparing the husband to Christ.

Although the command to the wife to submit herself and the command to the husband to love his wife function as complements, the two commands are based on two inseparable but different facts. Because the two commands depend on different facts, there is less reason to confuse submission and love; one cannot maintain, as the biblical feminists do, that there is no difference between the husband's love and the wife's submission. The command to the wife is based on the headship of the husband, which results from the creation order; the husband's command is based on the one-flesh relationship in marriage. In both cases, Paul touches the weak spots; he addresses the areas in which wives and husbands sin characteristically. Because of sin and the consequent disruption of the harmony of marriage, the wife tends to rebel against her husband; she tries to usurp his headship. And the husband in his struggle to maintain his position tends to abuse his wife—through blows, cruel words, etc. All of this is predicted in Genesis 3:16.

There are cases in which husbands kindly abdicate their roles as leader to their wives. Don't these husbands need to be told to rule their wives? There are cases in which wives completely submerge themselves in abject, servile obedience to their husbands. Don't these wives need to be told that they deserve to be treated as persons and that they have some rights? No. God's inspired instructions to husbands and wives bypass outward action and cut right to the heart of the matter. Wives should submit themselves to their husbands, and husbands should love their wives. It is the nature of sin to produce self-centeredness, selfishness, self-etc. in a person. The sinful nature in fallen humanity naturally demands its rights; it naturally seeks to put itself first. So the wife who submits in every external way still needs to be told to submit herself, and to acquire a gentle and submissive spirit; and the groveling husband still needs to be told to love his wife as Christ loves the church. If God's commandments are obeyed, marriage will assume its right order. Because of the natural egocentricity of sin, the Bible never encourages anyone to demand his or her rights.

All Christians in positions of authority are to "rule," not lording it over those under them, but with humility and service (Mark 10:42-45). The husband as head has the "right" to "rule" in this humble way; nonetheless, the Bible's way is not to demand one's rights but to fulfill one's duties. The Bible's instruction to the Christian is to give without expecting return, to put others first, and to love one's enemies (Matt. 5:39-42; Phil. 2:3-4). The husband's headship depends on his wife's voluntary submission to him, on her fulfillment of her duties. The Bible never commands the husband to rule his wife. In the requirements for elders and deacons, ruling one's household well is listed, but it is not a command. It is a by-product; that is, ruling his household well (that includes having a submissive wife) results from the husband's obedience to the command to love his wife. At the end of his chapter to husbands, Dr. Jay Adams writes:

> "Wait a minute," you say. "You were going to tell us how to control our wives. You have devoted all of this space to other matters, and you didn't say a word about how to control a wife." I have already

told you. If you can't see that, then let me spell it out for you. Paul tells us how to control our wives when he says to "love them." *Love* them. That is how you control a woman. You must love her. She is built that way. When she is fully loved, she is fully under control. Love her. If you don't believe me, just try it.[16]

This sounds almost like a Total Man principle. If you want to rule your wife, agape-love her. If you want your husband to love you, submit to him. That is the way marriage works. God's commands concerning marriage involve self-denial for both husband and wife, but of different sorts. The wife's submission establishes the God-ordained headship of her husband, and the husband's love insures the wife's best interests, her treatment as a person. Each one's obedience helps the other to fulfill his or her duty. Each also has the responsibility to exhort and encourage in love and humility the other to obey God's command to him or her.

There are disadvantages to being the head. Because the husband is the head of his wife, it is often assumed that he has the responsibility for his wife's behavior and beliefs. If she believes a wrong doctrine, some people consider the husband responsible and guilty before God. Such an assumption ignores individual responsibility. God says the soul that sins shall die (Ezek. 18:20), and each person will be judged according to his or her deeds (II Cor. 5:10). However, there is another biblical principle which applies especially to husband and wife because they are one flesh: a Christian is not to cause his brother or sister to stumble (Rom. 14:13). As we have said, husband and wife can help each other fulfill their duties; not to do so is sin. The wife can prevent her husband from holding office in the church, if she rebels against him. The man who cannot inspire submission in his wife is unfit to rule God's household. The paradox of Galatians 6:2, 5 pertains particularly to husbands and wives.

The husband as head has also been characterized as priest, because Christ is a priest. It has even been said that the wife can

---

[16]Jay E. Adams, *Christian Living in the Home* (Nutley, N.J.: Presbyterian and Reformed Publishing Co., 1972), p. 101.

approach God only through her husband; the hierarchy of I Corinthians 11:3 is a ladder one must climb to reach God. This sort of reasoning is why in some Christian homes, only the husband prays aloud at meals and family devotions. The husband as priest is a false title. The comparison of the husband to Christ in Ephesians 5 should not be carried so far as to make the husband like Christ in every detail; the main point of Ephesians 5 is that the husband should love his wife as Christ loves the church. In addition, the Bible teaches that all believers are priests (I Pet. 2:9) and that each believer has direct access to the throne of God because of the way made for us by Christ, the eternal high priest (Heb. 10:19–23). So both husband and wife have direct access to God through Christ. They are in every way joint heirs of God's grace.

Mutuality in Marriage

So far the emphasis has been on the distinctive duties of husband and wife, duties that maintain the authority structure of marriage in love. These instructions to husband and wife do not delineate the whole picture and cannot make sense without another factor—the mutuality of husband and wife. This mutuality has been obvious in the previous discussion—when the wife submits herself to her husband and puts him and his interests first and when the husband loves his wife in a self-sacrificing way and puts her and her interests first. Here we have the pictures of believers fulfilling the command: outdo one another in showing honor (Rom. 12:10). Both husband and wife should be concerned with how to please the other (I Cor. 7:33–34).

The Bible mentions one area in particular in which mutuality is the key: sex.

> The husband should give to his wife her conjugal rights, and likewise the wife to her husband. For the wife does not rule over her own body, but the husband does; likewise the husband does not rule over his own body, but the wife does. Do not refuse one another except perhaps by agreement for a season, that you may devote yourselves

to prayer; but then come together again, lest Satan tempt you
through lack of self-control (I Cor. 7:3–5).

Husband and wife share in each other's bodies because marriage
has made them one flesh; they are part of each other. The act of
intercourse demonstrates and reaffirms this oneness. Sex is an
essential part of marriage; abstinence is to occur only when both
partners agree. Both husband and wife should try to meet the
other's wishes in the area of sex. This means that sex is not to be
used as a reward or refusal as punishment. Fatigue or headaches
should not be regular excuses. Paul recognizes as normal that both
husband and wife need sex and either can initiate it. If the couple
agrees to refrain from intercourse for a time, the reason should be
prayer. This idea is rarely heard today. The fact that prayer takes
precedence over normal conjugal behavior indicates its great
importance for husbands and wives together. I Peter 3:7 affirms it;
the purpose of the husband's correct attitude towards his wife is so
that their prayers will not be hindered.

Sex is not to be considered an unpleasant duty to be performed.
Though the Victorian notion that nice women do not enjoy or
desire sex is dying, sex continues to be considered duty, or animal
behavior, or shameful by some. Perhaps sex retains these
connotations because of the way modern society has cheapened it.
Sex is a way to sell toothpaste and cars. Psychologists tell us sex is
just another drive, like hunger; and satisfaction of this drive, in or
out of marriage, is normal and healthy and not to be condemned.
Sex with anyone is justified and sanctified if one feels "love" for
that person at the moment.

But the biblical concept of sex is entirely different. Sex is a good
gift of God for the enjoyment of husband and wife; it is a source of
delight. It is fun; it is exciting. It is a way to express love. And it
permanently binds one person to another; therefore sex belongs
only in marriage.

This advice is given to the husband:

> Let your fountain be blessed,
>   and rejoice in the wife of your youth,
>   a lovely hind, a graceful doe.

> Let her affection fill you at all times with delight,
>> be infatuated always with her love (Prov. 5:18–19).

The clearest expression of the physical side of married love occurs in the Song of Solomon. Both husband and wife delight in each other's body without shame, as in the Garden of Eden before the fall. The wife begins, "O that you would kiss me with the kisses of your mouth!" (Song 1:2), and she longs for her husband, "O that his left hand were under my head, and that his right hand embraced me!" (Song 2:6). Her husband describes her longingly, rejoicing in her body.

> Behold, you are beautiful, my love,
>> behold, you are beautiful!
> Your eyes are doves
>> behind your veil.
> Your hair is like a flock of goats,
>> moving down the slopes of Gilead.
> Your teeth are like a flock of shorn ewes
>> that have come up from the washing,
> all of which bear twins,
>> and not one of them is bereaved.
> Your lips are like a scarlet thread,
>> and your mouth is lovely.
> Your cheeks are like halves of a pomegranate
>> behind your veil.
> Your neck is like the tower of David,
>> built for an arsenal,
> whereon hang a thousand bucklers,
>> all of them shields of warriors.
> Your two breasts are like two fawns,
>> twins of a gazelle,
>>> that feed among the lilies. . . .
> Your lips distill nectar, my bride;
>> honey and milk are under your tongue . . .
>>>> (Song 4:1–5, 11; cf. 7:1–9)

The wife takes the same delight in his body.

> My beloved is all radiant and ruddy,
>> distinguished among ten thousand.

His head is the finest gold;
   his locks are wavy,
   black as a raven.
His eyes are like doves
   beside springs of water,
bathed in milk,
   fitly set.
His cheeks are like beds of spices,
   yielding fragrance.
His lips are lilies,
   distilling liquid myrrh.
His arms are rounded gold,
   set with jewels.
His body is ivory work,
   encrusted with sapphires.
His legs are alabaster columns,
   set upon bases of gold.
His appearance is like Lebanon,
   choice as the cedars.
His speech is most sweet,
   and he is altogether desirable.
This is my beloved and this is my friend,
   O daughters of Jerusalem (Song 5:10–16).

Such frank sexuality has been a cause of embarrassment for some Christians, but God is not the perpetrator of such prudery.

The refrain, spoken by the woman, in the Song accentuates the mutuality of married love. "My beloved is mine and I am his" (Song 2:16; 6:3). The refrain is altered in 7:10: "I am my beloved's, and his desire is for me." "Desire" is the same word used in Genesis 3:16. Scanzoni and Hardesty comment on Genesis 3:16:

> Actually there is nothing morbid or pathogenic about the woman's desire—it is the same as man's for restoration of the communion with his mate and with his God. . . . The Song of Solomon, which gives us an ideal picture of marriage, says, "My beloved is mine and I am his. . . . I am my beloved's and his desire is for me" (2:16; 7:10).[17]

---

[17]Scanzoni and Hardesty, p. 35.

But they fail to note an important difference. In Genesis 3:16, in which the woman's desire is for her husband, the context is judgment; in Song 7:10, in which the man's desire is for his wife, the context suggests the ideal, the restoration of marriage as God intended it. In our discussion of Genesis 3:16, we have suggested that the "desire" of the woman is to control her husband, to usurp his headship. This interpretation is supported by the etymology of "desire," an exact parallel of language and syntax in Genesis 4:7, the context of judgment in Genesis 3 and the corroborating experience of marriage as a power struggle. The "desire" of the woman (Gen. 3:16) is sinful. The "desire" of the husband (Song 7:10) is not; it is proper, and his wife rejoices in it. How are we to understand the husband's "desire"? Is it to control his wife? In Song 2:16 and 6:3, the parallel phrases are antithetic; that is, the second clause clarifies the first by contrast: I am his, and he is mine. Two different but complementary ideas are expressed. In 7:10, the parallelism is probably synthetic; the second clause develops the idea in the first clause. The husband's desire for his wife is an extension of her belonging to him. (It is possible that synonymous parallelism is employed: "His desire [to possess] is for me"; there is a close association between the ideas of controlling and possessing.)

It seems obvious that the language of Song 7:10 is meant to recall Genesis 3:16; and given the notion of "paradise restored" in the Song of Solomon, it seems that Song 7:10b may be intended as a reversal of Genesis 3:16b. The wife's desire for her husband reflects the topsy-turvy order resulting from sin. Song 7:10b expresses the return of "desire" to its rightful owner, the husband; and thus it refers to the husband's headship. Song 7:10 could be roughly paraphrased: "I am my beloved's, and his desire is to be my head." It is significant that these words are spoken by the woman, not the man. He does not assert his right to rule; his wife gladly and lovingly restores it to him. She denies in herself the sinful tendency in women, resulting from the fall, to dominate her husband. Her statement is a recognition of his headship. The husband's "desire" involves rule, but the "rule" of the husband is exercised through self-sacrificing love. The mutuality of husband and wife, which is founded on their oneness and on their both being equally in God's image, is not damaged by the husband's headship.

Sex and Oneness

A change in attitude towards sex is occurring in Christian circles. Books, such as *Intended for Pleasure* by Ed and Gaye Wheat, are being candidly written about sex in Christian marriage. This development is healthy.

Scanzoni and Hardesty reflect this new openness in their brief discussion of sex.

> It's important for both spouses to maintain an openness of communication and not be afraid or ashamed to tell one another what they like and don't like about their sex life. This can be handled tactfully and lovingly without tearing the other person down. Many couples participate bodily in the intimacies of sex and yet feel strangely embarrassed and ill at ease about discussing it verbally with one another. So many difficulties could be overcome, and so many new joys and thrills could be experienced, if couples could only cultivate the habit of talking things over together and sharing deeply and honestly their innermost feelings.[18]

> . . . Husbands and wives can pray about their sex life together, just as they feel free to pray about any other area of life in which they sense a need for God's guidance and aid. Sex isn't a set-apart area of life, unrelated to one's Christian faith. It is something God has given and about which he cares.[19]

However, Scanzoni and Hardesty go on to speak of "an equality in the sexual relationship of a husband and wife"[20] and "egalitarian approach to marital sex."[21] They consider this sexual equality a part

---

[18]Ibid., p. 116.
[19]Ibid., p. 117.
[20]Ibid., p. 116.
[21]Ibid., p. 118.

of the complete equality between husband and wife. The implication is that the sexual equality between husband and wife can be expressed best only in egalitarian (headless) marriages, because only in these marriages are wives allowed to be total, fulfilled persons in their own right. Scanzoni and Hardesty are right when they say the Bible pictures the wife as one who enjoys sex, who expresses love physically as well as receives it. They are right when they say God did not intend for sex to be an act of conquest for men and surrender for women. Sex is rather a way of sharing oneself completely and of expressing physically the inner union of husband and wife. Yet, equality is not the best word to describe this relationship, and being a total, fulfilled person in one's own right is not the best goal for a married person. Equality suggests giving and getting an equal return; it suggests a balance sheet, rather than the Christian concept of total self-giving. In addition, two persons can be equal and have equal rights but share nothing. Mutuality or reciprocity is a better choice, because it indicates the unity and sharing that should be involved in marriage.

The mutuality of husband and wife in sex does not conflict with the concept of the husband as head of his wife. As we have seen, the husband has the authority to make decisions, but his primary duty is to love his wife so as to nourish and care for her; he is to have her best interests at heart. The wife is to submit herself to her husband, to help him execute his decisions, but her submission is not mindless, voiceless, or passive. In the Bible, the "roles" of and commands to husband and wife are different, but both include the duty to please the other and to do what is best for the other.

Being a person in one's own right contradicts the oneness of husband and wife. Oneness in marriage is more than a physical union in sex, though that is extremely important; it should involve a union of purpose, wills, and spirit. It means companionship (Mal. 2:14) and friendship (Song 5:16). It means that what benefits one benefits the other, and what hurts one hurts the other. Neither should function as an isolated individual. It does not mean loss of identity or personality for either. When husband and wife come together in body and soul, there is a wholeness that did not exist before. This new wholeness is implied in the creation of the woman; she was created to complete the man. Together they form one whole unit.

The oneness of marriage is permanent. Sexual intercourse establishes this permanent bond; that is, when a couple is joined through sexual intercourse, they become indissolubly one flesh (I Cor. 6:16). This union is an inescapable reality. That is why sex should take place only within marriage, and that is why divorce is prohibited.[22]

Marriage without divorce is a revolutionary concept. Today's society assumes that trial marriages, open marriages, cohabitation, serial marriages, etc. are modern inventions and that lifelong, faithful marriages are old-fashioned. But divorce was common in Jesus' time, so common, that when he made this statement

> Have you not read that he who made them from the beginning made them male and female, and said, "For this reason a man shall leave his father and mother and be joined to his wife, and the two shall become one"? So they are no longer two but one. What therefore God has joined together, let no man put asunder. . . . For your hardness of heart Moses allowed you to divorce your wives, but from the beginning it was not so. And I say to you: whoever divorces his wife, except for unchastity, and marries another, commits adultery (Matt. 19:4–6, 8–9).

his disciples responded in despair, "If such is the case of a man with his wife, it is not expedient to marry" (Matt. 19:10). Christian marriage is a hard saying. It has always been unpopular—from the Roman antinomians to the European Romantics to the flappers of the twenties to the present day.

---

[22]The only possible exceptions are divorce on the grounds of adultery (Matt. 19:9) and desertion by an unbeliever (I Cor. 7:15). It is possible that Jesus does not allow divorce in cases of adultery. The reverse of Jesus' statement is: if a man divorces his wife who has committed adultery, he does not commit adultery by marrying another—because his original one-flesh relationship has already been defiled by his wife's unchastity. Even if Jesus does allow divorce in cases of infidelity, he certainly does not encourage it; his emphasis is on the sanctity of marriage.

How can we meet Christ's requirements for marriage? Consider this example from the experience of Philip Yancey:

> One couple I talked to described a horrible two-year period of angry quarrels, temper tantrums, and walkouts. The wife, Beth Pestano, had come from a troubled family. Her father had left and her mother had died. Beth used the first few years of marriage to unleash her pent-up anxieties. She would fly into irrational rages over insignificant details. Somehow Peter rode out the violence of those first few years and continued to show her love. Today they have one of the happiest marriages I know of.
>
> I asked him, "Peter, how did you do it? What kept you from cracking in those long months of giving a lot and getting very little in return?" He then told me the story of his conversion, when God tracked him down after months of angry rebellion.
>
> "The most powerful motivating force in my life," he concluded, "was the grace of God in loving me and giving himself for me. When I hated coming home to face Beth, I would stop for a moment, think of God's sacrifice on my behalf, and ask him for strength to duplicate it."[23]

It can be done. There are two elements involved in Peter's ability to love his wife. He considered what God had done for him, and he knew God could and would enable him to love his wife. First, there is the example of God's love—God, who faithfully loved his people in spite of their repeated, flagrant disobedience (Hos. 11:1–9). It is no accident that the analogy of marriage is used to describe the relationship between God and his people (and Christ and the church), for marriage is to exemplify and demonstrate God's faithful love for his people. The greatest demonstration of God's love and forgiveness is Christ's death on the cross.

> While we were yet helpless, at the right time Christ died for the ungodly. Why, one will hardly die for a righteous man—though perhaps for a good man one will dare even to die. But God shows his love for us in that while we were yet sinners Christ died for us (Rom. 5:6–8).

---

[23]Philip Yancey, "Marriage: Minefields on the Way to Paradise," *Christianity Today,* 21:10 (February 18, 1977), 25.

But for Peter (above) and for each Christian, it is not just an academic example; it is an example experienced. The Christian knows that Christ died for him personally because God loves him. Each Christian has grieved the Holy Spirit countless times and has been forgiven innumerable times; and he knows God's love is sure and unchanging. He has seen God's love on the cross and felt it in daily forgiveness. And so, "we love, because he [God] first loved us" (I John 4:19); "if God so loved us, we also ought to love one another" (I John 4:11). "One another" includes one's spouse. Because we Christians have experienced God's love in Christ, we are commanded to love one another.

This idea brings us to the second point. God enables us to love, not with the gushy, sentimental, shallow love we see on TV, but with the kind of love God has for us—always forgiving, self-sacrificing, trustworthy and endless (John 3:14–18). Love for one another is part of the fruit of the Spirit (Gal. 5:22); it is a sign that one is born again (I John 3:14; 4:7–8). The child of God by nature loves. The Christian has an endless source of love in God that is his for the asking. So the Christian can meet the requirements of marriage. A corollary of the preceding is that the non-Christian is much less qualified to take the risk of marriage. Statistics bear this out: though the divorce rate is too high in Christian marriages, it is much lower in Christian marriages than in non-Christian marriages.

To Marry or Not to Marry

After hearing the stringent requirements for marriage (submission for wives, self-sacrificing love for husbands and total life-long commitment to each other for both), those still single may feel as Jesus' disciples felt—it is better not to marry. Jesus' response to this aversion to marriage is surprising.

> Not all men can receive this precept, but only those to whom it is given. For there are eunuchs who have been so from birth, and there are eunuchs who have been made eunuchs by men, and there are eunuchs who have made themselves eunuchs for the sake of the

kingdom of heaven. He who is able to receive this, let him receive it (Matt. 19:11–12).

He offers no defense of marriage, nor does he agree that marriage is to be avoided. Actually, Jesus says the same thing Paul says in I Corinthians 7:7–9, 25–38, a much misunderstood passage that gave Paul the reputation of a crusty old bachelor who hated marriage and/or women and that gave rise to a celibate clergy in the Roman Catholic church. Both Jesus and Paul affirm marriage as the normal or common state. Jesus warns that not all persons *can* remain single—only those to whom the precept (of singleness) is given, or as Paul would say, only those like himself to whom the gift (of celibacy) is given. To be able to remain single is a special gift; it is something extra. It involves a self-control that enables one to refrain from sexual intercourse and from lust.

That marriage is the normal or natural state is borne out by creation. In the beginning, God did not create single persons. God created a couple, husband and wife, because it was not good for the man to be alone (Gen. 2:18). One of God's first commands—to fill the earth—could not be obeyed apart from marriage; and the man needed the woman to help him in general. Marriage is not just a necessary evil; it is not just a way to control "lust" or passion, as some have deduced from I Corinthians 7:9, 36. God declared marriage good in Genesis 1:31; marriage was a part of God's original creation. Paul agrees, "So that he who marries his betrothed does well . . ." (I Cor. 7:38). The goodness of marriage cannot be doubted when one considers the analogy between marriage and the relationship of Christ and his church, beautifully written by Paul the bachelor (Eph. 5:25ff.), and between marriage and the relationship between God and his people (Hosea).

Paul's point in I Corinthians 7 is that one who remains single does better. Why?—because he or she has greater freedom to serve the Lord. Jesus mentions the same reason for remaining single—"for the sake of the kingdom." The gift of celibacy is given to promote God's kingdom, to further his gospel.

Before the fall, there was no conflict of interests between pleasing one's spouse and pleasing God. To do one was to do the other. But the entrance of sin and the consequent disruption of the husband-wife relationship have created a discrepancy between serving God and pleasing one's spouse. Neither husband nor wife *naturally* puts the interests of Christ's kingdom or of the other first. It is self first. And self often sees more concrete and direct benefits from pleasing one's spouse than from pleasing God. Buying your wife a new coat may seem "better," more gratifying, than tithing. And that self would prefer to be pleased by his or her spouse in many cases than to see that spouse serve God. Going to a movie with your husband seems "better," more fun, than staying home while he goes to choir practice.

More than a conflict of interests is involved; it is a matter of single or divided interests. The married man or woman has the God-given responsibility to please his or her spouse—not to gratify foolish desires but to do what is best for the other, and that responsibility takes time and effort. The single person does not have this concern. The single woman does not have to cook for husband and children; she does not have to take his suit to be altered. The single man does not have to paint the bedroom or take his children to the dentist. The single person can and should spend more time in the Lord's service—leading or attending Bible studies, staying late after work to talk to that fellow-worker with a problem. That is why he or she is given the gift of celibacy.

Instead of looking at singlehood as a burden to be borne or as punishment or as a means to gratify oneself and be able to do whatever one pleases, it should be received with thanksgiving to God as an opportunity; and it should be considered a great responsibility. The single person is specially devoted to the Lord. The single person is not one who has missed out or who lacks something; he or she is one who has a special position, one who has something extra. He is not to be pitied but respected. To be single is best. And it is time the church realized this fact in word and deed.

The single person has the same needs as everyone else—for love and companionship, but to meet such needs is more difficult than for the married who have spouse and children readily available. Nancy Hardesty's chapter on "The Single Woman" in *All We're*

Meant To Be discusses what these needs are and how they can be met with sensitivity and responsibility, with one exception in my estimation. The exception is masturbation. Hardesty implies that masturbation is an acceptable practice, that since the Bible says nothing about it, it is "morally neutral." She writes, "Particularly for the older single person (perhaps widowed or divorced) who is not just 'waiting for marriage,' masturbation can be accepted from God as a joyous release."[24] Though a Greek word for "masturbation" does not occur in the New Testament, I wonder if the stimulation of one's own body to orgasm, clearly sexual behavior, should be included under the heading of homosexuality, which the Bible condemns. The touching that leads to orgasm is intended to express deep love and commitment between husband and wife, and the orgasm itself is related to becoming one flesh. The release it brings should draw the two parties together in communion; it should fuse them together. Orgasm should not direct attention to self; it is not self-contained. It should be other-directed. All touching is meant to be a way of showing affection, but not all touching is sexual (that is, directed toward intercourse and orgasm). Sexual contact should be reserved for the marriage relationship, because it should be the expression of life-long love and commitment, and it performs the oneness. To talk in terms of love and commitment and becoming one flesh does not make sense when one speaks of one person. Sexual self-stimulation is unacceptable behavior.

What the single person needs is love, and that love needs to be expressed physically, but not sexually. "I have several friends, both men and women, who are not afraid to greet me with a hug,"[25] writes Hardesty. She calls these gestures precious. Several of Paul's letters end with the exhortation to greet one another with a holy kiss. This gesture was and is appropriate within the body of Christ because its members are to love one another, as members of one another.

---

[24]Scanzoni and Hardesty, p. 155.
[25]Ibid., p. 159.

Christian love and fellowship is especially important for the single person. The single Christian does not have husband or wife and children, but he has a family—the church. If he suffers, his fellow believers suffer. If he has a triumph, they are glad with him (I Cor. 12:26). What happens to him affects other people; he is loved. He is not alone. But the members of the church must realize this obligation to one another and especially to singles.

The Christian, single or not, knows that God loves him. God's love is freely given, unconditional and unchanging. It is I Corinthians 13 love. And Christ promised, ". . . and lo, I am with you always, to the close of the age" (Matt. 28:20). The Christian has God's constant love and companionship. Jay Adams has said:

> When God gives the gift of celibacy, He provides the grace to enable people to live in an incomplete manner. Their completeness must be found in Him.[26]

In other words, God takes the place of a spouse in the case of the single person and completes him (Gen. 2:18ff.). The single Christian is in a position in which he is forced to depend on God for love in a way that the married Christian is not. This dependency may be part of what makes the single person better able to serve the Lord with single-minded devotion.

To marry or not to marry depends on God's grace. Both conditions have difficult requirements which can be met only through God's grace: only by God's grace can husbands love their wives as Christ loves the church; only by God's grace can wives submit themselves to their husbands as is fitting in the Lord; and only by God's grace can the single person keep his desire under control. Both marriage and singlehood are honorable estates. Neither is to be disparaged. ". . . he who marries does well; and he who refrains from marriage will do better" (I Cor. 7:39). Singlehood is the better state, but it belongs only to those to whom God gives it; it is an extraordinary gift.

---

[26]Adams, p. 49.

EIGHT

FEMINISM AND FULFILLMENT

THE secular feminist movement has raised women's consciousnesses to ask the question, "Am I fulfilled?" Feminism has defined the meaning of existence as fulfillment; that is the goal. Betty Friedan in *The Feminine Mystique* defined the problem: modern women have a hunger that food cannot fill, a feeling that they are incomplete, left out, not alive. The woman has been told that her career, her reason for living, is marriage, family, and homemaking; but that is not enough.

> But by choosing femininity over the painful growth to full identity, by never achieving the hard core of self that comes not from fantasy but from mastering reality, these girls are doomed to suffer ultimately that bored, diffuse feeling of purposelessness, non-existence, non-involvement with the world that can be called *anomie,* or lack of identity, or merely felt as the problem that has no name.[1]

What is the answer? Friedan responds that women need a sense of identity and commitment to a larger purpose. How do women get these?

> The key to the trap is, of course, education. . . . But I think that

---

[1]Betty Friedan, *The Feminine Mystique* (New York: W. W. Norton, 1963), p. 172.

education, and only education, has saved, and can continue to save, American women from the greater dangers of the feminine mystique.[2]

Friedan sees full-time homemaking as a trap, a limit to personal growth, a waste of talents; the intelligent and able woman confined to the home will shrivel up and die. She considers homilies on the potential creativity in homemaking or on the importance of motherhood part of the deception intended to keep women in their place. Nevertheless, the facts she uncovered did not completely support her view of homemaking. After interviewing her college classmates from Smith (class of '42), Friedan discovered, "And yet most of these women continued to grow within the framework of suburban housewifery—perhaps because of the autonomy, the sense of purpose, the commitment to larger values which their education had given them."[3] Earlier, Friedan stated that education has kept women from adjusting to their role as housewife;[4] and still, because of her experience with her college classmates, she suggests education as the key to successful (fulfilling) homemaking. But for Friedan, the real answer for women's *anomie* is participation in a career outside of the home. Women do not need busy work outside the home, such as addressing envelopes, charity bazaars, etc.; women need something to commit themselves to, something that society recognizes as beneficial.[5] The real answer is meaningful work, and ideally for Friedan, this work in most, if not all, cases would be outside the home.

There are several problems with Friedan's (and the secular feminists') solution to the woman's dilemma.

Friedan defines a person's identity in terms of his work, as does our society. " 'In our masculine-oriented culture a person is worth the market value of his skills and personality. One's esteem depends not on the human qualities one possesses but on success in the

---

[2]Ibid., p. 344.
[3]Ibid., p. 346.
[4]Ibid., p. 296.
[5]Ibid., pp. 335–337.

competitive marketplace.' "[6] One derives one's sense of worth and purpose from one's job. Therefore, if one's job is unimportant or if one has no job, one feels unimportant, worthless, without purpose. One's work need be worthy of total commitment and valued by society, if one is to feel worthwhile. Housework does not meet this standard; it cannot give one identity.

As Christian women, should we accept the world's system of evaluation? No, a person should not be defined in terms of an occupation. Such an evaluation springs from a pragmatic or utilitarian philosophy, which does not account for a person's character, his relationships with others, or less commercial abilities, such as the ability to listen to another's problems. One lawyer may be satisfied to be known primarily as a lawyer, but another lawyer may find more satisfaction in being known as the little league baseball coach.

Friedan seems to assume that work outside the home is fulfilling, worthwhile. She condemns housework because it is repetitious (how many dishes do you wash?) and boring; such a dull routine stifles a person's growth. She seems unaware that almost all jobs have boring, repetitious aspects and that many jobs are boring and repetitious in essence—more than are exciting and fulfilling. Consider how many people work in assembly lines or as typists. Somebody has to do these things (and somebody has to do housework). Few jobs give one the opportunity to increase one's knowledge, pursue one's interests or implement one's ideas. Consider how many college graduates "use" their majors. The ex-housewife seeking a meaningful job may end up behind a typewriter typing meaningless (to her) combinations of numbers and letters. She may end up caring for and teaching another's children instead of her own, wiping another's tables, washing another's dishes, etc. The only difference is that she is paid. Even if she finds a "good" job, she may find that after a year or so, the excitement wears off; as she catches on to the routine, the sense of purpose is lost in continuous

---

[6]Judith M. Bardwick, *Psychology of Women* (New York: Harper & Row, 1971), p. 166, quoted by Scanzoni and Hardesty, p. 187.

and tedious red tape, the joy fades as a fear of failure or replacement creeps in, and she feels no more fulfilled than she did before she started. The person who expects automatic and lasting fulfillment from a job will be disappointed.

However, any work, including housework, can be enjoyed. The key is attitude—how you do it. In an article about Dorothy Sayers, Cheryl Forbes says:

> "Whether it is possible for a machine-worker to feel creatively about his routine job," she [Dorothy L. Sayers] says, "I do not know; but I suspect that it is, provided and so long as the worker eagerly desires that before all things else the work shall be done." Or, as the author of Ecclesiasticus says, the craftsman "watches to finish the work." Each of us can have that attitude. The typist looking (almost lovingly) on clean, error-free letters, reports, or manuscripts, neatly stacked and assembled. A secretary who efficiently schedules and guides her supervisor's day for the greatest productivity. The grocery clerk who rapidly and accurately checks out foodstuffs. Or the waiter who enhances the pleasure of a well-prepared meal by cheerful, courteous service. A housewife who knows that cleaning is a never-ending job and proudly views shining floors and polished tables. All these are jobs considered by our society as menial, yet they can be done creatively and can produce satisfaction.[7]

To the Christian, each task is important and purposeful. Why? Every job that brings order out of chaos reflects God's first creative act and has significance as part of the expression of God's image in humanity. Every task is to be done for God's glory and in his presence. Paul's explanation of how the body of Christ functions (I Cor. 12) is relevant here. God has given each member of Christ's body various gifts to perform various jobs, some of which seem less "honorable" (cf. I Cor. 12:22–26) than others. Nonetheless, every job must be done if the body is to function properly, and so each member and each member's task are important. In addition, knowing that one is doing what God has appointed for him to do is a source of fulfillment; there is no larger purpose in life.

---

[7]Cheryl Forbes, "Dorothy L. Sayers—For Good Work, for God's Work," *Christianity Today*, 21:11 (March 4, 1977), 18.

Friedan also refers to larger values, but she is not clear as to what they are. Perhaps what she has in mind is that a hospital's cleaning crew should remember that they are contributing to the health of patients, that one should consider and remember how his or her job contributes to the good of society. The good of society is a worthy aim, perhaps the worthiest, according to the secularist. Such a goal raises a question the secularist cannot satisfactorily answer, "Why should I help others?" Perhaps because this question is not often asked, "for the good of society" is not the motivating force for most workers. For most, questions of high ideals, lofty purposes or even self-fulfillment do not come up, because most people work because they have to—to feed themselves and their families, etc. With such pragmatic motivations, finding a job, any job, is often the important thing, not the job's fulfillment potential or its contribution to a higher purpose.

At this point, it becomes obvious that Friedan is addressing an elite, an elite in terms of finances, education and talents or intellect. Only such an elite would be qualified for "meaningful" careers; only an elite would be inclined toward or able to afford further education. Friedan does not address the problems of the majority.

Friedan mistakenly sees *anomie* as the woman's problem. As a result, she sees the solution as something men have: freer access to meaningful work. She avoids the fact that men (and women) with important, worthwhile jobs still suffer from lack of fulfillment or *anomie*. It is a case of "the grass is always greener on the other side."

What is fulfillment and how does one find it? Generally, fulfillment involves feeling complete, content, useful, at peace; it means feeling that life has meaning, and you have a part in it. The need to be fulfilled is universal, but how it is handled varies. Some give up and live in resigned disappointment; they consider its pursuit adolescent, something one gets over with age and maturity. Some try every "new" thrill in a frenzied effort to find "the real thing." Some think they have it; and then in some crisis, in sickness or at the ultimate crisis, death, they find that what they had will not fill the bill.

Friedan's answer is that meaningful work will bring fulfillment.

There are other suggestions—love, one's children, the acquisition of material things, art. Those who advocate a shorter workweek must see personal fulfillment in leisure time.

From a Christian perspective, none of these goals is sufficient. Ecclesiastes, which is a critique of secularism, effectively dooms the world's search for fulfillment, including feminist hopes. The preacher pronounces, "I have seen everything that is done under the sun; and behold, all is vanity and a striving after wind" (Eccl. 1:14). There is nothing in the created world to give fulfillment; when the world is considered an end in itself (secularism), when it is thought to be all there is, life makes no sense and yields no satisfaction. The two facts of life, evil and death, deprive life of its meaning. Not stopping with generalities, the preacher enumerates man's vain attempts at fulfillment. He has tried wisdom (Eccl. 1:16–18; 2:14–16), pleasure (Eccl. 2:1–11), "meaningful work" (Eccl. 2:10–11, 18–23), wealth (Eccl. 4:7–8; 5:10–17), and none of them satisfy. All is vanity, futility.

Ecclesiastes systematically destroys all of humanity's false hopes. But he hints at something better:

> Every man also to whom God has given wealth and possessions and power to enjoy them, and to accept his lot and find enjoyment in his toil—this is the gift of God. For he will not much remember the days of his life because God keeps him occupied with joy in his heart (Eccl. 5:19–20).

Joy and enjoyment are possible, but they are not produced by acquiring the right job (or finding one's true love, etc.). Joy is a gift of God; the only way to have joy is to receive it from God. In spite of all the negative things he has said, the preacher affirms, "Yet I know that it will be well with those who fear God, because they fear before him" (Eccl. 8:12).

C. S. Lewis describes the universal search for fulfillment:

> Most people, if they had really learned to look into their own hearts, would know that they do want, and want acutely, something that cannot be had in this world. There are all sorts of things in this world that offer to give it to you, but they never quite keep their promise. The longings which arise in us when we first fall in love, or first

think of some subject that excites us, are longings which no marriage, no travel, no learning, can really satisfy. I am not now speaking of what would be ordinarily called unsuccessful marriages, or holidays, or learned careers. I am speaking of the best possible ones. There was something we grasped at, in that first moment of longing, which just fades away in reality. I think everyone knows what I mean. The wife may be a good wife, and the hotels and scenery may have been excellent, and chemistry may be a very interesting job: but something has evaded us.[8]

The Christian response to this desire, this need for fulfillment is: "If I find in myself a desire which no experience in this world can satisfy, the most probable explanation is that I was made for another world."[9] That is, the Christian knows he is made for heaven, to know and be known by God. Perfect communion with God is the only thing that will satisfy human beings. All earthly blessings are only shadows of the real thing; they point to it, but they should not be mistaken for it. The preacher indicates the universal need for God: God has put eternity into man's mind (Eccl. 3:11). Augustine calls it the God-shaped vacuum.

Even Christ speaks to the problem of fulfillment:

Then Jesus told his disciples, "If any man would come after me, let him deny himself and take up his cross and follow me. For whoever would save his life will lose it, and whoever loses his life for my sake will find it. For what will it profit a man, if he gains the whole world and forfeits his life? Or what shall a man give in return for his life? (Matt. 16:24–26).

The person whose interests and efforts are spent trying to make his life meaningful by buying nice clothes, meeting the right people, visiting the right vacation spots, taking the right courses or even defending the right causes, will not succeed. He who would save his life, keep it and use it for himself (self-fulfillment) will lose it; he will not find happiness and he will ultimately lose his life at death.

---

[8]C. S. Lewis, *Mere Christianity* (New York: Macmillan, 1960), p. 119.
[9]Ibid., p. 120.

But the person who gives up his life, who gives up all the world's ways to fulfill himself, who does not see his own satisfaction as the ultimate good, and who puts Jesus Christ and his kingdom first, will find true and infinite happiness; and his life will never end. Real fulfillment is possible only for those who know the God of the Scriptures; and to those, fulfillment is possible in whatever circumstances they find themselves.

Knowledge of Jesus Christ meets every desire of the human heart. The Christian's identity is primarily that of a Christian; he knows he has value because he is created in God's image and has been bought at an awful price. His existence has a purpose because every Christian has the task of spreading Christ's gospel and every Christian is given gifts to perform a function in the body of Christ (I Cor. 12:7ff.). To the Christian belong peace (Isa. 26:3; John 14:27), joy (Phil. 4:4), and contentment (Phil. 4:11–13) that does not depend on external conditions. In addition, the Christian knows that this world is not the final reality; the Christian's sure hope is a heavenly city, in which his joy will be complete and untarnished.

The goal of the Christian life is not self-fulfillment. It is not even the use of our God-given talents *per se*. Though our talents are not to be buried, they are to be used according to God's will (this means that even if a woman is a good speaker, an able exegete, and a wise counselor, she is not to be a minister). God's choice for our talents may not seem wise according to the world's standards; it may involve losing one's life for Christ's sake. According to Judas, the woman who anointed Jesus with costly oil misused her resources; Jesus thought it was a beautiful act. The goal of Christian living is righteousness, holiness, conformity to Christ's image. This is Paul's major concern (II Cor. 11:2; Col. 1:28). For the Christian, satisfaction is found in obedience to God.

The Christian woman should not be deceived by feminist dreams and promises. Women will not automatically become immune to *anomie* when they are given equal opportunities in the work world. Meaningful work will not cure their ills nor satisfy their longings. The Christian who lacks fulfillment lacks it because he or she is sinning by not fixing his or her mind and trust on Christ, the only one who fulfills. To recognize that satisfaction comes from God frees persons to do their own work, without worrying about whether or not it is fulfilling them or is of cosmic value. One does not have to feel guilty if he or she lacks the desire or talents to become a doctor, lawyer, minister, or college professor. The feminists have made many women feel ashamed and guilty to be "only housewives." Motherhood has been degraded to only a biological necessity, which science should and is about to eliminate. In the Christian scheme, there is room for both women who work at home and women who work outside of it. The primary work directive for the Christian is that everyone work. The idle housewife who spends the mornings on the phone and the afternoon in front of the TV munching chocolates has no justification. The homemaker, like those who work outside the home, is to work; as Ecclesiastes 9:10 reminds us, "Whatever your hand finds to do, do it with your might. . . ."

What all this means is that the Christian woman or man has fulfillment apart from job or any other temporal source. It means that whatever one does, whether it is cancer research or changing diapers, it has significance. How? As we have said before, it is significant when it is done for God's glory (I Cor. 10:31). Paul's exhortation to slaves, who for the most part had menial jobs, was: "Whatever your task, work heartily, as serving the Lord and not men, knowing that from the Lord you will receive the inheritance as your reward; you are serving the Lord Christ" (Col. 3:23–24).

NINE

WOMEN AND THE CHURCH

SHOULD women be "admitted" to the pulpit, to the "top" office in the church? Should women be ordained as ministers, elders, or priests (depending on one's denomination)? This question has elicited the biblical feminists' deepest concern. Scanzoni and Hardesty ask:

> Ordination is relevant to women who feel called to the official ministry, and many women in all branches of the church do feel this call of God upon their lives. Can the church continue to deny them opportunity to respond to this call?[1]

Men and women are joint heirs of God's grace, spiritual equals. Why should an order of inequality rule in the church, ask the feminists.

What Is Ordination?

What ordination means is a more basic question. The biblical picture is not well-defined. Elders were ordained (Acts 14:23; Titus 1:5), but exactly what that meant is uncertain. I Timothy 4:14 gives us the

---

[1]Scanzoni and Hardesty, p. 177.

most information about ordination, though the word "ordination" is not used.

> Do not neglect the gift you have, which was given you by prophetic utterance when the elders laid their hands upon you.

Ordination involves the possession of a divine gift, which was given to Timothy by means of ($\delta\iota\alpha$) prophecy, and the laying on of hands by the elders. Prayer is also included (Acts 14:23; cf. Acts 6:6).

The important aspect of ordination for our discussion is the fact that it is the recognition of the specific gift(s) that a person has for a specific task in the church. Ordination does not confer authority or anything else; it is the church's recognition of what God has given. Thus, ordination to the ministry (in biblical terms, to the office of elder or pastor-teacher) is not a right to be fought for; it is a matter of grace, what God has given.

Some feminists, such as Letty M. Russell, have questioned anyone's ordination to the ministry.

> In the light of the one ministry of Jesus Christ in which both [men and women] are called to participate, the question ought not to arise, Why should *women* be ordained as clergy? They are already part of those who have inherited Christ's ministry of suffering service (Mark 10:43–45; I Peter 4:10). The question ought to arise, Why should *men* or anyone else be ordained to a special clerical status when all share the one calling of the whole people?[2]

This trend toward the removal of clergy-laity distinctions is another example of the secular movement (including the feminist movement) away from authority structures of any kind. The church must not allow this trend to become a reality. Why?—because God has commanded a hierarchy in his church. In the apostolic church the hierarchy was:

---

[2] Letty M. Russell, *Human Liberation in a Feminist Perspective* (Philadelphia: Westminster Press, 1974), p. 173.

apostles
prophets
teachers
workers of miracles
healers, helpers, administrators, speakers in various kinds of tongues
(I Cor. 12:28).

The Corinthian church resisted the idea of hierarchy, just as modern man does. That is why Paul wrote several chapters concerning the church as the *body* of Christ. Like the human body, the church needs different functioning units, persons with different gifts. Each person, like each part of the body, is important and dependent on the others. Some gifts may seem more important than others, but each is essential to the proper functioning of the whole. It is pride, the status-seeking pride of the old nature, that has assimilated the world's values, that incites the foot to try to become an eye, or an administrator to try to become a teacher. Paul informs the Corinthians that more important than one's gifts or one's position in the church is love. Because of love, the hierarchy in Christ's body is not like that in the world. Jesus told his disciples:

> You know that those who are supposed to rule over the Gentiles lord it over them. . . . But it shall not be so among you; but whoever would be great among you must be your servant, and whoever would be first among you must be slave of all. For the Son of man also came not to be served but to serve, and to give his life as a ransom for many (Mark 10:42–45).

The elders who were appointed in every town (Titus 1:5) were to rule (I Tim. 3:5; 5:17), but they were to rule in this way:

> So I exhort the elders among you, as a fellow elder and a witness of the sufferings of Christ as well as a partaker in the glory that is to be revealed. Tend the flock of God that is your charge, (exercising the oversight) not by constraint but willingly, not for shameful gain but eagerly, not as domineering over those in your charge but being examples to the flock. And when the chief Shepherd is manifested you will obtain the unfading crown of glory (I Pet. 5:1–4).

The humility of the elders does not change their authority over the congregation, as the writer of Hebrews makes clear:

> Obey your leaders and submit to them; for they are keeping watch over your souls, as men who will have to give account. Let them do this joyfully, and not sadly, for that would be of no advantage to you (Heb. 13:17).

In Scripture a group of church leaders to whom the congregation owes obedience is established. The oneness of Christ's body, every believer's union with Christ in his suffering and glorification, and the fact that each believer is given a particular gift (or ministry or service) for the edification of the body do not contradict or undermine the hierarchy God has founded for the government of his church. As long as the church is run according to God's rules, there will be an elders-(clergy-)laity distinction.

As we have previously said, ordination is the church's recognition that an individual has the gifts for a particular service. This service is not exclusively the office of elder or pastor. Some denominations ordain deacons, as did the early church. A common understanding of Acts 6:1–6 is the ordination of the church's first deacons. In considering whether or not women should be ordained to the ministry, the issue is the office of elder, minister, or pastor-teacher, not ordination itself. If women can be deacons (as we believe), their ordination to the diaconate is proper. In the early church women were ordained as deacons, but this ordination is irrelevant to the case for the ordination of women to the *ministry*. This section is concerned primarily with the ordination of women to the ministry, to the office of elder or pastor-teacher.

Invalid Arguments

There are bad arguments on both sides of the question of women's ordination to the ministry. The biblical feminists have appropriately attacked those false arguments against the ordination of women as ministers as follows:

(1) The argument based on the nature of women. Simply, this argument is: women are inferior to men. The Roman Catholic version is that women cannot receive the indelible character of ordination.

Paul Jewett affirms that this inferiority is taught by Paul in I Timothy 2:11-15, a case in which his Christian vision loses out to his rabbinic training.

> Women, according to the author [of I Tim.], are to take a subordinate role to men in the teaching office of the church. While men may teach women, women should not aspire to reverse this relationship, for they are inferior in their gifts, so far as the teaching office is concerned. This inferiority is inferred from the fact that the male (Adam) was created first; and it is an inference for which the author of I Timothy finds corroboration in the further fact that the woman, not the man, was approached and seduced by the tempter. The thought seems to be that the tempter approached the woman because he knew that she did not have the same critical acumen as the man.[3]

We must repeat that Jewett has misinterpreted Paul here because he falsely assumes that submission necessarily implies inferiority. Paul bases his prohibition on two objective facts of history (creation and fall) without maligning or demeaning the nature of woman. However, in the history of the church, the misunderstanding that Paul Jewett espouses has found ample expression.

Scanzoni and Hardesty react to this misunderstanding.

> What they are saying is that for one sex, half the human race, sexual differentiation is a handicap so crippling that no amount of personal talent, intelligence, piety, or even divine enabling can make them fit ministers of the gospel.[4]

The nature of woman is not a compelling argument against the ordination of women. Scripture does not teach that women are inferior or incapable in any way. We have suggested in chapter 6 that there is no essential or ontological difference between men and women; they are of the same substance and spirit. But there is what may be called a functional (economic) difference between men and women in the home and in the church.

---

[3]Jewett, pp. 60–61.
[4]Scanzoni and Hardesty, p. 171.

Another aspect of this argument is that a woman in the pulpit is more distracting to the men in the congregation than a man is to a woman. One wonders how anyone can seriously propose such a reason. One objection to this argument is that there are attractive young male pastors who have flocks of women who hang on their every word, and at seminary every young man is warned against counseling women alone. It is a male myth that women are not "distracted" by men. Another objection is that the wrong is not the fault of the one in the pulpit (usually), but of the weakness of those in the congregation. And another is that if women are such a distraction, they should be excluded from all participation in worship. Maybe that is why the Jews of Jesus' day confined women to the outer court, out of sight and hearing and out of mind.

(2) The argument from the nature of God. God is spoken of in masculine terms. Jesus was a male. The minister represents Christ, so he must be male. Although the use of masculine terms with reference to God is significant and although Christ's incarnation as a man is theologically necessary (see chapter 5), this argument is insufficient to exclude women from the ministry. It would be difficult, if not impossible, to prove from Scripture that the minister or elder or pastor-teacher was to represent Christ to the congregation. It has been said that the priest in the Old Testament represented the people to God and the prophet represented God to the people (note that God did not allow female priests, but he did allow prophetesses); but the office of minister is not the equivalent of either of these offices.

In addition, an argument from the nature of God against women's ordination can be balanced by one for it—both male and female are in God's image.

Scripture does not forbid the ordination of women to the ministry on the basis of God's nature, and neither should the church.

(3) The argument from biblical example. Jesus chose only men to be his apostles, he set the example for the church. This argument is also inadequate. As many feminists have pointed out, the apostles were also all Jews. Should all ministers be Jews? Who is to decide

which choices and actions of Jesus are normative and which are not? The proponents of women's ordination can also appeal to the discontinuity of the apostolate. It no longer exists; it was necessary only for the founding of the church. The office of the elder or pastor-teacher is a different office and existed contemporaneously with that of the apostle.

(4) The argument from tradition. Throughout the history of the church, women have not been ordained to the ministry. In fact, in the past women became ministers only in sects or heretical groups like the Montanists. Although the practice of God's people throughout history is important and deserves careful consideration, it does not possess absolute, unquestionable authority. The argument from tradition against women's ordination to the ministry stands only if it is based on Scripture.

The Argument against Women's Ordination to the Ministry

There is only one sufficient argument against women's ordination: scriptural prohibition. The case against the ordination of women should be confined to this one argument; it should not be based on tradition, speculations about the nature of women, extra-scriptural deductions from the nature of God or from biblical examples. A clear prohibition against the ordination of women to the ministry is I Timothy 2:12. Whether this passage is specifically intended to prohibit women from being elders[5] or not can be debated; even if it does have a more general application, it still forbids women from becoming elders or pastor-teachers, because the specified duties of this office are teaching (I Tim. 3:2) and ruling (I Tim. 5:17). The reason women are not allowed to teach or exercise authority over men is not because God is our Father or Christ is the Son or because Jesus chose men for apostles or because women are inferior. Women cannot do these two things because (1) the man was formed first and (2) the man was not deceived but the woman was. Whether or

---

[5]See pp. 125–126.

not these reasons seem fair or reasonable to us is irrelevant; they are God's reasons.

We know that the temporal priority of the man in creation is the reason for the husband's headship and the wife's consequent submission, and we have seen that the position of the man as head affects the way men and women are to worship God (I Cor. 11:3–16). According to the Scriptures, the order of creation is significant in two areas: marriage and the church. In both areas women are not to be the authority, the leader. To say this much is not to imply that all women are to be submissive to all men. In the church, the women are not told to submit themselves to all the men of the church, nor are all men given the right to teach and exercise authority (be elders) by virtue of their masculinity. I Timothy 2:12 means that the teaching and ruling office(s) of the church is not accessible to women; and only those men who meet the qualifications of I Timothy 3:1–7 can aspire to that office.

Why the creation order applies to the church as well as the home is not made clear; and guesses, such as to preserve the husband's headship or to image the relationship between Christ and the church, are only guesses.

The choice of an all-male apostolate is the result or expression of the principle in I Timothy 2:12–14, of the subordination (which merely means ordering under) of the woman in the church. We know that the choice of *men* as apostles is significant because of I Timothy 2:12–14. To have chosen a woman as an apostle would have contradicted the principle of the woman's subordination in the church (I Cor. 14:34). Scriptural principles tell us how to interpret biblical examples, not the reverse. I Timothy 2:12–14 is not to be dismissed as a proof-text, one isolated section that is out of agreement with the rest of Scripture. Though biblical examples, such as the male apostolate, taken by themselves, should not be generalized into principles, they can be mentioned as support of a principle. The principle of the woman's subordination in the church is buttressed by biblical history from beginning to end. Only men could be priests and elders in the Old Testament. Men were prominent as patriarchs, kings, prophets, judges, and authors of Scripture (all known authors were men). Only men were chosen as apostles; only men are mentioned in Acts as evangelists and missionaries. The principles involved in the commands to women in I Corinthians 11:3-16 and I Corinthians 14:34-35 confirm the prohibition in I Timothy 2:12-14. Even the commands that teach the headship of the husband (Num. 30:1-15; Eph. 5:21-33; Col. 3:18-19; I Pet. 3:1-7) lend support because they agree on the significance of the creation order and maintain that hierarchical relations are not contrary to God's plan.

Arguments for Women's Ordination

What evidence do the proponents of women's ordination to the ministry have? Is there any reason to change our conclusion that women should not be ordained to the ministry?

The feminists cite the participation of women in the New Testament church as evidence that women can and should be ordained. Scanzoni and Hardesty write: "From the beginning women participated fully and equally with men."[6] It is true and noteworthy that women have played a prominent role in the Christian church. They are valued as converts, in contrast to Judaism; they prophesy; they are fellow-workers in the gospel (Phil. 4:2-3; Rom. 16:3, 6, 12). There is no reason to suppose that women's labor in the gospel was only nonverbal or menial; Priscilla's instruction of Apollos illustrates differently. However, there is no indication that women did everything that men could do. "Fellow-workers," a word given much weight by feminists, is an imprecise term; what the duties of a fellow-worker were would be difficult to determine. When we consider the New Testament record, we find no female elders[7] or

---

[6]Scanzoni and Hardesty, p. 60.

[7]In I Timothy 5:1-2, neither male nor female elders (officers of the church) are in consideration; Paul mentions four age groups—older and younger men and older and younger women. In I Timothy 3 the office of elder is designated by "bishop" ($\dot{\epsilon}\pi\iota\sigma\kappa o\pi o\nu$); in I Timothy 5:17 and 4:14, the official elders ($\pi\rho\epsilon\sigma\beta\upsilon\tau\epsilon\rho o\iota$) are mentioned; that officers of the church are meant is clear from the context. In 4:14 the body of elders is mentioned; in 5:17ff. "elders" is modified by ruling and their work is said to be teaching and preaching.

apostles. Women taught children and other women; there is one example of a woman teaching a man (Priscilla in Acts 18:24ff.) individually. But there are no examples of women teaching the assembly of saints or even a miscellaneous group of people. In addition, there is the unmistakable command in I Timothy 2:12: "I permit no woman to teach or to have authority over men; she is to keep silent." There is no biblical example of disobedience to Paul's command to women.

In the New Testament church, there was at least one female διακονον (deacon) and προστατις (patron), Phoebe (Rom. 16:1–2). Most likely, she was a deacon and a patron or perhaps administrator; she had an important part in the church. Phoebe is an example of what women can do in the church, but she does not aid the case for the ordination of women to the ministry.

Tradition is cited by advocates of women's ordination as well as opponents; but it does not support women's ordination to the ministry. Though women have done many deeds for Christ's gospel, including martyrdom, the Christian church historically has not ordained women to the ministry.[8] Women have been ordained as deacons, an office not forbidden to them by Scripture. There was also an influential order of widows in the early church. But neither of these "offices" entails the same functions as that of the minister (elder)—to teach and to rule. Tradition witnesses to the activity of women but not to their ordination to the ministry.

There are other arguments for the ordination of women, such as the preaching of women has been honored by God, women have the necessary gifts or times have changed and now women are able to get the necessary training and would be accepted as leaders of the church. All of these arguments are based on experience; they ignore God's word. We know that God is able to bring good results from wrong doing (such as converts from women's preaching, cf. Phil. 1:15–18), but that does not justify disobedience. We are to judge

---

[8]Ambrosiaster said the custom of the ordination of women to the clergy was a Montanist error (*Comm. in Eph. ad Tim. P.L.* XVII, 493), cited by *Acts and Reports of the Reformed Ecumenical Synod,* "Supplement No. 4: Women and Office," (Amsterdam, 1968), p. 150.

whether or not a person has the gifts (or call) to the ministry by examining the Scriptures, which prohibit a woman from teaching and exercising authority over men, two duties that a minister or elder must perform. Advances in women's education do not change Paul's instructions. In fact, one wonders how changed our time is: the same feminists who use the existence of untrained, ignorant women in Ephesus as an explanation for I Timothy 2:11–14 laud the talents of Priscilla, who spent some time in Ephesus, as one who exhibited "such gifts to the extent that many have suggested her name as the author of Hebrews."[9] There were some capable women, even in Ephesus, in Paul's day.

The changing times do not affect God's unchanging word; in fact, the church should be especially wary about changing its policies to follow the world's lead, because the church and the world are two opposing orders based on two very different foundations. The church knows that God exists and that the world and all that is in it are his; obedience to God should be the church's motivation. Secularism denies God's existence and operates as if humanity is the only one to be considered. The church must be in the world as a witness to Christ, but not of it. Paul wrote, "Do not be conformed to this world but be transformed by the renewal of your mind, that you may prove what is the will of God, what is good and acceptable and perfect" (Rom. 12:2).

The universal priesthood of believers is another argument for the ordination of women to the ministry. Jewett reasons:

> . . . if individual priesthood rests upon the general priesthood of the laity, then women, who, like men, are incorporated by baptism into the body of Christ and so made "to be priests unto his God and Father" (Rev. 1:6), are equally qualified to become priests in the individualized meaning of the term. Whatever difference one may postulate between the priesthood in its general and in its individual form, this difference implies *nothing* for men that it does not imply

---

[9]Scanzoni and Hardesty, p. 62. One wonders how the theory that Priscilla wrote Hebrews could possibly be substantiated or even proposed since little is known about her and no samples of her writing exist.

for women. In fact, since the church is the bride of Christ and therefore feminine to him, one could just as well reason that the universal priesthood of all believers should find its individual expression in the woman *rather than* in the man, an inference which the theologians, as males, have never drawn.[10]

In response to such reasoning, it should be stated that there is no continuity between the office of elder or pastor-teacher and the office of priest, which was part of the Old Testament economy that ceased when Christ performed his once-for-all sacrifice (Heb. 7:11–10:25). The duty of the priest was to offer sacrifices for the people's sins; only the priest could enter the Holy of Holies, and he could enter only once a year and with blood (Heb. 9:7–8). The Old Testament sacrifices were not efficacious; they did not clear the guilt of sin away (Heb. 9:9). But when Christ came, he offered himself, the perfect sacrifice, to which the Old Testament sacrifices pointed; this sacrifice accomplished eternal redemption for those who believe in him (Heb. 9:12). Christ's sacrifice was *once,* for all (Heb. 9:25–28; 10:12–14). The office of priest is obsolete because Christ is our eternal and great high priest, who eternally intercedes for us. As a result, the believer may now approach God's throne and enter into the Holy of Holies (Heb. 10:19–22), which formerly only the priest could do for us (typically). The priesthood of believers is primarily understood as the offering of ourselves as spiritual sacrifices to God.

> . . . and like living stones be yourselves built into a spiritual house, to be a holy priesthood, to offer spiritual sacrifices acceptable to God through Jesus Christ (I Pet. 2:5; cf. Rom. 12:1).

The universal priesthood of believers involves our access to God's presence by Christ's blood and our spiritual sacrifices of ourselves to God.

The office of minister has little in common with that of the Old Testament priest, whose primary function was to offer sacrifices for sin. The minister's duties include teaching God's word, church

---

[10]Jewett, p. 164.

government (including the administration of the sacraments) and caring for (pastoring) the congregation. The universal priesthood of believers does not qualify one for church office; it is not the foundation or source for any present church office. It is a doctrine irrelevant to the question of women's ordination.

Perhaps the most common argument for women's ordination to the ministry is that not to ordain women wastes the church's resources. God has given each member of his body gifts to be used for the building up of the body to the glory of God (I Pet. 4:10; Eph. 4:7–16). There are a variety of gifts, and none are labelled "for men only," as Scanzoni and Hardesty point out. Scripture does not suggest that gifts of teaching, wisdom, knowledge, and administration are always given to men and gifts of helping and service only to women. They explain:

> "To each is given the manifestation of the Spirit for the common good" (1 Cor. 12:7). The decision to use or to squander our gift is not a purely personal one, but something that has ramifications for the entire Body. If anyone hides her talent or uses it for purely selfish ends, the Body is weakened, handicapped. But if each uses her gifts to build up the Body, then all benefit.[11]

That is true. However, the same Spirit who apportions gifts to whom he wills (I Cor. 12:11) is the author of the Scriptures which include I Timothy 2:11–14. It is foolish to suppose the Holy Spirit would contradict himself. The Holy Spirit does not call women to the office of elder (though a woman may have the gift of teaching); to do so would be a contradiction.

Of course, some Christian feminists answer that Paul did not really mean that women should never teach or exercise authority over men. His concern was to eliminate false teaching in the church. Such an understanding goes against the obvious sense of the words. (For a critique of this approach, see pp. 122–123.)

But there are some women who feel called to the ministry. To determine whether or not one has a "call" to the ministry is a

---

[11]Scanzoni and Hardesty, p. 177.

difficult thing. One must start with the Scriptures and examine him- or herself in their light. For a woman who feels she has the call, an examination of the Bible should show her that her feelings have misled her. Women are forbidden to exercise the office of elder in I Timothy 2:11–14. Some women want to become ministers out of pride, ambition, etc., but a woman's motives may not be "bad." She may have certain gifts that seemingly qualify her (by the world's reasoning) for the ministry, such as gifts for teaching, public speaking, exegesis, and counseling. The Holy Spirit does give such gifts to women, and it is wrong for the church to waste them. But they should not be employed in the office of elder.

There are several lists of gifts in the New Testament, and some of them are hard to define. In Ephesians 4:11, some of the gifts of the Spirit are that some should *be* apostles, prophets, evangelists and pastor-teachers, that some should "hold" these "offices." It would seem that the gift of being a pastor-teacher would be different from the gift of teaching. Women might have the gift of teaching, but women would never be given the gift of being pastor-teacher.

Galatians 3:28 forms the foundation for all of the biblical feminists' arguments for sexual equality, including women's access to the ministry; Galatians 3:28 is THE proof-text. Dorothy R. Pape concludes:

> Thus [on the basis of Gal. 3:28] any discrimination on the ground of being "female" is ended among Christians. . . . But the logical conclusion would appear to be that in the Christian community or church, especially, there can be no justifiable discrimination merely on the ground of sex.[12]

In other words, being a woman cannot disqualify one from the ministry.

But does Galatians 3:28 really address the problem of discrimination on the basis of sex? Is it concerned with the abolition of all distinctions (except biological) between the sexes?

---

[12]Dorothy R. Pape, *In Search of God's Ideal Woman* (Downers Grove: InterVarsity Press, 1976), pp. 202–203.

The integrity and authority of the Scriptures weigh against such an understanding of Galatians 3:28. I Corinthians 11:2-16; 14:34-35; Ephesians 5:22-33; Colossians 3:18-19; I Timothy 2:11-14; and I Peter 3:1-6 teach that there are different "roles" or functions for men and women in the church and in marriage.

Galatians 3:28 in context also argues against the biblical feminists' use of it. In Galatians, Paul discusses the relation of faith and law. Justification by faith, not obedience to the law, is the way of salvation. In Galatians 3:23-29, Paul affirms that *everyone* who believes in Christ is justified and shares in Christ's benefits. The main thrust of verse 28 is oneness, and the basis for that oneness is Christ. The unity of Christ's body includes diversity (I Cor. 12:4-6); it does not imply homogeneity nor the obliteration of distinctions. The unity of Christ's body does mean unity of purpose (i.e., the glory of God through the spread of the gospel and the maturity of the church) and genuine love for one another (I Cor. 13). Galatians 3:28 abolishes the hostilities between the three pairs of categories, and it provides for each believer's equal standing as a child of God and heir to God's promises, regardless of nationality, social status, or sex. All believers are equally important in God's kingdom, but that does not give every believer the right to become an eye (I Cor. 12:14-30). (See pp. 140-142 for a more complete discussion.)

What Women Can Do in the Church

Though the feminists' arguments for the ordination of women to the ministry should not be allowed to nullify the scriptural prohibition, they do raise a point to which the church should respond. From the disappointments of their own experience, Scanzoni and Hardesty write:

> The church does actively discourage women. If they report that the Holy Spirit has given them gifts for changing diapers, corralling seven-year-olds, baking cakes, or rolling bandages, the church has a place for them. But if their gifts are administration, accounting, theological investigation, or public speaking, forget it. . . .

... One well-known woman missionary was permitted to speak only to the women of a certain church. But her speech was recorded and immediately played for the men assembled elsewhere in the building!

If women are supposed to keep silence in the church, why do we let them sing solos, play musical instruments, and even lead choirs? ...

And why are women allowed to write Bible studies, Sunday school quarterlies, magazine articles, and books which instruct men as well as women?[13]

The church is confused about what women can and cannot do. In this confusion and in reaction to the secularly stimulated cry for sexual equality, some churches hold tightly to the old ways, which in many instances "fence" the law and prohibit women from doing things the Bible would allow them to do. The biblical passages that should determine what part women are to take in the church (I Cor. 11:2–16; 14:34–35; I Tim. 2:11–14) are difficult to exegete. Because of this difficulty, rather than wrestling with today's application of them, church leaders take the prohibitions at their most compre- hensive application; just to make sure the commands are being observed, they make them forbid more than they actually do. As a result, some denominations have no female directors of Christian education or choir directors; and some individuals maintain that women cannot teach in colleges or hold any position, ecclesiastical or secular, where men must obey their orders. Most of these churches have not compared women's silence in the church with singing in the choir; if it is brought to their attention, they may forbid women to sing. In the middle ages, choirs were composed only of men and boys for this very reason.

Other churches capitulate to the world's demands and remove all distinctions between men and women. Other churches, without serious reference to biblical injunctions, randomly allow women to perform some functions but not others. Tradition may be the deter- mining factor in many churches.

What is needed is the proper understanding of I Corinthians

---

[13]Scanzoni and Hardesty, pp. 178–179.

11:2–16; 14:34–35; and I Timothy 2:11–14. We have concluded that women are expected to pray and prophesy[14] in the assembly of the saints as long as their heads are covered, that the command to silence refers to not asking questions during the period of instruction (I Cor. 14:34–35), and that I Timothy 2:12 is intended to eliminate women from the office of elder (that is, women cannot occupy the official teaching-ruling office in the church). Unfortunately, these exegetical conclusions constitute only the first step. The differences between the modern worship service and the New Testament worship service and the variations in modern church government make it difficult to apply these passages to today's women. While it should be clear that the office of elder (to use the biblical designation) or minister is closed to women, today there are other offices that did not exist in the early church—boards of directors, treasurers, Sunday School teachers, denominational officers, committee chairpersons. Are these automatically open to women because they are not mentioned in the New Testament? Or is each position to be evaluated by these standards: women should not teach or exercise authority over men?

It may be a surprise that I am inclined to think that the two activities in I Timothy 2:12 are not to be used as criteria for other jobs, because they refer particularly to the office of elder. Teaching and exercising authority are inseparable for the elder; that is, the elder has the authority to teach and to "enforce" his teaching by means of church discipline. If I Timothy 2:12 does refer to the office of elder, the authority forbidden to women would not be authority in general but the authority to rule the church, to exercise church discipline. If Paul is only forbidding eldership to women, other jobs in the church could be opened to women. Women could have a say about the use of funds, church property, and the like; this sort of authority hardly compares to the authority (and responsibility) the

---

[14]The question of whether or not prophecy still exists is not within the scope of this book. If it has ceased, an act equivalent to prophecy would be the reading of Scripture. The Scriptures are God's direct word to the church, and so its reading would not violate the prohibition against women's teaching and exercising authority over men.

minister of God has over human souls (cf. I Tim. 4:16; Heb. 13:17), to teach others God's truth and correct them so that they might grow in God's grace. The kind of authority administrative officers have, even when it extends to the choice of programs, etc., is not the authority over individuals' doctrine and life that the minister has.

One caution must be sounded concerning the opening of all other offices to women. In some cases, administrative officers, boards of trustees and even deacons may have assumed some of the duties of the minister or elder. In such cases, it would perhaps be better to re-allot those duties to the minister or elders, rather than refuse the jobs to women. This situation raises the question of church government. Is there one form of church government that is biblical and that should be normative for the Christian church? There are no easy answers, but this writer thinks that the more church government conforms to the biblical picture, the easier it will be to see how Scripture applies and to find solutions for problems such as what women can do in the church.

The above understanding of I Timothy 2:12 also opens the door to female Sunday School teachers on all levels. Can women teach a mixed adult Sunday School class? is one of the most common questions asked (at least in groups opposed to the ordination of women). This question presents greater difficulty than that of administrative officers because the Sunday School teacher in many cases appears to be doing exactly what the minister does in his sermons. And some point out that the adult Sunday School class is more like the instruction period of the early church than modern worship services. The similarity lies in the fact that in Sunday School classes and in the ancient worship service, there was interaction between teacher and class or congregation; there were questions from the floor. Our Sunday School class resembles the situation in I Corinthians 14:34–35, where women are told not even to ask questions. However, the nature of the Sunday School must be defined before we can proceed.

Popularly, the Sunday School is not considered part of the regular worship service (except in the general sense that all we do should be done to God's glory and so is considered part of our worship). It is optional; not every church member attends nor is his absence from Sunday School a cause for church discipline or even rebuke. For that reason, if no other, the Sunday School should not be equated with the ecclesia gathering, where all of God's people are to assemble. The Sunday School teacher does not have the authority to enforce his or her teaching; it is nonofficial, informal teaching, for the most part, that resembles the mutual teaching all believers are to engage in (Col. 3:16), rather than the official, binding teaching of the minister, which the congregation is told to obey (Heb. 13:17). Thus the Sunday School teacher's work is not the same as the minister's.

The origin of the Sunday Schools is pertinent. It is a recent development; it was begun in 1781 by Robert Raikes in England to instruct poor children, to teach them to read and to reform their rough conduct. It was so successful that it spread rapidly. Note that the institution was begun outside the church by an individual.

The major difference between what the Sunday School teacher does and what the minister does is the authority behind it. The fact that the Sunday School teacher teaches on Sunday, the day of worship, and in the church should not obscure this difference. To do full justice to the authority of the Scriptures, this distinction should be made clear so that those involved would know that the command in I Timothy 2:12 is being honored.

To what extent can women participate in the worship service, the official ecclesia meeting of the body? This question raises hosts of other questions about the format of church services, what elements does the Bible require, what was the apostolic "church service" like, are we to imitate it? The "woman" question challenges the traditional worship service, partly because the passages dealing with women's participation are part of sections dealing with the entirety of the ecclesia meeting (I Cor. 11–14), and partly because women with raised consciousnesses want to use their gifts, and this desire raises the broader question of how each Christian's gifts are to be used.

To answer how women can participate in the traditional church service of today is not so difficult because it has essentially become a one-man show. The minister usually does all the praying, Scripture-reading and teaching. Women may participate with the whole congregation in reciting the Lord's prayer, singing hymns (and anthems) and reading responsive readings. These traditionally accepted activities are sanctioned by proper exegesis of I Corinthians 11:2–16; 14:34–35; and I Timothy 2:11–14. Women can pray and prophesy in the assembly. Reading Scripture, as in the responsive reading, falls in the category of prophecy because it is God's inspired word, not a human interpretation of it. The silence commanded for women in the church is always related to learning so that women should be silent during the instruction period, that is, the sermon. Absolute silence is not the point. As for singing, there is no indication that women are *not* to sing, and Colossians 3:16 suggests that everyone sings. It may be argued that singing is teaching, and so women should not sing. The words of hymns and psalms are instructive. If one wanted to go to extremes, prayer and even facial expressions are instructive; one would have to silence women completely (which is contrary to I Cor. 11:2–16) and to cover women's faces entirely (not just heads as in I Cor. 11:2–16) to prevent her from giving any instruction in the assembled congregation. But the primary purpose of singing or prayer is not instruction. The silence commanded of women refers to the time in the worship service specifically intended for instruction; in modern services, that is the sermon.

In addition, the women of the congregation participate corporately in most modern worship services. It is unlikely that Paul's prohibition was intended to eliminate female voices from the whole group during corporate reading, prayer, recitation, and singing. When everyone is saying the same thing, it would take a great stretch of the imagination to interpret that activity as a woman's participation in instruction as forbidden in I Corinthians 14:34–35 or I Timothy 2:11–12.

The real problems of the woman's participation arise in a more informal worship service, as pictured in the New Testament, one in which everyone contributes. One problem is that what the covering of I Corinthians 11:5 is must be determined. It is possible that in corporate prayer and Scripture-reading, women's heads should be

covered; but there is no doubt that women should cover their heads
when they pray or read Scripture individually in the assembly. Paul
does seem to have individual prayer and prophecy in view in I Corinthians 11:2–16, for he says each (or every) man who prays and each
(or every) woman who prays; and prophets were to speak one at a
time (I Cor. 14:29–32). I Corinthians 11:2–16 regulates leading in
prayer and prophecy in the congregation.

There are other questions involved in an informal service: can a
woman give her testimony, can a woman missionary give her
report, can a woman share her prayer requests or praises, can a
woman ask questions after the sermon? This writer cannot answer
(or even ask) all the questions. But it seems that if a woman can
pray, she could make prayer requests. And in services in which there
is a discussion period after the sermon, women cannot ask questions;
that situation would be similar to the one discussed in I Corinthians
14:34–35. In the cases of personal testimonies and missionary
reports, the answer is less clear. However, if the silence of women in
the church is directly related to instruction, not in a broad sense but
in the narrow sense of authoritative teaching, personal testimonies
and missionary reports would be appropriate, if they were not
substituted for the sermon. It is women's participation in the
authoritative instruction, the sermon and its discussion, in the
assembly that is forbidden.

Luther, who did not have feminist inclinations, seems to agree
with this limited definition of the woman's silence.

> Through St. Paul the Holy Spirit Himself determines the role women
> are to play in the worship services—they are to keep silent, that is,
> they are not to preach. . . . As for the rest, women can and should
> "pray, sing, praise and say Amen, and read and teach one another in
> the household, admonishing, comforting, and also expounding the
> Holy Scriptures" as well as they possibly can.[15]

The question of women's participation in the church has been
formulated this way: cannot women do everything a layman can do?

---

[15]Martin Luther quoted by Brunner, p. 9.

After all, men are not qualified by virtue of being men for the office of elder; all men are not authorized to teach/rule over others in the church. It is tempting to answer "yes" on the basis of I Timothy 2:11–14 alone. However, I Corinthians 14:34–35 seems to imply that any man could ask questions, that only women are excluded from that discussion. So the question should be answered "yes," with the exception of any participation in a question-answer period that is a part of the official instruction in the assembly.

Hypothetical questions about women's participation are always raised. What if there is a situation in which there are no men qualified to be elders, but there is a woman who is trained, as on a mission field? Most importantly, we must affirm that God's rules cannot be accommodated to fit what appears to us to be the exceptional case. Nonetheless, it is presumptuous (and untrue as experience demonstrates) to assume that since God has ordained to rule and teach his church by men, he will always provide able men to perform those functions.

Elisabeth Elliot, after the massacre of her husband and several other missionaries, was the only "able" (theologically trained) person left who could speak the language of the Auca Indians. Her solution was to hold Bible classes and to "teach" a sermon to one of the Auca men who had potential before the worship service. She refused to give the message of the official worship service. To some, her action may seem legalistic, obeying the external form of the law but getting around it. Some would say that she was really teaching and exercising authority over men, only through someone else. But is this the case? Does not her solution resemble Priscilla's and Aquila's? That couple did not usurp Apollos' place as a teacher of God's word; they instructed him privately, and he continued his ministry. Elisabeth Elliot was engaged in privately training Auca men who could eventually assume the office of elder in the church. Her course of action seems to be the best answer to the exceptional situation.

If the prohibitions of I Corinthians 14:34–35 and I Timothy 2:11–14 are understood as specifically concerned with the official instruction of the assembly and with the office of elder, then a wide range of activities are accessible to women (many of which have been open for quite a while). Women can be Sunday School superintendents, Sunday School teachers on all levels, administrative officers, church paper editors, treasurers, writers (magazine articles, Sunday School literature, tracts, systematic theologies, hymns, commentaries, etc.), counselors, choir directors, committee chairpersons. Women's gifts and talents should be employed in the church and they can be without opening ordination to the ministry to them.

On the subject of what women may do in the church, two "offices" need special attention: evangelist and deacon. "Evangelist" is mentioned as one of Christ's gifts to the church to perfect God's people for the work of ministry, along with apostles, prophets, and pastor-teachers, in Ephesians 4:11. We know that Philip (Acts 21:8) and Timothy (II Tim. 4:5) were evangelists, but what distinguished the evangelist is not stated. The pastor-teacher is subsumed under elder (the elder is to teach and to pastor or shepherd God's people, I Pet. 5:2-3). But is the evangelist an elder? The noun $εὐαγγελιστής$ occurs only in Acts 21:8; Ephesians 4:11 and II Timothy 4:5; the verb $εὐαγγελίζω$ occurs frequently, and it is most frequently translated preach or preach the gospel. Who are those who "evangelize"?—angels, Jesus, John the Baptist, the twelve apostles, Paul, Philip, Barnabus. In the New Testament, no woman is portrayed as "evangelizing" or preaching ($κηρύσσω$ or $καταγγελλω$). This evidence is most inconclusive, yet it suggests that the office of evangelist is not open to women. If we consider Timothy as an example of an evangelist, we see a man who both teaches authoritatively and who has responsibility for the elders and the people of the church. He is told to "preach the word, be urgent in season and out of season, convince, rebuke and exhort, be unfailing in patience and in teaching" (II Tim. 4:2). If such is the position of an evangelist, the office is closed to women. However, we do not know if Timothy's authority to teach and to discipline depends on his being an evangelist or on his close relationship with Paul or even on some other gift or office. Philip the evangelist travelled as he preached the good news; he resembles the modern concept of the evangelist, a preacher who is not connected with a local church and who goes from town to town (like Billy Graham), an itinerant pastor-teacher. Philip was empowered to baptize (Acts 8:38), an act expressing the authority of the church.

Can women be evangelists? The biblical data is scarce, but what there is suggests a negative answer. There are two basic ways to conceive of the office—as an elder not attached to a local congregation or as a "glorified" witness (and we are all to witness to our Lord). It seems that the former understanding is closer to the biblical picture, if we consider who "evangelized." The main function of the evangelist would be authoritative teaching or preaching. He also has the authority to baptize. He differs from the pastor-teacher in that he is not associated with a specific church and possibly he deals mainly with non-Christians. Permit two hypothetical questions: how could a church ordain someone (i.e., a woman) who could never address the assembly at the worship service to the office of evangelist; and if the evangelist's task is to start new churches, how could she function if she could not preach at the worship services and exercise church discipline?

To forbid this office (as a type of elder) to women would not put an end to women missionaries. As we have indicated with the example of Elisabeth Elliot, women missionaries should not act as elders to a mission church by preaching, exercising discipline, or administering the sacraments (baptism and the Lord's supper). For this reason, it is best that a missionary team include an ordained elder. Nonetheless, there are many contributions a trained woman missionary can make, as Elisabeth Elliot would testify. She can instruct the people through Bible studies and individually. We must remember that one does not have to be an ordained evangelist to tell the good news to others; the witnessing activity of women is not diminished.

In chapter 4 we indicated that the biblical evidence favors women deacons. I Timothy 3:11 is best understood as referring to female deacons rather than to deacons' wives: the witness of the early church (The Greek Fathers and Theodore of Mopsuestia) confirms this interpretation. In A.D. 111, Pliny, Governor of Bithynia, questioned two maidservants who were called deaconesses (minis-trae). This reference may be to an office in the church.[16] In the third and fourth centuries there are clearer references to deaconesses. In the Didascalia (early third c.) and the Apostolic Constitutions (late 4th c.), the function of the deaconess is described. She was to assist the clergy in the baptism of women, minister to the poor and sick, particularly women, and help in the instruction of female catechu-mens; she was to act as an intermediary between the clergy and the women in the congregation. She was also to visit women in pagan households. The office of deaconess disappeared in the West in the fourth century and in the East in the twelfth century.

The functions of the deacon, though not clearly delineated in Scripture, focus on material, physical service. The qualifications for deacons (serious, not double-tongued, sober, not greedy, not slander-ers) are appropriate for one dealing with financial, administrative, and social service. The office arose out of a need for fair distribution of food to needy widows (Acts 6:1-6). The deacon does not teach or rule in the official sense. The tasks of the deaconess today would be the same as in the third century, including the financial and adminis-trative aspects of those services.

It has been suggested that women should participate in the diaconal ministry only in an auxiliary way. According to George W. Knight, III:

> . . . because there is no clear Scriptural evidence for women occupying the office of deacons, they [the church] make full use of the gifts and services of women in the diaconal task in an auxiliary capacity. . . .[17]

Women could be deaconesses, but that role would not be considered a church office and it would not allow women to initiate diaconal work but only to help the men in it. This theory is based on a forced understanding of I Timothy 3:8-13.

---

[16]A. F. Walls, "Deaconess," in Douglas (ed.), *NBD*, p. 298.
[17]George W. Knight, III, *The New Testament Teaching on the Role Relationship of Men and Women* (Grand Rapids: Baker Book House, 1977), p. 68.

> They [women] are mentioned in the midst of the description of
> deacons because it is perfectly proper for them to be involved in the
> diaconal ministry, which does not involve inherently, ruling and
> teaching. [So far so good.] It is also striking that the office of deacon
> is described not in both male and female terms or without any
> reference to sex, but in male terms, and the reference to women or
> wives appears in the midst of that description. It would seem there-
> fore that the office of deacon is an office for men only, but that at the
> same time women are to be involved in that diaconal area.[18]

Surely, this interpretation is making too much of too little. Actually,
the facts of exegesis cited above, though they are not definitive,
suggest that women did hold the office of deacon. Why else would a
reference to women be sandwiched between two commands for
deacons? The inclusion of "likewise" indicates the same status for
the group women as for the groups, elders and deacons, that is,
church office. There is nothing in the text to suggest that women in
verse 11 have a different relation to the church or that women have
a secondary, auxiliary function. The requirements for "deacons" in
verse 8 are comparable to those for "women" in verse 11. Commands
applying to both men and women are sometimes put only in masculine terms, such as in Exodus 20:17; similarly, women could be
included in the masculine noun "deacon." In order to make it clear
that women were included as deacons, Paul would have to refer to
them by sex. The feminine noun "deaconess" does not occur in the
New Testament; so Paul inserts "women" in the middle of the
section on deacons.

Ministering to physical needs is an important part of the church's
witness to the world. Jesus said to the Jews, ". . . even though you do
not believe me, believe the works . . ." (John 10:38), and to his
disciples, "Truly, I say to you, as you did it [fed the hungry, gave drink
to the thirsty, welcomed the stranger, clothed the naked and visited
the sick and the imprisoned] to one of the least of these my
brethren, you did it to me" (Matt. 25:40). These duties belong to
every Christian but to the diaconate in particular. It is the deacon's

---

[18]Ibid., p. 48.

responsibility to seek out those with needs and meet those needs in the name of Christ. Though the deacon's emphasis is on material needs, the help provided by the diaconate does not lack spiritual dimensions. The work of the deacon is to be done in the name of Christ, and that means witnessing to the unbeliever and comforting and exhortation for all of the needy.

What can women do in the church? In the worship service, the ecclesia gathering, the woman may participate fully, with the exception of taking part in the instruction period. She may not lead the instruction (preach) or ask questions if discussion is included in the teaching period. The silence commanded of women in the ecclesia is relative; it pertains to teaching. Women who are covered may lead in prayer and prophecy (including Scripture-reading). Regarding church office, the woman may not become a minister, pastor, elder or evangelist, for these offices involve teaching and ruling (I Tim. 2:11–12). She may become a deacon; administrative offices are open to her. To answer the question of women's participation in the church completely, more basic questions concerning church government, the format of worship and the duties of the laity must be raised and answered. The church not only wastes the gifts of women; it wastes the gifts of the laity as a whole, and it often misuses the gifts of the clergy. To function properly, the church must employ the gifts of all members in obedience to God's commands; we are to use our gifts but in the way prescribed by God's word.

TEN

SUMMARY

HOW much progress have we made? To some, it will undoubtedly seem that this author and the Bible come out on the side against women. Some will still maintain that it is unjust and unfair to make distinctions on the basis of sex. It will seem to some that God, like so many chauvinist employers, has passed over the women when he was looking for persons to fill positions of authority and prestige. Where do women stand?

We have discovered three biblical principles that are established in Genesis 1–2, undergirded by Old Testament legislation, assumed by Jesus and explained by Paul.

(1) Men and women are equally in the image of God. Both are to rule the earth as God's vice-regents. Sin has the same effect on them; both have the same need for salvation. Male and female believers share the benefits of salvation equally; both are being conformed to Christ's image. Scripture does not teach psychological or personality differences between men and women. This principle can be termed ontological equality or equality in being. It means men and women are equal as persons, and men and women should treat one another with kindness and respect, as persons made in God's image.

(2) Wives are to submit themselves to their husbands, and women are not to teach or exercise authority over men in the church. The

woman's subordination to her husband and in the church is not based on merit or lack of it. It is not based on any sort of superiority inherent in the man or inferiority inherent in the woman. It is based on God's appointment. God chose to create two sexes, to create the man first to establish his headship in the family and potentially in the church, and to create the woman after, from, and for the sake of the man to establish her position in the family and the church, just as God chose to plant the tree of the knowledge of good and evil in the garden and to forbid the eating of its fruit to the man and woman. Why God chose to confer headship on the man is not clarified in the Bible; one possible explanation, suggested by Ephesians 5:22ff., is to demonstrate the relationship between Christ and the church to believers and to the world. This difference between men and women can be termed economic or functional subordination. It means that though men and women are equal in personhood, God has ordained a difference in function. Men function as heads of their wives and may become elders in the church if they meet the qualifications in I Timothy 3:1ff. Women submit themselves to their husbands and may not become elders in the church (they may not teach and rule in the church).

These two principles exist in some tension and may be described as one of the antinomies of Scripture. Yet, a third principle holds the first two together and eases the tension between them.

(3) Husband and wife are one flesh, and believers are one body in Christ. Husband and wife become one flesh—in reality, mysteriously and irreversibly. Therefore, what benefits one benefits the other and what harms one harms the other. The same is true of the union of believers, including male elders and lay women. In such unions, there should be no place for envy or rivalry, because each has an essential, divinely appointed task to perform for the benefit of all (I Cor. 12:14–31). Loving oneness is the key to understanding and accepting the woman's position in marriage and church. For those who persist in thinking that women are second-rate citizens in God's kingdom, there are two more scriptural principles:

(1) God has ascribed honor to the place of subordination. That is part of the reason the husband is commanded to honor his wife in

I Peter 3:7. Jesus himself was not ashamed to take the form of a servant, to humble himself. We are commanded to have the same mind as Christ (Phil. 2:5), and we are warned, "God opposes the proud, but gives grace to the humble" (I Pet. 5:5). It is pride and rebellion against God that moves Christian women to refuse to fulfill their positions in marriage and the church. This rebellion is part of the judgment in Genesis 3:16.

But biblical feminists speak in the names of equality, not pride, and justice, not rebellion.

(2) It is God and God alone who determines what justice is. There is no external (to the Bible), autonomous, Platonic standard of justice to which men and gods must submit and by which we can edit the Scriptures. Justice is defined by God's word, not by human reason. Therefore, it is just and fair that women cannot be elders in the church, even though an equal partnership of the sexes in marriage and in the church may seem like a better idea to many persons.

Today, there is a forbidden fruit, just as there was in the garden. That fruit is role interchangeability in marriage and the church. Christian women, like Eve, are being tempted with half truths (such as subordination implies inferiority) and are being told that God (or the Bible or the church) is depriving them of something quite arbitrarily. (We forget that God's commandments are for our own good.) In some instances Christian women are deceived into thinking that God's word forbids more than it does; they think they must not even touch the tree with the forbidden fruit. And like Eve, Christian women are guilty of sinning against their creator by discussing with other creatures whether or not God's law is fair.

Let us resist temptation and say with the Psalmist:

> The law of the Lord is perfect, reviving the soul;
> the testimony of the Lord is sure, making wise the simple;
> the precepts of the Lord are right, rejoicing the heart;
> the commandment of the Lord is pure, enlightening the eyes;
> the fear of the Lord is clean, enduring for ever;
> the ordinances of the Lord are true, and righteous altogether.
> More to be desired are they than gold, even much find gold;
> sweeter also than honey and drippings of the honeycomb.
> Moreover by them is thy servant warned;
> in keeping them there is great reward (Ps. 19:7–11).

BIBLIOGRAPHY

Acts and Reports of the Reformed Ecumenical Synod, "Supplement No. 4: Women and Office," Amsterdam, 1968, pp. 144–160.

Acts of Synod . . . , Grand Rapids: Board of Publications of the Christian Reformed Church, 1973, pp. 519–539.

Adams, Jay E. *Christian Living in the Home.* Nutley, N.J.: Presbyterian and Reformed Publishing Co., 1972.

Alexander, John F. (interviewer). "A Conversation with Virginia Mollenkott," *The Other Side,* 12:3 (May–June, 1976), 21–30, 73–75.

——————. "Some Incoherent Thoughts on Scripture," *The Other Side,* 12:3 (May–June, 1976), 8–11.

Alford, Henry. *The Greek Testament, with a Critically Revised Text, a Digest of Various Readings, Marginal References to Verbal and Idiomatic Usage, Prolegomena, and a Critical and Exegetical Commentary.* Chicago: Moody Press, 1958.

Allis, Oswald T. *The Five Books of Moses.* Nutley, N.J.: Presbyterian and Reformed Publishing Co., 1949.

Andrews, Gini. *Your Half of the Apple: God and the Single Girl.* Grand Rapids: Zondervan, 1972.

Bahnsen, Greg L. *Theonomy in Christian Ethics.* Nutley, N.J.: Craig Press, 1977, pp. 97–116.

Bailey, Derrick Sherwin. *Sexual Relation in Christian Thought.* New York: Harper & Brothers, 1959.

Barton, George Aaron. *A Critical and Exegetical Commentary on the Book of Ecclesiastes* (International Critical Commentary). New York: Charles Scribner's Sons, 1909, pp. 146–147.

Bedale, Stephen. "Notes and Studies: The Meaning of κεφαλή in the Pauline Epistles," *The Journal of Theological Studies,* new series, V, (1954), 211–215.

Berkhof, L. *Systematic Theology.* Grand Rapids: Eerdmans, c1941, pp. 328–9.

Birney, Leroy. *The Role of Women in the New Testament Church.* Pinner (Middlesex): Christian Brethren Research Fellowship, 1971.

Bonar, Andrew. *A Commentary on Leviticus.* London: Banner of Truth Trust, reprint 1972.

Bruce, Michael. "Heresy, Equality and the Rights of Women," *The Churchman,* 85:4 (Winter, 1971), 246–262.

—————————. and Duffield, G. E., eds. *Why Not? Priesthood and the Ministry of Women.* Abingdon (Berkshire): Marcham Manor Press, 1972.

Brunner, Peter. *The Ministry and the Ministry of Women.* St. Louis: Concordia Publishing House, 1971.

Bruns, J. Edgar. *God as Woman, Woman as God.* New York: Paulist Press, 1973.

Burtness James H. "An Interview with the Rev. Barbara Andrews," *Dialog,* 10 (1971), 123–129.

Calvin, John. *Commentaries,* I (Genesis). Grand Rapids: Eerdmans, 1948.

—————————. *Commentaries on the Epistles of Paul to the Galatians and Ephesians.* Grand Rapids: Eerdmans, 1948.

—————————. *The Epistle of Paul the Apostle to the Hebrews and the First and Second Epistles of St. Peter.* Grand Rapids: Eerdmans, 1963.

—————————. *A Harmony of the Gospels: Matthew, Mark and Luke,* II. Grand Rapids: Eerdmans, 1972.

Christenson, Larry. *The Christian Family.* Minneapolis: Bethany Fellowship, 1974.

Collins, Sheila D. "Toward a Feminist Theology," *Christian Century*, 89 (August 2, 1972), 796–799.

Conzelmann, Hans. *I Corinthians*. Philadelphia: Fortress Press, 1975.

Culver, Elsie Thomas. *Women in the World of Religion*. Garden City: Doubleday & Co., 1967.

Daly, Mary. *Beyond God the Father: toward a Philosophy of Women's Liberation*. Boston: Beacon Press, 1973.

Dana, H. E. and Mantey, Julius R. *A Manual Grammar of the Greek New Testament*. New York: Macmillan Co., 1955.

The Deaconess: a Service of Women in the World of Today. Geneva: World Council of Churches, 1966.

Dodd, C. H. *New Testament Studies*. Manchester: Manchester University Press, 1953, pp. 129–142.

Douglas, J. D., ed. *New Bible Dictionary*. Grand Rapids: Eerdmans, c1962. *NBD*

Driver, G. R. "Notes and Studies: Theological and Philological Problems in the Old Testament," *Journal of Theological Studies*, 47 (1946), 157–160.

Elliot, Elisabeth. *Let Me Be a Woman: Notes on Womanhood for Valerie*. Wheaton: Tyndale House, 1976.

————————. "Why I Oppose the Ordination of Women," *Christianity Today*, 19:18 (June 6, 1975), 12–16.

Ermarth, Margaret Sittler. *Adam's Fractured Rib*. Philadelphia: Fortress Press, 1970.

Fellersen, Elizabeth, ed. *Toward Christian Marriage: a Chalcedon Study*. Nutley, N.J.: Presbyterian and Reformed Publishing Co., 1972.

Fischer, Clare Benedicks, Brenneman, Betsy and Bennett, Anne McGrew, eds. *Women in a Strange Land: Search for a New Image*. Philadelphia: Fortress Press, 1975.

Forbes, Cheryl. "Dorothy L. Sayers—For Good Work, for God's Work," *Christianity Today*, 21:11 (March 4, 1977), 16–18.

Foster, A. Durwood. "God and Woman: Some Theses on Theology, Ethics, and Women's Lib," *Religion in Life*, 42 (1973), 42–56.

Friedan, Betty. *The Feminine Mystique*. New York: W. W. Norton, 1963.

Goldberg, Steven. *The Inevitability of Patriarchy*. New York: William Morrow & Co., 1973/74.

Grassi, Joseph A. *The Teacher in the Primitive Church and the Teacher Today*. Santa Clara: University of Santa Clara Press, 1973, pp. 113–129.

Grosheide, F. W. *Commentary on the First Epistle to the Corinthians*. Grand Rapids: Eerdmans, 1953.

Guthrie, D. et al., eds. *New Bible Commentary: Revised*. Downers Grove: InterVarsity Press, c1970.

Guthrie, Donald. *The Pastoral Epistles: an Introduction and Commentary*. Grand Rapids: Eerdmans, 1957.

Hardesty, Nancy. "Women: Second Class Citizens?" *Eternity*, 22:1 (January, 1971), 14–16, 24–29.

Harinck, C. "The Biblical View of Women in the Church," *The Banner of Truth*, 39:5 (May, 1973), 15–16.

Harkness, Georgia. *Women in Church and Society*. Nashville: Abingdon Press, 1972.

Hendriksen, William. *New Testament Commentary: Exposition of the Gospel according to Matthew*. Grand Rapids: Baker Book House, 1973.

Hengstenberg, Ernest W. *A Commentary on Ecclesiastes*. n.p.: Sovereign Grace Publishers, 1960, pp. 181–190.

Henry, Matthew. *Commentary on the Whole Bible . . .* , III, New York: Fleming H. Revell Co., n.d.

Hodge, Charles. *An Exposition of the First Epistle to the Corinthians*. Grand Rapids: Eerdmans, 1956.

_____. *Systematic Theology*. II, Grand Rapids: Eerdmans, 1968, p. 388.

Hooker, M. D. "Authority on Her Head: an Examination of I Cor. XI.10," *New Testament Studies*, 10 (1963–64), 410–416.

Hurley, James Bassett. *Man and Woman in 1 Corinthians: Some Exegetical Studies in Pauline Theology and Ethics*. A dissertation submitted to Cambridge University for the Degree of Doctor of Philosophy, June, 1973.

Isaksson, Abel. *Marriage and Ministry in the New Temple*. Copenhagen: C. W. K. Gleerup Lund, 1965.

Jaubert, Annie. "Le Voile des Femmes (I Cor. XI.2–16)," *New Testament Studies*, 18 (1971–72), 419–430.

Jeremias, Joachim. *Jerusalem in the Time of Jesus: an Investigation into Economic and Social Conditions during the New Testament Period*. Philadelphia: Fortress Press, 1969.

Jewett, Paul K. *Man as Male and Female*. Grand Rapids: Eerdmans, 1975.

Johansson, Nils. *Women and the Church's Ministry*. Uppsala: Pro Veritate, 1972?.

Keil, C. F. and Delitzsch, F. *Commentary on the Old Testament in Ten Volumes*. Grand Rapids: Eerdmans, n.d.

Knight, George W., III. *The New Testament Teaching on the Role Relationship of Men and Women*. Grand Rapids: Baker, 1977.

Lake, Alice. "Are We Born into Our Sex Roles or Programmed into Them?" *Woman's Day* (January, 1976), 22, 24, 92–94.

Leitch, Elisabeth Elliot. Speaking at Wheaton College, May 2, 1975, *The Other Side*, 12:3 (May–June, 1976), 50.

Lenski, R. C. H. *The Interpretation of St. Paul's Epistles to the Colossians, to the Thessalonians, to Timothy, to Titus and to Philemon*. Minneapolis: Augsburg, 1937.

——————. *The Interpretation of St. Paul's Epistles to the Galatians, to the Ephesians and to the Philippians*. Minneapolis: Augsburg, 1937.

——————. *The Interpretation of St. Paul's First and Second Epistles to the Corinthians*. Minneapolis: Augsburg, 1961.

Leupold, H. C. *Exposition of Ecclesiastes*. Columbus, Ohio: The Wartburg Press, 1952, pp. 171–178.

Lewis, C. S. *Mere Christianity*. New York: Macmillan, 1960.

Lindsell, Harold. *The Battle for the Bible*. Grand Rapids: Zondervan, 1976.

Louthan, Robert B. *The Atoning Efficacy of the Sacrifices of the Mosaic Legislation*. A thesis submitted to the faculty of Westminster Theological Seminary . . . , Philadelphia, 1959.

Luther, Martin. *Luther's Commentary on Genesis, I.* Grand Rapids: Zondervan, 1958.

Machen, J. Gresham. *What Is Faith?* Grand Rapids: Eerdmans, 1925.

Mack, Wayne. *The Role of Women in the Church,* Cherry Hill, N.J.: Mack Publishing Co., c1972.

Maier, Walter A. "Some Thoughts on the Role of Women in the Church," *The Springfielder,* 33:4 (March, 1970), 33–37.

"Marabel Morgan: 'Preferring One Another': an Interview," *Christianity Today,* 20:24 (September 10, 1976), 12–15.

Martin, Faith. "God's Image in the Christian Woman," *Covenanter Witness,* 41:13 (June 18, 1975), 6–7.

Martin, William J. "I Corinthians 11:2–16: an Interpretation," in *Apostolic History and the Gospel: Biblical and Historical Essays Presented to F. F. Bruce on His 60th Birthday,* ed. by W. Ward Gasque and Ralph Martin. Grand Rapids: Eerdmans, 1970, pp. 231–241.

Mead, Margaret. *Sex and Temperament in Three Primitive Societies.* New York: William Morrow and Co., c1963.

Millett, Kate. *Sexual Politics.* Garden City: Doubleday & Co., 1970.

Mitchell, John. "Was Phoebe a Deacon—No?" *The Presbyterian Guardian,* 42 (November, 1975), 134–135.

Mollenkott, Virginia. "A Challenge to Male Interpretation: Women and the Bible," *The Sojourners,* 5:2 (February, 1976), 20–25.

——————. *Women, Men & the Bible.* Nashville: Abingdon, c1977.

Morgan, Marabel. *The Total Woman.* Old Tappan, N.J.: Fleming H. Revell, 1973.

Mount, Eric. "The Feminine Factor," *Soundings,* 53:4 (Winter, 1970), 379–397.

Murray, John. "The Attestation of Scripture," in *The Infallible Word: a Symposium* by the members of the faculty of Westminster Seminary. Philadelphia: Presbyterian and Reformed Publishing Co., 1946, pp. 1–54.

——————. *Divorce.* Philadelphia: Presbyterian and Reformed Publishing Co., 1972.

——————. *Principles of Conduct.* Grand Rapids: Eerdmans, 1957.

Naumann, Martin J. "Natural Orders," *The Springfielder,* 33:4 (March, 1970), 4–9.

Neufeld, E. *Ancient Hebrew Marriage Laws*. London: Longmans, Green & Co., 1944, pp. 163–175, 231–249, 88–117.

Olthuis, James H. *I Pledge You My Troth: a Christian View of Marriage, Family, Friendship*. New York: Harper & Row, 1975.

Packer, J. I. *Evangelism and the Sovereignty of God*. Chicago: InterVarsity Press, 1967.

Pape, Dorothy R. *In Search of God's Ideal Woman*. Downers Grove: InterVarsity Press, 1976.

Peritz, Ismar J. "Woman in the Ancient Hebrew Cult," *Journal of Biblical Literature*, 17 (1898), 111–148.

Prohl, Russell C. *Woman in the Church*. Grand Rapids: Eerdmans, 1957.

Ramsay, W. M. *The Cities of St. Paul: Their Influence on His Life and Thought*. New York: A. C. Armstrong and Son, 1908.

Reynolds, Stephen M. "Hair in Scripture: a Critique of Two Recent Studies and a Proposed Solution to the Problem," *The Reformation Review*, 21:21 (January, 1974), 65–71.

Ridderbos, Herman, *Paul: an Outline of His Theology*. Grand Rapids: Eerdmans, 1975.

Roetzel, Calvin J. *The Letters of Paul: Conversations in Context*. Atlanta: John Knox Press, 1975.

Roon, A. van. *The Authenticity of Ephesians*. Leiden: E. J. Brill, 1974, pp. 275.–279.

Ruether, Rosemary Radford. *New Woman/New Earth: Sexist Idealogies and Human Liberation*. New York: Seabury Press, 1975.

Russell, Letty M. *Human Liberation in a Feminist Perspective*. Philadelphia: Westminster Press, 1974.

Sayers, Dorothy. *Are Women Human?* Downers Grove: InterVarsity Press, 1971.

Scaer, David P. "May Women Be Ordained as Pastors," *The Springfielder*, 36:2 (September, 1972), 89–109.

Scanzoni, Letha and Hardesty, Nancy. *All We're Meant to Be*. Waco: Word Books, 1975, c1974.

Schaeffer, Francis, "Schaeffer on Scripture," *Christianity Today*, 19:23 (August 29, 1975), 29.

Scroggs, Robin. "Paul: Chauvinist or Liberationist?" *Christian Century,* 89 (March 15, 1972), 307–309.

Spencer, Aida Dina Besançon. "Eve at Ephesus (Should Women Be Ordained as Pastors according to the First Letter to Timothy 2:11–15?)," *Journal of the Evangelical Theological Society,* 17:4 (Fall, 1974), 215–222.

Stanton, Elizabeth Cady. *The Original Feminist Attack on the Bible (the Woman's Bible).* New York: Arno Press, 1974.

Stendahl, Krister. *The Bible and the Role of Women: a Case Study in Hermeneutics.* Philadelphia: Fortress Press, 1966.

——————. "Women in the Churches: No Special Pleading," *Soundings,* 53:4 (Winter, 1970), 374–378.

Stonehouse, N. B. "The Authority of the New Testament," in *The Infallible Word: a Symposium* by the members of the faculty of Westminster Seminary. Philadelphia: Presbyterian and Reformed Publishing Co., 1946, pp. 92–140.

Surburg, Raymond F. "The Place of Woman in the Old Testament," *The Springfielder,* 33:4 (March, 1970), 27–32.

Swidler, Arlene. *Woman in a Man's Church.* New York: Paulist Press, 1972.

Swidler, Leonard. "Jesus Was a Feminist," *Southeast Asia Journal of Theology,* 13:1 (1971), 102–110.

Tavard, George H. *Woman in Christian Tradition.* Notre Dame: University of Notre Dame Press, 1973.

Terrien, Samuel. "Toward a Biblical Theology of Womanhood," *Religion in Life,* 42:3 (Autumn, 1973), 322–333.

Tertullian. "On the Apparel of Women," *The Ante-Nicene Fathers,* ed. by Alexander Roberts and James Donaldson, IV. Grand Rapids: Eerdmans, 1956, pp. 14–26.

Thayer, Joseph Henry, tr. & rev. *Greek-English Lexicon of the New Testament Being Grimm's Wilke's Clavis Novi Testamenti.* Grand Rapids: Zondervan, 1962.

Toy, Crawford H. *A Critical and Exegetical Commentary on the Book of Proverbs* (International Critical Commentary). New York: Charles Scribner's sons, 1916, pp. 542–550.

Trible, Phyllis. "Eve and Adam: Genesis 2–3 Reread," *Andover Newton Quarterly,* 13:4 (March, 1973), 251–258.

_____ . "Good Tidings of Great Joy: Biblical Faith without Sexism," *Christianity & Crisis,* 34:1 (February 4, 1974), 12–16.

Vaux, Roland de. *Ancient Israel: Its Life and Institutions.* New York: McGraw-Hill Book Co., 1961, pp. 16–40.

Vos, Clarence J. *Woman in Old Testament Worship.* Delft: N. V. Verenigde Drukkerijen Judels & Brinkman, n.d.

Vos, Geerhardus. *Biblical Theology.* Grand Rapids: Eerdmans, 1971, pp. 37–55.

Warfield, Benjamin Breckinridge. *The Inspiration and Authority of the Bible.* Philadelphia: Presbyterian and Reformed Publishing Co., 1948.

Weeks, Noel. "Of Silence and Head Covering," *Westminster Theological Journal,* 35 (1972–73), 21–27.

Weiser, Artur. *The Old Testament: Its Formation and Development.* New York: Association Press, 1961.

Wessel, Helen. *Natural Childbirth and the Christian Family.* New York: Harper & Row, 1963.

Yancey, Philip. "Marriage: Minefields on the Way to Paradise," *Christianity Today,* 21:10 (February 18, 1977), 24–27.

Yates, Gayle Graham. *What Women Want: the Ideas of the Movement.* Cambridge: Harvard University Press, 1975.

Young, Edward J. *Studies in Genesis One.* Philadelphia: Presbyterian and Reformed Publishing Co., 1964.

_____ . *The Word Is Truth: Some Thoughts on the Biblical Doctrine of Inspiration.* Grand Rapids: Eerdmans, 1957.